Contents

Section Three : Formalising the Informal

Section Four : FACE Development Papers

Preface

The 2008 FACE Annual Conference was held at York St John University. The theme of the Conference was *Challenging Isolation – the role of lifelong learning.* FACE Conferences have a reputation of being welcoming, informative and provocative. 2008 was no exception. The Conference provided a lively forum for all concerned with lifelong learning, access and widening participation. The papers in this publication give a flavour of our conference discussions.

Section I addresses the theme of Empowering Learners. Here the diversity of FACE member experience is clearly evident. Empowerment is considered in the context of prisons in Ireland, Maori and Pacific learners in New Zealand, student writers in cyberspace, and in other settings.

Section II addresses the timely issue of Work Related Learning, including papers on the perceived meaning of vocational learning, of work based learning in the voluntary sector, and the work based learning needs of the isolated worker.

Section III has the theme of Formalising the Informal in education. Papers here explore the educational achievement of Looked After Children, of foster parents, and of adults in community based education. The research reports in Section IV have been supported by the FACE Development Fund.

I offer my grateful thanks to colleagues, staff and students at York St. John University for hosting the conference with such style, care and passion. Thanks too to our editorial group. My warmest thanks go, of course, to all our contributors. I thank you for sharing your practice in such an open and thought-provoking way, and in helping us all to gain a greater understanding of the role of lifelong learning in challenging isolation.

Professor John Storan,
FACE Chair.

Section One:

Empowering Learners

Exploring prisoners' experience of education in Ireland – a life history approach

Jane Carrigan, St. Patrick's College, Dublin, Ireland.

Introduction

This paper offers a rationale for a doctorate study in the area of prisoner education in Ireland and provides a contextual background for such work. Through examination of the historical and current environment of prisoner education in Ireland and the different models at work, various questions on the nature of prison in general and prisoner education specifically emerge. The established links between prison and educational disadvantage will be detailed and the basis for choosing a life history approach will be documented.

In Ireland and internationally both the penal system and indeed the education system have been popular subjects for many policy makers, journalists and academics. This research will attempt to link the two institutions of education and prison by interviewing male prisoners attending schools in prisons and will explore how one institution operates within the other. The decision to concentrate on male prisoners was two-fold. Firstly, the Irish prison population is overwhelmingly male -with the average number of female prisoners in Ireland just over 3% (Irish Prison Service Report, 2006). Secondly there is overwhelming evidence to suggest that men are underrepresented in literacy and basic education programmes (Learning for Life, 2000; Owens, 2000; OECD report Education at a Glance, 2000). The Economic and Social Research Institute's Annual School Leavers' Survey reported that 64% of early school leavers are boys and according to the OECD (Education at a Glance, 2000) those who receive the most formal education are more likely to avail of education and training as adults. It is in this context that I want to interview men who have decided to participate in educational classes, particularly literacy and basic education classes, within the confines of the prison.

Much of the research involving prisoners in Ireland has been quantitative in nature and while this is necessary to gain statistical understanding of issues, I hope to build on work already completed and to adopt a learner centred approach to the issue of learning in a penal institution. It is anticipated that this research may have implications not just for those studying or working within the prison system but for those who are working with students who are or have been marginalised.

Historical and Current Context of Prisoner Education

There is general agreement that in the eighteenth century in Western Europe there was a departure from concentration on retribution to one of rehabilitation and reform of the criminal (Kelly, 1992; Foucault 1975; Coyle 2005). Mutilation, hanging, drowning, burning, decapitation and the use of public stocks, once features of medieval Europe's system of punishment, are no more (Peters, 1995). Prisons therefore, as we know them today, are relatively modern inventions, having been in existence for less than three hundred years (Foucault, 1975; Rothman, 1995; Coyle, 2005; Gutterman, 1992; Carey, 2005). There has also been increasing acceptance in Europe that punishment of prisoners consists of their denial of liberty and should not involve extra punishments (Council of Europe, 1987, Coyle, 2005). This in itself has marked a radical change in how prisons have operated in Western Europe. One of the most progressive changes introduced into the prisons at the beginning of the 19th century was education, although this was often religious in nature and clearly designed to reform the soul (Carey, 2005; Duguid, 2000).

Higgins (2004) argues that debates over prison education mirror society's debates about why offending behaviour takes place and what should be done about it. As such education in prison is influenced by political debates and policies regarding crime. Davidson (1995) echoes this view and contends that schooling in prison is caught up in the 'power and politics of crime and social control'. Higgins (2004) identifies two opposing positions. The first one is an 'education as corrections model' which centres on the belief that crime is an outcome of individual pathology and that education should address the characteristics in offenders that led them to offend. The second one is that crime is the outcome of oppressive social structures and that education should enlighten prisoners so that they will see their place within these structures. As Higgins readily admits neither of these positions is entirely satisfactory with the first position ignoring or diminishing the role that social structures play and the second providing a very narrow view of education and its potential.

Warner (2002) draws attention to two models of education in use in prisons that roughly correspond to Higgins' two outlined positions. The first is a European model whose philosophy is contained in the Council of Europe report on Education in Prisons (1990). It states that 'the primary aims of prison education services must be to facilitate the right to learn which all men and women have and which is a key to their human development'. This model adopts an adult education approach that has a holistic view of education and espouses the principles of participation in that the adult learner has a say in what to learn and how to learn. In effect it recognises that the adult learner in prison is a learner first and foremost. The report acknowledges that tension can exist between the prison regime and the pursuit of education. An adult education ethos encourages participation and choice whereas the prison regime is concerned with control. The second model is what Warner terms 'an Anglo-American model'. Warner (2002) argues that this model is based on negative stereotyping, vengeful attitudes and a massive increase in the use of incarceration. He argues that mandatory education programmes, which are becoming increasingly common in US prisons, are 'anathema to good adult education policies'. Furthermore, with mandatory classes, Warner states that education can be seen as part of the punishment. An essential principle of adult education, according to Warner, is that the learner should have a say in his/her education.

The philosophy of adult education in prisons contained in the Council of Europe 1990 report clearly argues that prison education should mirror education that is available in the community. While Irish prisons currently offer a broad curriculum Costelloe and

Warner (2003) draw attention to the popularity of short term offender behaviour courses that are fashionable with some policy makers in America and increasingly the UK. While such courses undoubtedly have an economic attraction to service providers, the education they deliver is clearly narrowly defined.

The Situation in Ireland

Learners in Irish prisons are there on a voluntary basis. The latest Irish prison service report (2006) notes that 54% of prisoners were involved in some education, with more than half of that figure (29% of the entire prison population) intensively involved in education i.e. attending more than 10 hours per week of classes. The teachers are not employees of the prison service and the emphasis is not on exams but rather participation.

In 1972 Vocational Education Committees (VEC) became involved in teaching in the prisons. A Committee of Inquiry into the Penal System was established in the 1980s and the subsequent report (The Whitaker Report, 1985) acknowledged that the involvement of the VEC in prison education was 'a most important step'. However the report also stated that the progress that had been made since 1972 had regressed-'educational provision has not kept pace with the greatly increased numbers entering prisons nor is it likely to do so unless there is a formal policy decision in this regard'. The report acknowledged that education in prison provides the opportunity for increased self-esteem and self-improvement, which it sees as realistic objectives. It stated however that the possible rehabilitative effects of education and training are offset by what it called the 'triple depressant of overcrowding, idleness and squalor which dominates most Irish prisons'.

In *The Whitaker Committee Report 20 years On* (2007), a number of commentators from various section of Irish society where asked to reflect on the Whitaker Report and current conditions in Irish prisons. One of the commentators, Dr. Paul O'Mahony, noted that the Whitaker Report was not an isolated critique of the prison system in Ireland, other reports, most notably the MacBride

Commission (1980) had been extremely critical of conditions in the prison. The MacBride Commission had acknowledged that the relatively high crime rate among a small section of society 'may be due more to a failure in education and learning than to an innate propensity for crime'.

The link between prison and educational disadvantage

The link between poor educational attainment and imprisonment has been noted in a number of studies (O'Mahony, 1997; Dillon, 2001; Seymour and Costello, 2005). O'Mahony's study in particular illustrated the relatively homogenous nature of who we imprison in Ireland and drew attention to the fact that prisoners, as a group, tended to come from backgrounds of extreme deprivation. He noted that the characteristics of the prisoners he interviewed are the same for most developed countries; 'they tend to be young, urban, undereducated males from the lower socio-economic classes'. 80% of his sample had left school before the age of 16 with 29% reporting that they had difficulty reading and writing and 21% admitting to functional illiteracy. Only a quarter had taken public state exams and O'Mahony states that of those who had taken exams, many had done so through the prison education system. This figure is at odds with the figures from outside the prison – in the community almost 80% of young people in Ireland now complete upper second level education. This, according to O'Mahony, indicates that the majority of prisoners have failed at the education system and that the education system in turn has failed them.

The International Adult Literacy Survey (Morgan et al, 1997), which was conducted in Ireland in 1995, revealed that nearly one quarter of the population in Ireland has literacy levels rated at the lowest level (Level 1). In the survey participants were asked to complete a number of literacy tasks and were subsequently given a score according to five levels. Level 1 indicated a poor level of literacy e.g. difficulty in comprehending instructions on a bottle of medicine while levels 4 and 5 demonstrate higher literacy skills with an ability to decipher complex information. The high number of people at the lowest level of literacy would later be a catalyst for more funding for the adult education sector in Ireland. Denny et al (1999) attributed this relatively low level of literacy (25%) to a cohort effect – the presence of an older age group who had less access to secondary education due to fees being required prior to 1966. In this national survey, it was found that the older you were the more likely you were to have lower levels of literacy. Importantly for the purposes of this paper, they also note that of the thirteen original countries who took part, all were instructed to exclude residents in prisons, hospitals and psychiatric institutions.

A number of years later the survey was replicated in prisons in Ireland and revealed a worrying discrepancy between literacy rates in prison and the community. Both surveys gave participants a 'screening test' that measured literacy at an elementary level – participants had to complete two out of the six tasks at this level before being allowed to proceed. In the prison survey however, due to the number of prisoners who were unable to complete this screening test, a level called 'Pre Level 1' was introduced – the presence of which is indicative of the low levels of literacy. Table 1 illustrates the results at each level of literacy and reveals that half the prison population is at Level 1 or below.

Levels of Literacy Within Irish Prisons

	Males	Females	All
Pre-Level 1	22.7	16.7	22
Level 1	30.1	36.7	30.8
Level 2	18	16.7	17.8
Level 3	14.1	13.3	14
Level 4/5	15.2	16.7	15.4

Table 1.1 (The Prison Adult Literacy Survey as cited in Morgan, 2003)

The prison literacy survey indicated that a significant number of prisoners have almost no literacy skills and a large number of prisoners have limited skills that would make it difficult for them to meet the challenges of modern life. A comparison between the two surveys illustrated that the Irish prison population has a much larger group with very poor literacy skills compared to the general population. In the general population survey approximately 25% of people scored at Level 1 – this compares to 52% of the prison population who scored at Level 1 and Pre-Level 1. A survey of the general population had revealed that those over 45 years did less well on the literacy tests. However in the prison survey the opposite was the case with two fifths of those in the oldest age group scoring at the highest level. The survey also noted that young males, in particular, did seem to have relatively poor literacy skills.

A Life History Approach

This paper seeks to provide a context for doctorate work currently being undertaken in the area of prisoner education. The research has been designed using a rights based approach that recognises the rights of the individual. The 'right to learn' is noted in the Council of Europe report on Education in Prisons (1990). In line with this rights based approach a phenomenological strategy will be used. A phenomenological approach focuses on how life is lived and as such concentrates on people's perceptions, attitudes, feelings and emotions (Denscombe, 2003). It can be seen in direct contrast to positivism which is concerned with objective measurement. There are a number of advantages to this type of research as acknowledged by Denscombe; not least that it is a humanistic style that embodies the notion of respect for people. This is an important aspect to this study.

Researchers agree that the popularity of the life history approach has at times fallen in and out of favour amongst researchers over the course of the twentieth century. The first significant use of life history was Thomas and Znaniecki's (1918-1920) landmark study 'The Polish Peasant in Europe and America' in which the life record of a Polish immigrant Wladek Wisniewski is presented (Goodson and Sikes, 2001). Life history research seemed to reach its peak in the 1930s and as a method was promoted by the Chicago School sociologists who collected life histories in 1920s and 30s. Life history as a method, however, was marginalised in the 1940s and 50s when surveys and statistical research was favoured (Goodson and Sikes, 2001; Chase, 2005). Chase (2005) notes that the liberation movements of the 1960s and 70s helped to reinvigorate the life history method e.g. the collection of slave narratives. Since the 1970s the method has had a renaissance particularly in educational studies (Goodson and Sikes, 2001; Antikainen, et al, 1996). Antikainen et al's (1996) study is of particular interest to my research. Their study deals with the place and meaning of education and learning in people's lives in Finland. Using a life-story approach, forty-four thematic interviews were conducted in which participants were asked about the place and meaning of education and learning in their lives. Antikainen noted that 'educational institutions have had a central role both in the individualisation of socialisation ....and in the institutionalisation of the life-course' (p.9). He states that researching a life story is one way of studying identity and concepts of memory, meaning and language. The advocacy potential of a life history approach is clear - life stories allow a participant to reveal an image of his/her self-identity – and give meaning to their experience. As Becker (2002) notes, a life history emphasises the value of a person's own story.

A life-history approach also has the potential to empower participants and the literature reflects its use with groups who have tended to be marginalized; including the elderly, people with a learning disability and people who have been institutionalized. Atkinson (2004) states that the ability of a life history approach to facilitate reflection and insights makes it a powerful research method leading her to conclude " historical awareness –of one's own history and the history of others-is an important step towards empowerment and, therefore, towards inclusion....Life story research can change people's lives. It can and does empower people."

Challenges

There are however many challenges, to both the researcher and participants, in life history interviewing. Munro (1998), for example, illustrates the complexity of such an approach:

> *I know that I cannot 'collect' a life. ....Instead, my*
> *understanding of a life history suggests that we need to*

attend to the silences as well as what is said, that we need to attend to how the story is told as well as what is told or not told, and to attend to the tensions and contradictions rather that succumb to the temptations to gloss over these in our desire for 'the' story.

The approach also poses many practical concerns, issues that are heightened by the environment of the prison. These issues include ethical matters, the well being of participants, the setting of the interview and the role of the researcher in narrative analysis. Wicks and Whiteford (2006) reflected on their use of a life-history approach in a study that sought to analyse the experience of Australian women who were over 65 years. They acknowledge the burdens that may be placed on participants such as being able and willing to spend time being interviewed. They also argue that participants need to be 'psychologically robust' as the telling of experience may evoke both positive and negative memories. This has particular resonance for my study and as part of the research design protocol there will be liaison with the prison authorities in order to ensure that support is available to participants. The success of this approach will be examined in the pilot study.

In conclusion a life history approach allows voices to be heard, in particular it can allow voices that have previously been silenced, to be heard. Adults attending literacy or basic education classes in the community have experienced educational disadvantage. Adult students in the prison system are, I would argue, even more marginalized. Adopting a life history approach has clearly many advantages; it allows people to become conscious of their own actions and influences that have helped or indeed hindered them. It has the capacity to empower people. The postmodern move away from grand narratives and towards the subjective has favoured approaches such as a life history. Dhunpath (2000) goes further and argues that he sees the life history approach as 'the only authentic means of understanding how motives and practices reflect the intimate intersection of institutional and individual experience in the postmodern world' (544).

References

Antikainen, A., Houtsonen, J., Huotelin, H., Kauppila, J. (1996) *Living in a Learning Society, Life Histories, Identities and Education*. London: Falmer Press.

Becker, H.S. (2002) 'The Life History and the Scientific Mosaic'. In D. Weinberg (ed.) *Qualitative Research Methods*. Oxford: Blackwell.

Carey, T. (2005) *Mountjoy: the story of a prison* (2nd edition) The Collins Press.

Chase, S.E. (2005) 'Narrative Inquiry: Multiple Lenses, Approaches, Voices'. In N.K. Denzin and Y.S. Lincoln (eds) *Handbook of Qualitative Research*. 3rd Edition. Thousand Oaks: Sage.

Commission of Inquiry into the Irish Penal System (Chairman: Sean MacBride) 1980 Report. Dublin: The Commission.

Costelloe, A., Warner, K. (2003) *Beyond 'Offending Behaviour': The Wider Perspectives of Adult Education and the European Prison Rules*. Paper presented to the 9th EPEA International Conference on Prison Education, Langesund, Norway.

Council of Europe (1987) *European Prison Rules* Rec No. R (87) 3 of the Committee of Ministers to Member States on the European Prison Rules. Strasbourg: Council of Europe.

Council of Europe (1990) *Education in Prison* (Council of Europe, Strasbourg).

Coyle, A. (2005) *Understanding Prisons* . Open University Press.

Davidson, H. (1995) 'Possibilities for Critical Pedagogy in a "Total Institution": An Introduction to Critical Perspectives on Prison Education'. In Bergin and Garvey (eds) *Schooling in a "Total Institution"*.

Denny, K., Harmon, C., McMahon, D., Redmond, S. (1999) 'Literacy and education in Ireland'. *The Economic and Social Review,* Vol. 30, No. 3, pp. 215-26.

Denscombe, M. (2003) *The Good Research Guide* (2nd Edition) Open University Press.

Department of Education and Science (2000) *Learning for life: White Paper on adult education.* Dublin: Government Publications.

Department of Justice (1985) *Report of the Committee of Inquiry in to the Penal System [The Whitaker Report].* Dublin: Government Publications.

Dhunpath, R. (2000) 'Life history methodology: "narradigm" regained'. *Qualitative Studies in Education* Vol.13, No.5, pp. 543-51

Dillon, L. (2001) *Drug use among prisoners: An exploratory study.* Dublin: The Health Research Board

Duguid, S. (2000) *Can Prisons Work? The Prisoner as object and subject in modern corrections.* University of Toronto Press.

Foucault, Michel (1975) *Discipline and Punish, The Birth of the Prison.* Penguin Books.

Goodson, I., Sikes, P. (2001) *Life History Research in Educational Settings.* Buckingham: Open University Press.

Gorby, S., McCoy, S., and Watson D. (2006) 2004 *Annual School Leavers' Survey of 2002/2003 Leavers.* Dublin: ESRI and Department of Education & Science.

Gutterman, M. (1992) Prison objectives and human dignity: Reaching a mutual accommodation. *Brigham Young University Law Review*, 1992 (4), 857-916.

Higgins, J. (2004) 'Sharing sociological stories: reflections on teaching sociology in prison'. *International Journal of Lifelong Education Vol.23, No. 3,* pp.243-57.

Irish Prison Service Annual Report (2006).

Kelly, J.M. (1992) *A Short History of Western Legal Theory.* Oxford: Clarendon Press.

Morgan, M and Kett, M. (2003) The Prison Adult Literacy Survey Results and Implications. Published by the Irish Prison Service.

Morgan, M., Hickey, B., and Kellaghan, T. (1997) *International adult literacy survey: Results for Ireland (A report to the Minister for Education).* Dublin: Government Publications.

Munro, P (1998) *Subject to Fiction: Women Teachers' Life History Narratives and the cultural politics of Resistance.* Buckingham: Open University Press.

O'Mahony, P. (1997) *Mountjoy prisoners: A Sociological and criminological profile.* Dublin: Department of Justice.

Organisation for Economic Co-operation and Development (OECD) (2000) *Education at a Glance.* Paris: OECD.

Owens, T. (2000) *Men on the Move: A Study of Barriers to Male Participation in Education and Training Initiatives*, Dublin: AONTAS.

Peters, E.M. (1995) 'Prison Before the Prison: The Ancient and Medieval Worlds' in *The Oxford History of the Prison*, Oxford University Press.

Rothman, D.J (1995) 'Perfecting the Prison: United States, 1789-1865' in *The Oxford History of the Prison*, Oxford University Press.

Seymour, M. and Costello, L. (2005) *A study of the number, profile & progression routes of homeless persons before the court and in custody.* Centre for Social & Educational Research, Dublin Institute of Technology.

The Whitaker Committee Report 20 Years on. (2007) Published by the Katherine Howard Foundation.

Warner, K. (2002) 'Penal policy and the adult education of prisoners'. In O'Mahony P. (ed.). *Criminal Justice in Ireland.* Dublin: Institute of Public Administration.

Wicks, A. and Whiteford, G. (2006) 'Conceptual and practical issues in qualitative research: Reflections on a life-history study'. *Scandinavian Journal of Occupational Therapy,* 13: pp. 94-100.

Ka Whangaia, Ka Tupu, Ka Puawai.

(That which is nurtured grows then blossoms).

Ko Karioi te maunga	Karioi is my mountain
Ko Waikato te awa	Waikato is my river
Ko Whaingaroa te moana	Whaingaroa is my harbour
Ko Kirikiriroa taku kainga	Hamilton is my birthplace
Ko Nga Kete	My place to stand is
Wānanga te marae	called Nga Kete Wānanga
Ko Whare Takiura o	I work at Manukau Institute
Manukau te wahi mahi	of Technology
Ko Catherine Dickey toku ingoa	My name is Catherine Dickey
No reira tena koutou katoa	Greetings to you all.

E. Catherine Dickey. Manukau Institute of Technology

Whakaatu / Introduction

2010 is fast approaching and here in Aotearoa New Zealand, at Manukau Institute of Technology the numbers of non-traditional or marginalised adult learners who successfully complete courses has yet to reach the targeted levels set by the New Zealand Tertiary Commission in 2002. This is in spite of the variety of approaches to reinforcing retention and levels of success that are provided by this institution through foundation/bridging courses, culturally appropriate academic and pastoral support, learning centres and strategies used to actively recruit 'non-traditional' or 'marginalised' students.

This paper, *Ka whangaia, ka tupu, ka puawai (That which is nurtured grows then blossoms)* seeks to describe and evaluate a different approach to retention and success. An approach that first values the life experiences of the non-traditional or marginalised student as a learner, that is based in a supportive community within which they could learn and develop the academic skills they need, contemporaneously within each of their papers in their degree work. Hours of contact with lecturers were not increased, based on the belief that these students already had within them life experiences from which the necessary academic skills for degree completion, could be established.

In 2002, the Government of Aotearoa New Zealand recognised the need for action to increase New Zealanders' participation in the global economy. It wanted Aotearoa New Zealand to be a knowledge society in which diversity was valued, where people had thoughts and innovations that could be world-changing, where people wanted to stay and work and where there was continual investment in the future through focussing on global developments and the acquisition of new skills and knowledge. To achieve this vision, six national goals were established: "economic transformation, social development, Māori development, environmental sustainability, infrastructural development and innovation" (Ministry of Education, 2002a:10). One of the sectors involved in moving towards these goals is tertiary education.

For some groups in Aotearoa New Zealand, current and past education provisions, including the tertiary sector, have failed to meet their educational needs. As a result, we have individuals and groups in New Zealand who are unable to participate positively in an economy based on knowledge. In 2006, for example, of all the 25 to 64 year olds in Aotearoa New Zealand, non Māori and non Pacific people had 22% of the Bachelor's or above degrees, whilst Māori and Pacific peoples had only 8.4% and 7.6% respectively, in spite of attending the same schools and theoretically, having the same educational opportunities (Ministry of Education, 2005:3). This result suggests that because of educational underachievement, whole sections of the community are not represented equitably in the work force. These individuals do not have the human capital described by Schuller (Cited by Armstrong, 2000:3) as "the economic behaviour of individual…". The underlying implication is that when one invests in knowledge and skills, one has better opportunities for economic returns. It is in this particular context, that Manukau Institute of Technology and *Ka Whangaia, Ka Tupu, Ka Puawai* has the opportunity to make an educational difference in its community, within the Tertiary Education Strategy (2002a).

Established in 1970, in Manukau City - the city with the greatest concentration of Maori and Pacific population in New Zealand, Manukau Institute has as its objective, the desire 'to provide quality accessible education across a broad range of disciplines at certificate, diploma and applied degree level to meet the vocational needs of students and develop the skills that the Institute's community needs for the knowledge society' (Manukau Institute of Technology, 2007: 26). Underpinning this, is the recognition of the place of the *te reo* (Māori language) version of the Treaty of Waitangi, the partnership document signed in 1840 between Māori and non Māori. Under the Treaty, the Institute has an obligation to 'meet Māori educational needs and aspirations emphasising participation, achievement and success'(33). In a similar way, because of its geographical position, the Institute has a particular responsibility for people from Pacific nations, to provide them with culturally appropriate and effective educational opportunities that lead to retention, and educational success that fulfills Pacific aspirations. Within the Institute's catchment area, there is a multiplicity of diverse, cultural, family realities. Often these families inhabit the lower rungs of socio-economic status, whose experience in education, for a variety of reasons is limited and often negative. As a result, there are many people in the district who are, or could potentially be second chance learners. Attracting and retaining these individuals, in this institute, in a context that respects their unique world views and counters hegemonic processes in education, is both a challenge and an opportunity. The context chosen needs to be one where these students' lived realities, will be able to find expression. Metaphorically speaking, this context can be described to be like the *Kahikatea.*

The *Kahikatea* is a large tree with shallow roots. If it grows apart from others it can easily fall down. By growing in groves, the roots interlace and give each other strength and support. Ideologically, within the Māori paradigm the tree metaphorically represents the extended family. More importantly it highlights that if the Institute was to attract the right people to undertake the new degree, a bicultural Bachelor of Social Work (BASW), then creating a learning context symbolised by *kahikatea* was important. The aim was to create a learning environment where the students and staff could support each other.

E hara taku toa, i te toa takitahi ēngari he toa taku tini
(My strength is not from myself alone, but from the strength of the group)

This degree has been developed in direct response to, and in consultation with, Tangata Whenua (Māori) and Tauiwi (non Māori) from the community that the Institute serves. This was a collaborative relationship to address the social environment that exists in the region. A region where issues like poverty, criminal activity and abuse, fail to be dealt with appropriately because many of those charged with undertaking this work have very different worldviews from those they are expected to assist. The number of workers had to be increased and the training needed radical changes. With more than 161 ethnicities, come the associated social challenges that such diversity may exhibit. Social workers were in great demand and their work was mostly amongst the communities of these non-traditional or marginalised students. Being mindful of this, there was an imperative to attract and retain men and women who could most appropriately meet the social challenges of the district, that is, individuals who themselves were from the non-traditional or marginalised populations; some of the same individuals that appear in the negative education statistics.

In June 2006, it was decided to convene focus groups of students who were currently in certificate courses in social services and were considering, somewhat apprehensively, moving into degree study in 2007. The students were asked to respond to three questions: What does moving into a degree mean to you? What barriers/concerns do you have about progressing to the degree next year? How do you think the Institute can assist? Comments such as,

> 'No-one in my extended family has a degree. I'll be the first…it's a big responsibility. I'm comfortable at MIT but I'll need heaps of academic writing help! I want to get a qualification fast. I'll be the first to keep my mana as Māori.

(What do you mean? Keep your mana?)... I know that I'll get sorted academically in a way that won't 'put me down'. It's about epistemology- my way of knowing. Big word for me the fourth form dropout! (laughter) They (Manukau Institute of Technology) think about us and the way we understand things.'

'...some words that lecturers use like 'deficit theorizing, trauma, implementation'-some are sort of special words for the subject but others... are not in my world. I should have known 'trauma'.'

'I got kicked out of school real early and now want to show my community that people can change and can make a positive contribution to my community.'

'When you keep on being told you are just another 'dumb Māori' over time you begin to believe it. My greatest challenge will be to get my head and emotions in the right place so that I can believe I can do it.'

The responses from these groups were analysed and then related to the espoused theories of a number of academics world wide who have explored concepts relating to adult and lifelong learning principles. Stephen Brookfield (2000:2) debated the use of the terminology 'adult education' versus 'lifelong learning.' He contended that what was 'distinctive about the adult dimension in lifelong learning' could be generalised to four strands; 'the capacity to think dialectically, the capacity to employ practical logic, the capacity to know how we know what we know and the capacity for critical reflection'. Of these four strands, it is the fourth, 'the capacity for critical reflection, when it encompasses both emotive and cognitive processes', that resonated most with the cohort of BASW students. We found that the student responses in their focus groups (2006; 2007; 2008) contained notions or attributes similar to those that have been described by Brookfield (2000) of 'impostorship, cultural suicide, incremental fluctuation, community and lost innocence'.

At this point there is a need for a pause Brookfield's strands. Lee (1994, cited by Ruwhiu & Ruwhiu, 2005:8) "pointed out that cultural knowledge and empowerment involved the strategy of embracing one's own culture and using it to understand and make sense of new knowledge and other people". For Tangata Whenua and other Polynesian peoples, wellness concerns more than the physical. To be 'well' in these worldviews requires that all aspects of an individual's life be in balance; *taha wairua* (spiritual), *taha tinana* (physical), ta*ha hinengaro* (mental and emotional) and *taha whanau* (family). The importance of this interconnectedness of human attributes for Tangata Whenua and other Polynesian people therefore requires a different approach to education and training with a more culturally appropriate social worker (Ruwhiu, 2005; Durie, 1998).

At Manukau Institute of Technology, we have some difficulty with the terminology used by Brookfield (2000). Terms like 'impostorship, cultural suicide and lost innocence' become negatively personalised in our context where a person's collective ethno-cultural identity (Fig.1) is extremely important.

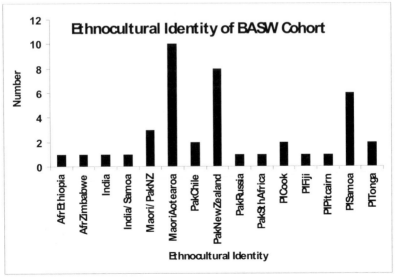

Figure 1: Ethnocultural Identity of BASW Cohort.

One does not want to personalise these notions because it is more about the system than the student. It is as a result of their interactions with this system or process for learning, one in which many have had limited or unsatisfactory experiences, that students can relate to what Brookfield (2000) is saying. In consequence the experiences described by the students during focus interviews, will be framed using Māori concepts expressed through proverbs or phrases. The use of these proverbs or phrases accommodates the worldviews of the students in the cohort.

First, 'impostorship' for us is better described by the following proverb, *E nohotia ana a waho, kei roto he aha.* This literally means that one cannot tell from the outside what is contained within. Thus, when the students explain that at times they feel that they have no place in this system/process of learning, one poignant reason for this as expressed by the respondents, was that they often lack experience of any formal learning process. Students therefore lack congruence with the system/process they find themselves in.

The second, being the traumatic feeling described by Brookfield as, 'cultural suicide' can be assessed by the statement, *Whanau tu mokemoke.* This suggests the feeling of being isolated from those root cultural supports that surrounded the student before they committed to the learning processes involved in the BASW programme. This process of learning separated respondents from those support networks that were part of their previous world.

The third thematic terrain from their responses *Tururturu a tai. Tururu a uta* is what we call 'incremental fluctuation'. This phrase is metaphorically, the feeling of the *surging of the tide.* As students journey through the system they have times when they feel they are moving forward and at other times they think they are going backwards.

Fourth, there is the 'changing world' or *Te ao hurihuri* which we use as the substitute descriptor for 'lost innocence'. Here, students acknowledge that this system/process that they are now in expects them to interrogate the beliefs and values that, until entering the institution, were considered by them as 'truths'. For some, having to reflect on these long held beliefs, can lead to a real loss of part of their identity.

Finally, there is the importance of 'community.' For Māori, community means people - *he tangata, he tangata, he tangata.* Very few of the students in the group give their reason for becoming a social worker in individualistic terms. They credit the community around them as their motivation and soon attribute success on the course to both hard work and their interactions with their staff and student colleagues.

In a comparable way, the students accurately discussed components of Mezirow's (2003) 'transformative theory of adult learning' without knowing that was what they were talking about. Similarly they described Bron's (2005) notion of 'floating', Alheit's (1995) 'biographical learning' and through their utterances, the need for what Tinto (2001) called 'educational communities' in which to create a context for success.

This information was used to provide students with a degree programme that valued their prior life experiences as a base from which to grow. The programme had 'academic foundation education', embedded or provided concurrently in each of the papers. Administratively the programme allowed for the cohort to stay together or at times, to work in ethnically based caucus groups and use their own languages. These non-traditional' students, as mentioned earlier, the majority of whom came from a depressed socio-economic geographical area, are older than the school leaver tertiary student. Many had unsatisfactory or short experiences of secondary schooling and, in general, come from backgrounds that did not consider tertiary education as an option. Hegemonic discourse over time has convinced them, and their families that they do not have the intellect or attributes required, nor do they need a tertiary education. For these students unequal power relationships in education (Bishop et al, 2003) had been their lived reality and this prevented them, as Mason Durie (2001) observed, from 'participating in the global community'.

Although Durie was specifically referring to Māori, there is an urgent need to empower all marginalised students so that they may gain qualifications that will assist their crossing the borders to become true "citizens of the world" (Ministry of Education, 2002). These students from Manukau's 161 plus self identified ethnic groups had huge mental, social and emotional borders to cross before they could even enter the gates of an institution. Some of these 'borders' include a fear of more failure in an education system/process. There is also a lack of understanding about how these large institutes operate, as well as the barrier of stereotypical views that are prevalent about different ethnocultural groups of people, as well as issues of welfare dependency. They have even more challenges to stay there and complete a qualification when contrasted with those who have had success throughout their schooling and consider it normal to progress to tertiary education on completion of compulsory schooling .

For these western defined non traditional or marginalised students, the teaching team has to constantly look at how the programme meets the needs of the diverse realities of both Tangata Whenua (Māori) and Tauiwi (non Māori). In addition, the bipolity expressed in Te Tiriti o Waitangi (Treaty of Waitangi) needs to be visibly present in the content of the different courses. By strengthening of this bipolity, multiculturalism emerges. Lessons learnt on the bicultural journey of the implementation of the articles of the Treaty of Waitangi are resulting in more appropriate ways of working with the diversity that exists in Aotearoa New Zealand.

Tohu (The Bachelor of Applied Social Work-Bicultural)

At this point, more information is required about the unique, bicultural degree programme that these students are pursuing. The foundation on which this was established, is explained in the *Programme Approval Document* (2006: 54) in the following way:

> *The Tahuhu (ridgepole) of the BASW is underpinned*
> *by the following Whakatauki:*
> *Iti rearea teitei Kahikatea ka taea*

In establishing the philosophy as the tahuhu for the BASW, we are acknowledging that any knowledge has a base from which it emanates and develops just as a backbone helps to support the physical self and a ridgepole the frame of a whare. Therefore the tahuhu is essential not only as a source, a beginning point but also as a form of support to the tikanga and kaupapa that follows.

It is very appropriate in a tangata whenua worldview to begin to construct the tahuhu through whakataukī. 'Whakataukī are often quoted to sum up a situation or make a succinct point.' (Karetu, 1975, p.50). This encapsulates the understandings of relationships through which processes become evident.

Therefore in this respect the context of time, the tikanga or worldview and the interconnectedness of whakawhānaungatanga and tuhonohono, are all integral to the notions of person, practice and profession, which form the basis of social work in Aotearoa New Zealand.

The whakataukī refers to the Rearea, which is one of the smallest birds in Te Urewera, however it is able to reach the lofty heights of the Kahikatea tree, one of the tallest found within Te Urewera.

This pukorero describes achievement irrespective of how daunting the task might be and exemplifies relationships despite the existence of difference.

*Kahikatea is also significant as it models the concepts of whānau and manaaki. The root system of this tree is very shallow and therefore if it were to grow on its own, it would be easily toppled by the wind. That is why the Kahikatea is found growing in groves, where the root systems of **the collective intertwine giving support to** each other and gaining strength from their unity. Therefore with tautoko anything is achievable. The small Rearea and the giant Kahikatea achieve a balance as their unique differences develop fluidity and a natural harmony that allows each to grow in their own space, place and time.*

The representation of difference and value of relationships is evident in the honouring of two distinct world views within the degree programme, Te Ao Māori and Te Ao Tauiwi world as defined by Te Tiriti O Waitangi. This is a central and pivotal theme to the Bachelor in Applied Social Work programme. However the recognition of other world views existent within Aotearoa New Zealand today, such as Pacific Peoples and immigrant groups, is also present (pp.51-52).

The programme consists of 22 courses, eight in Year One and seven in Years Two and Three. All courses need to be completed. The courses in each of the three years are in general terms, focussed on 'the self', 'the student as the practitioner' and lastly 'the student as the professional.'

Having considered some of the theoretical imperatives underpinning this approach to Social Work education, is this theory being manifest in positive learning for the participants? Are these participants, who are in the programme because they were deemed to have life experiences, attributes and potential needed to become social workers, able to perform academically at the appropriate level? Many of these students were accepted into the programme with little knowledge and experience of 'academic writing.' Has the learning in context, of 'academic writing skills' proved to be sufficient?

Let's look at the student make-up, their results and their evaluation of the academic writing skills provided.

Tauira kōrero (Information about the students).

There are 41 students in the BASW Year One cohort whose cultural identity (using the government's identifiers) can be seen in Figure 2 below.

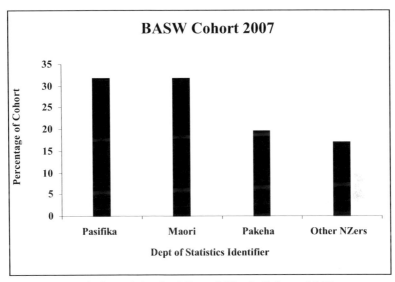

Figure 2: Bachelor of Applied Social Work Cohort 2007

This compares favourably with the Institute figures relating to enrolment, particularly in the Tertiary Education Commissions' 2002 targeted retention groups.

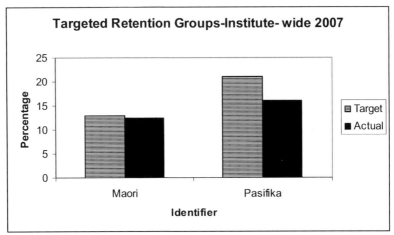

Figure 3: Targeted and Retention Groups. Institute-wide, 2007.

Their ages range from 18 to 57.

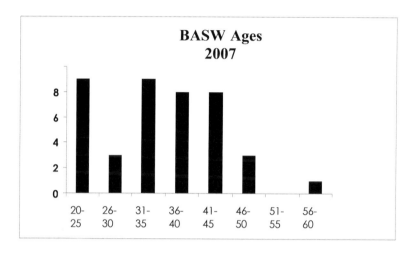

Figure 4: Age of Bachelor of Applied Social Work Cohort

Tukunga Iho (The Results).

At the end of the first year, four failed to complete. Of the four, three had reasons beyond their control that led to their withdrawal.

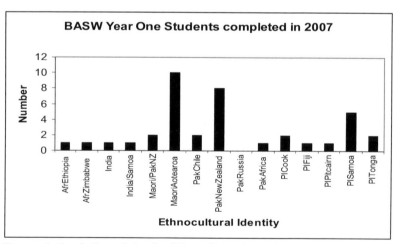

Figure 5: Bachelor of Applied Social Work Students who completed in 2007.

The Institute uses a grade system from A+ to F for each course. Those students who finished the year, that is 39(out of 43) passed every course.

Arotake e Tauira (Evaluation by students)

At the end of 2007, students were asked to evaluate the academic support given during their learning experience that year.

Students were asked to respond to the following statements:

The in-class preparation for future assignments was relevant and useful.
35 out of 40 students strongly agreed with this statement, and 5 agreed.

The once a week writing class in Semester One contributed to my success this year.
35 out of 40 students strongly agreed with this statement, and 5 agreed.

The idea of concurrent academic upskilling is a good idea.
35 out of 40 students strongly agreed with this statement, with 1 agreeing.

The email availability for formative feedback was relevant and useful.
36 out of 40 students strongly agreed with this statement, with 4 agreeing.

The availability of one on one academic help was very important to me.
36 out of 40 students strongly agreed with this statement, with 4 agreeing.

Rubrics help you complete your assignments more easily.
34 out of 40 students strongly agreed with this statement, with
2 agreeing. A further 4 students disagreed.

Whakamutunga / Conclusion

Is the approach working? Already the retention and success rates
exceed the Institute's expectations. The Institute wanted a retention
and success rate of twenty per cent Māori and Pacific students. In
BASW, this number is exceeded (see Figure 5). In terms of the
Government of Aotearoa New Zealand and the Tertiary Education
Commission's (2002) strategy requirements for the New Zealand
knowledge society, this programme is innovative; it is reversing the
negative educational experiences of these non traditional and
marginalised students and as a professional & academic degree it is
indeed developing skilful bicultural social work practitioners. Most
importantly, the students want to be in class, and their families are
beginning to see that tertiary education is a positive and achievable
option for their *whānau* (family).

Ki Hea? / Where to?

Twice in 2007, focus groups were convened and written evaluations
sought on their student- learning experiences. At the end of 2008,
the focus groups will be reconvened. In addition, individual students
have initiated a project to tell their own stories of their journey. In a
collaborative relationship we are analysing these experiences to
clearly identify what support was needed for them and what else
would be useful and relevant, to continue their success. The
emphasis in this relationship is for the students to make sense of
these educational experiences, interactions, and relationships, using
their own ways of theorising and explaining. Information from the
students' projects will then be used collaboratively to inform
learning approaches being used in the BASW programme.
Mā pango, mā whero, ka oti mahi.
(By black and by red the work is done)
No reira tena koutou katoa.

References

Alheit, P. (1995) 'Biographical learning. Theoretical outline, challenges and contradictions of a new approach in adult education.' In Peter Alheit et al. (eds) (1995) *The biographical approach in European adult education.*Wein:verban Weiner Volksbildung.

Armstrong, Paul. (July 2000) 'Never Mind the Quality, Measure the Length', *Working Papers of the Global Colloquium on Supporting Lifelong Learning* Online. Milton Keynes, UK: Open University. Available from http//:www.open.ac.uk/lifelong-learning (accessed 10 April 2008).

Bishop, R. (1996) *Collaborative research stories: Whakawhanaungatanga.* Palmerston North: Dunmore Press.

Bishop, R., Berryman, M., Richardson, C., & Tiakiwai, S. (2003) *Te kōtahitanga: The experiences of year 9 and 10 students in mainstream.* Research Report. Wellington: Ministry of Education.

Bron, A. (2005) 'Understanding learning processes through adult education theory.' In M'hammed Sabour & Leena Koski (eds). *Searching for meaning of education and culture.* (pp.181-192). Joenssu: University Press.

Brookfield, S. (2000) 'Adult cognition as a dimension of lifelong learning.' In J. Field & M. Leicester (eds), *Lifelong learning: Education across the lifespan.* Philadelphia: Routledge Falmer Press. Downloaded from http://www.open.ac.uk/lifelong-learning/papers /393CD0DF-000B-67DB-0000015700000157_StephenBrookfieldpaper.doc.

Durie, M. (1998) *Whaiora: Māori health development.* Auckland: Oxford University Press.
Durie, M. (2001) A framework for considering Māori education advancement. Opening paper. *Hui Taumata Mātauranga.* Turangi, Taupo: Department of Māori Studies, Massey University.

Manukau Institute of Technology (2007) *Annual Report 2007*.
Manukau: Manukau Institute of Technology.

Manukau Institute of Technology (2006) *Bachelor of Applied Social
Work Course Approval Document.* Manukau: Manukau Institute of
Technology.

May, S. (2002) *Accommodating multiculturalism and biculturalism
in Aotearoa/New Zealand.* Hamilton: University of Waikato.

Mezirow, Jack. (2003) 'Changing perspective: Theory and practice
of transformative learning.' In Tom Hagström (ed.). *Adult
development in post-industrial society and working life.* Stockholm:
Ministry of Education, Stockholm University.

Ministry of Education (2005) *Tertiary Education Strategy 2007-
2012.* Wellington: Ministry of Education.

Ministry of Education (2002) Programmes and platforms for Maori
educational achievement. Keynote address by Mason Durie at *Hui
Taumata Matauranga.* Turangi Taupo, 9-11 November, 2001.

Ministry of Education (2002a) *Tertiary Education Strategy.*
Wellington: Ministry of Education.. From
http://www.minedu.govt.nz accessed on 23 January 2008.

Ruwhiu, Pirihi Te Ohaki (Bill) and Ruwhiu, Leland A. (2005) Ko te
pae o te atua mai i nga whakaaro hohonu nei, hei oranga mo te ira
tangata. *Te Koromako* (Hotoke),1-20.

Tinto, V. (2001) *Developmental Education Learning Communities.*
Accessed on 12 January 2008 from http://soeweb.syr.edu/
academics/grad/highereducation/vtinto.cfm.

Developing Skills for Independent Learning for Access to Higher Education Students

F. Nieto, N. Davy, Westminster Kingsway College, A. Dimitriadou, Westminster Kingsway College and Institute of Education, University of London

This paper reports on an investigation that was carried out into how Access to Higher Education teachers at an inner London further education college implemented the development of independent learning and developing learner autonomy, the use of information technology and critical thinking in their teaching practices.

Access to HE programmes developed in the late 1970s as an alternative route to University level study for mature (+21) students. They were developed by partnerships between Universities or Polytechnics and neighbouring Further Education Colleges (FEC), sometimes with Local Education Authority (LEA) involvement. Access courses offered clear progression routes to named awards at the receiving Higher Education Institute (HEI). From their inception they were predicated on the assumption that the traditional qualification route into University level education – A levels – used teaching and learning practices and models which were perhaps inappropriate for mature learners (Parry, 1986).

Researchers in the 1980s (Woodrow, 1988, Parry, 1986) argued that Access courses are characterised by their focus on student and on the process of learning and skills development rather than being subject or institution based. 'Unlike the banking of knowledge under an A level regime the Access intention is to develop content both as a vehicle for improving study and communication skills and as a necessary foundation for further study' (Parry, 1986: 46).

However, although there are some generally agreed purposes for Access courses – targeting under-represented groups, providing progression pathways, fostering FE/HE collaboration, developing alternative models of teaching and learning – local management and delivery means it is difficult to capture what models and practices of teaching and learning are actually adopted by FEC based Access to HE teaching teams; 'there is considerable diversity among Access courses in their aims, curricula and client groups' (Hayes et al, 1997: 27).

Moreover, in comparison, for example to BTEC courses that have a strong assessment-led teaching and learning philosophy, which is clearly written with back-up training available, there is comparatively limited structured *advice* on teaching skills for independent learning (SIL) provided to local Access to HE teaching teams. In their general introduction about Access courses Open College Network – London Region describes study on the programmes as being, 'Learning to develop ideas, write essays and make notes are all important parts of Access programmes. In addition, you are introduced to subjects that will be covered more fully in the degree and diploma programmes' (OCNLR: 2008). The Quality Assurance Agency (QAA: 2006) provides similar advice. Additionally, in the OCNLR course specification documentation that local providers are required to complete, there is no requirement that local teams report on the course's underlying teaching and learning strategies in relation to SIL.

Unfortunately, although there have been many studies of Access students' perceptions of their experience of access courses - including teaching and learning (examples include: Betts, 1999; Gibson and Waters, 2002; Waller, 2004; Burke, 2004) - there has been relatively little research into the teaching and learning practices of general education and access teachers in FEC (Lucas, 2004).

The vast majority of Access teachers come from the 'general education' tradition in FEC (Lucas, 2004), graduate educated, with a clear subject specialism. In the case of this study four of the six teachers interviewed came from an A level teaching background, experienced in teaching students with a narrow range of abilities. Evidence from studies of 'subject specialist' secondary and University teachers indicate that those with a strong subject orientation tend to emphasise the importance of knowledge transmission over different forms of pedagogy in their teaching practices (Lucas, 2004); and to be teacher-centred and curriculum driven (Biggs, 2003).

However, Access courses stress the importance of skills development; particularly SIL, critical thinking and developing the capacity for autonomous learning – all attributes seen as vital for success in a mass higher education system (HEFCE, 2003; QAA, 2001).

This project initially examined key course documents – course specification, lesson plans, schemes of work, tutorial programmes - and learning resource centre (LRC) input to ascertain teachers' approaches and practices. These documents indicate that SIL such as note taking, essay writing, research skills and critical thinking are taught in the communication module and are progressively developed in the subject units, but only formally assessed in the former. Internet research skills and effective use of the college's virtual learning environment (VLE) is delivered by the LRC and in the IT core skills module. Near the end of the programme learners complete an oral presentation assessment and a simulated exam to develop and test exam technique. SIL then are developed in both subject and core skills units (CSU), formally assessed in the CSU, with several skills assessed during an oral presentation towards the end of the programme.

Secondly, the interrogation of these secondary documents was followed by individual interviews to explore the interpretation of these documents in practice.

Accordingly, this research has focussed on what teaching and learning practices and strategies are deployed by Access teachers in teaching concepts such as SIL and critical thinking.

Thirdly, a small group of ex-Access students, completing their first year of HE study, was convened to ascertain their preparedness for applying SIL and critical thinking, in preparation for further research.

Methodology

The project deployed a case study approach exploring the access course delivery of one inner city London College. The rationale behind this approach is that it enables the investigation of a phenomenon within its real-life context (Yin, 1989: 23) and strengthens the validity of the findings through triangulation (Yin, 1989; Singleton and Straights, 1999), as previous research in this subject has been scarce.

The design was based on a mixed-method approach, deploying one to one semi structured interviews with teachers, a focus group with former Access to HE students and documentary analysis of schemes of work, assessment plans and course validation documents as its principal methods of investigation. The design of the interview schedule was based on the Delphi approach (Brown, 1968), in which Access to HE experts were consulted in developing the questions.

The project started in February 2008 and data were collected and analysed between April and May. All research participants were fully briefed about the purpose of the research project before their participation, and informed consent was sought in all instances. In addition, research participants were not subjected to any form of physical or psychological harm and anonymity and confidentiality has been kept throughout the research.

Finally, the analysis of the interviews and documents was based on a combination of analytic and diagrammed coding (Lofland and Lofland, 1995), which enabled a focused analysis on skills development. All data were analysed with NVivo 2 (Gibbs, 2002).

Findings

The development of SIL and critical thinking is to a large extent driven by an interpretation of unit learning outcomes and formal assessment methods reported in the course specification. Thus, the development of SIL (such as note taking, critical thinking and reading texts critically, and use of information and communication technology (ICT) skills) are developed and assessed in subject specific and core skills modules by students critically engaging with textual information in which they are encouraged to experiment with different learning modes. Although a variety of learning skills are assessed, it is primarily essay writing, oral presentation skills and exam rehearsal that are most prominently emphasised and assessed.

In particular, skills development is divided into three phases: the first phase places an emphasis on initial skills development focussed on future assessment; the second phase, preparation for level three assessment. Learners' success in these two phases determines their readiness for the third phase, which is preparation for HE study. Within this model, a major emphasis is placed on teachers supervising learners to read texts critically, using critical thinking and note taking as the major teaching and learning methods, as the essential prerequisites for the development of essay writing skills; a minor emphasis is placed at this stage on learner autonomy and the use of ICT skills within the subject modules. The figure below depicts the relationship between teaching and learning, SIL, critical thinking and ICT skills.

Figure 1: The relationship between skills development and learning outcomes

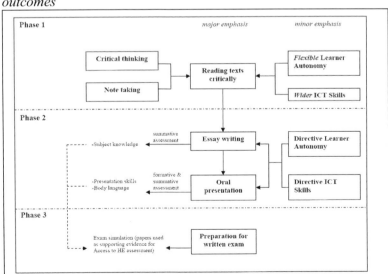

There was a consensus amongst Access to HE teachers interviewed. Their approach was to emphasise note-taking and critical thinking in the first few weeks of the programme and then to encourage learners to engage with textual information available on the web or in printed sources. Critical reading in turn is taught as a developmental process, emphasis being placed on comprehension followed by analytical engagement with textual information in style, length and format. The purpose of these practices is to develop the skills that facilitate directive reading, necessary for essay writing. The aim is to allow students to develop a directive approach to note taking, which is also practiced through different forms, such as note-taking during lectures, video or from printed sources. In addition, the development of critical thinking skills is being encouraged through the examination of positive or negative aspects of an issue filtered through the theoretical perspectives of a subject-specific issue.

At the same time, objectivity, as one element of learner autonomy, is developed using ICT skills for retrieving and filtering subject-specific information. The intention is to create a learning culture in which learners are encouraged to develop objectivity through the application of their views and experiences on subject-specific content, as well as through the exchange of ideas and experiences within small groups for the production of individual work. Peer learning support networks are not formally developed, although small group work is encouraged that can lead to their development. Basic ICT skills are taught in the IT core skills sessions. Subject sessions support IT skills development by encouraging the use of the Learning Resource Centre for research purposes and secondly, treating the Internet as a resource. However, teachers do not put emphasis on teaching learners how to identify sources of information and tend to see this as a role for the staff of the Learning Resource Centre. Thus, the teacher's role is related to teaching learners how to assess and filter such information for subject-specific purposes. In a teacher's words:

> 'The Virtual Learning Environment is when I can see that they can go to sites where they can learn and be taught things without the presence of a teacher. [...] Some of the things we do [...] is more competently shifting information

and making sense of the vast array of information, where there is too much information'. (Interview with A, 21.04.08)

Moving on to the second stage of skills development, essay writing per se is again taught through a model based on building blocks of combined knowledge, in which the quality of the textual body is gradually improved. Learners' work is primarily assessed on subject knowledge, although there is an advice section on the assessment feedback form indicating quality of written English and ability to source. All teachers reported emphasising academic style writing and the use of bibliographical references, the avoidance of plagiarism and the critical processing of information acquired from the Internet. Again, an emphasis is placed on the development of strategies of how to develop an argument, where learners are encouraged to list their opinions backed up by evidence, rather than descriptive text. As one teacher put it:

> 'Looking at the evidence, students are inclined to have opinions, so it [essay writing] is about learning the value of opinions'. (Interview with E, 30.04.08)

In turn, the knowledge produced in a subject-specific essay is further assessed in oral presentations. The assessment aim of oral presentations is not focused on the content of the presentation itself, but on presentation and communication skills. As an assessment method it also provides students with the opportunity to open up their work for debate within their peer network.

Within this stage, ICT skills and learner autonomy is highly directive. Blackboard, the college's VLE (Visual Learning Environment) is increasingly being used as a learning tool by some teachers, in which documents are deposited and learners are also encouraged to use the Internet. In addition, teachers expect all work submitted to be word-processed, skills the learners have learnt in the IT core skills sessions. Whilst in the previous phase learners were encouraged to work independently and develop their objectivity, in this phase time-management skills are important as the work schedule and deadlines frame the work to be produced. In addition, feedback is more directed in the assessment feedback forms and

Individual Learning Plans are developed in which teacher and learner negotiate the latter's achievement and identify areas for improvement. If learners contest their teachers' final decision on the quality of the work submitted there is an appeals procedure. In this respect, learner autonomy is partly encouraged through the learner's active involvement in his/her learning and assessment plan and partly through their defence of their submitted work in oral presentations in front of their peers. Even though learners' conceptions of the purpose of oral presentations vary, one teacher referred to it as 'the ultimate sign of learner autonomy'.

Although teachers' views on the development of SIL were similar, there were some differences in the consistency of the agreed practices. For instance, whilst one teacher built flexibility into the work schedule to account for issues that many adult students face, such as childcare needs and employment, another teacher viewed this practice as a weakness of the programme. While the former teacher justified his views as enabling learners to achieve the course, the latter questioned the effectiveness of the teachers' team-working efforts.

> 'It is important that they [the learners] gain what is required by the end of the course, but it is not necessary that they do every single assignment at the specific time'.
> (Interview F, 2.04.08)

> 'So, in a way, within the team, we can be our own worse enemy – giving mixed messages [to students]'.
> (Interview A, 21.04.08)

Finally, the third phase of skills development of the Access to HE course includes preparation for written examinations. The examination does not always contribute to the formal assessment but aims to prepare students for examination conditions experienced at HE level. Thus, there is an emphasis on the development of SIL such as revision, planning and time management in order to increase students' confidence as prospective HE students. As a teacher explained:

'Students are often overwhelmed by exams because [they] may come in with a fear of exam; it might have been something that they have brought from their early schooling. So I think we have to be very careful about how we do it.' (Interview with E, 30.04.08)

Instead, the exam papers are used as supporting evidence to the formal assessment criteria of the programme; they are an opportunity for students to experience not only formal exam conditions, but also to rehearse the exam preparation process within their informal peer networks.

In this respect, this third phase can be regarded as bringing together all the sets of skills developed and knowledge acquired through their development during the academic year are being brought together through this informal/formal assessment. It is during this phase that the learner starts to develop an understanding of the demands, as well as the strategies required, for successful study at HE level.

Discussion

Overall, teachers' interpretations of their documented practice indicate that they are aware of the model they are applying, although not surprisingly there are differences of emphasis and nuance. Moreover, they are attempting to develop skills and a concept – learner autonomy – that is often used but not clearly defined.

> *A major consequence of the failure to define independent learning adequately in the context of higher education is that there has often been an inability to discriminate between independent study as a learning activity and as a capacity to be developed. As a result the process by which a student becomes self-capable of self-directed study is left to serendipity.* (Knight, 1996: 35)

Thus, there are variations in the interpretation of learner autonomy and its subsequent application in practice. These variations are evident in the course's documentation, its reported teaching and learning practices of the skills required in higher education learner autonomy. For example, ICT is not always clearly integrated into the delivery of the subject units and time management is only 'taught' through the assessment deadline rules. The development of peer networks is not clearly formalised and all teachers do not regularly use the VLE. There is also limited evidence that skills developed in the CSU and LRC inputs into the programme – Internet research and the use of subject specific gateways and academic journals – are reinforced in formal subject unit assessments.

However, there is clear evidence that the teachers are aware of the need to develop SIL and critical thinking and have put into place structures that develop these skills throughout the programme. Moreover, in several cases – essay writing skills, critical reading and note taking – practice mirrors structure; there is a clear phased development of skills.

Additionally, there is a strong emphasis on an oral presentation that is meant to bring together and assess many of the SIL developed previously. The exam simulation also provides an opportunity to rehearse exam technique skills and prepare for a popular University assessment mode. All these skills are seen to determine a successful University readiness learning experience.

Consequently, there is a tendency for the development of SIL and learner autonomy to evolve around the individuality of the adult learner and his/her needs, rather than on an agreed pedagogic model or practice:

> 'We do encourage students to think about how they organise their own lives and their work around their college life, because often with Access students there is a problem with the demands from home life and demands of study'.
> (Interview with E, 30.04.08)

So, although the teaching team has a model that most sign up to, in practice there are variations based both on individual teachers' assumptions of adult learner needs and preferred teaching and learning styles.

There is also an issue relating to the role of skills development within the subject units; is it the case that teachers teach skills necessary for the understanding of the subject or the corollary; that the delivery of the subject drives skills development? The latter approach is usually associated with 'general education' pedagogic traditions; the former more linked with adult and community education (Lucas, 2004). This report indicates that the teaching team probably deliver a hybrid model drawing from both traditions. This could be the strength of the programme, although it could lead to confusion for the learners if different teachers use significantly different models of teaching and learning.

However, the evidence indicates that although the majority of the team come from a general education background and traditions they have adapted their teaching to meet the needs of the client group. Their teaching and learning practices emphasise skills development as much as transmission of knowledge; student orientation over teacher-centred-ness; a constructivist rather than a student deficit model. Indeed, many of their practices chime with the philosophy of the early Access movement.

Overall then, the report indicates a group of staff that are delivering a hybrid teaching and learning model based on skills development/knowledge transmission within an access course tradition informed by relatively limited outside structural advice. SIL and critical thinking are clearly identified as important skills to be developed, although there is evidence of some difference between the teaching team in terms of how these skills could be interpreted and taught.

Conclusions

This report has explored Access teachers' structures and perceptions of delivering SIL within the context of an inner London FE college. It is clear that with the ever increasing vocationalism of the adult FE sector and withdrawal of support for adult general education that Access to HE courses are under threat. This report indicates that this course team have responded to the needs of its client group and are in general delivering the skills needed for HE study. It is also clear that this area of FE is under researched, in particular the long tradition of general education courses and its associated discourses and practices.

References

Betts, S. (1999) 'From Access through HE: a gendered journey'. *Journal of Access and Credit Studies*, 1(2), pp.124-136.

Biggs, J. (2003) *Teaching for quality learning at university*. Buckingham: Open University Press.

Brown, B.B. (1968) *Delphi Process: A Methodology Used for the Elicitation of Opinions of Experts*. RAND. P-3925. Available at http://rand.org/pubs/papers/2006/P3925.pdf, accessed on 8/06/08.

Burke, P.J. (2004) 'Women accessing education: Subject, policy and participation'. *Journal of Access Policy and Practice*, 1(2) pp.100-118.

Dentith, K. (2008) Access to Higher Education statistics summary (2005-06). Internal report, Access to Higher Education.

Gibbs, G.R. (2002) *Qualitative data analysis: Explorations with NVivo*. Buckingham: Open University Press.

Gibson, K., Waters, J. (2001/2002) 'Mature students perceptions of Access: perspectives from a qualitative longitudinal study'. *Journal of Access and Credit Studies*, 3(2) pp.155-166.

Hayes, K., King, E., Richardson, J.T.E. (1997) 'Mature students in higher education: III. Approaches to studying in access students'. *Studies in Higher Education*, 22(1) pp.19-31.

HEFCE (2003) *Supporting HE in FECS: A guide for tutors and lecturers*, HEFCE.

Knight, P. (1996) 'Independent Study, independent studies and 'core skills' in higher education'. In Tait, J. and Knight. P. (eds), *The management of independent learning*. London: Kogan Page in association with SEDA.

Lofland, J. and Lofland, L. (1995) *Analyzing social settings: A guide to qualitative observation and analysis*. Third edition. Belmond, CA: Wadsworth Publishing Company.

Lucas, N. (2004) *Teaching in Further Education: New Perspectives for a Changing Context*. London: Institute of Education, University of London.

OCNLR (2008) *General Information about Access Programmes*, available online at http://www.ocnlr.org.uk/default.aspx?id=95. Accessed on 5/06/08.

Parry, G. (1986) 'From patronage to partnership' *Journal of Access Studies*, 1(1) pp.43-53.

QAA (2001) *The Framework for Higher Education Qualifications in England, Wales and Northern Ireland*. Available online at http://www.qaa.ac.uk/academicinfrastructure/FHEQ/EWNI/default.a sp. Accessed on 26/02/08.

QAA (2006) *The Access to Higher Education Diploma and credit specifications*. Available online at http://www.accesstohe.ac.uk/home/publications/creditspecifications draft06/default.asp. Accessed on 1/06/08.

Singleton, R.A. and Straits, B.G. (1999) *Approaches to Social Research*. Third edition, Oxford: Oxford University Press.

Waller, R. (2004) 'I really hated school and couldn't wait to get out!: Reflections on a wasted opportunity amongst Access to HE students'. *Journal of Access Policy and Practice*, 2(1) pp.24-43.

Woodrow, M. (1988) 'The access course route to higher education'. *Higher Education Quarterly*, 42(4) pp.317-334.

Yin, R. (1989). *Case study research: Design and methods*. Second edition, Newbury Park, CA: Sage.

The Journey of Student Writers in Cyberspace.

Tony Wailey, Susana Sambade, London College of Communication, University of the Arts

We discuss here a strategy for using established creative writing techniques *where the writing is an end in itself*, as a means of bringing writing into the skill set of art students. The popularity of Creative Writing as an outlet for imaginative self-expression certainly needs to be approached with caution. Its use in cultural studies, sociology or psychotherapy, for example, has been the subject of serious investigation in the past few years. The opportunity to see writing as creative output in *itself*, and *not* in service to the creation of an artefact (project research) or even as a means of recording the creative process (reflective analysis) is one not only worth exploring further, and in cyberspace, it also enhances ideas of what constitutes cultural capital.

> *In cyberspace, we chat and argue, engage in intellectual discourse, perform acts of commerce, exchange knowledge, share emotional support, make plans, brainstorm, gossip, feud, fall in love, find friends, lose them, play games and metagames, flirt...We do everything people do when people get together, but we do it with words on computer screens, leaving our bodies behind...Our identities commingle and interact electronically, independent of local time or location.* (Rheingold in Preece, 2000: 11)

This paper will focus on a group of elective courses in Creative Writing, which were offered to all second year students attending a visual based degree, at the London College of Communication (LCC). During this elective students are set the task to write a poem inspired by one of the images shown at an exhibition within the college. The poems are then recreated in the 3-D virtual reality space *Second Life* enabling the LCC student-writers, and others from institutions around the world, to participate in the task, to visit the exhibition and write poems to the images. In cyberspace a previous exhibition with student-writers' poems acts as a form of guidance and exemplar. A writers' club was set up to enable our LCC student-writers to recreate, in cyberspace, a community of practice and to invite other institutions to participate in discussions about the suitability of poetry to image.

Overview

The research was conducted in three stages. Stage one involved establishing the lecturers' expectations of what learning outcomes the students would achieve during the creative writing course. Students' writing experience and their motivation in choosing the creative writing course were factors to be considered. Stage two consisted of student-writers attending the classes, visiting the exhibition physically at LCC, and then virtually in *Second Life*. *Second Life* enables students to participate in the writers' club and to interact with student-writers from other institutions around Europe. Stage three of the research focused on discovering the effect of the 'in-between worlds' on student-writers' experience and if the writing course, synchronous and asynchronous, met their expectations.

Stage One

During stage one both lecturers' and students' expectations of the creative writing were established.

Lecturers' expectations
The lecturers expected the student to acquire skills and knowledge to become professional writers. The following were the skills and knowledge they found the most important:

> Be self-disciplined.
> Become a professional reader.
> Know that creativity needs constraint.
> Understand constructive criticism/feedback.

Accept that writing is a mild obsession.
Recognise that professional writing involves sacrifices.
Engage with a variety of work to make ends meet.
Find the kind of writing that suits an individual voice.
Know that to get published you need luck.

Overall the lecturers expected to develop in the students' the ability to find their own voice, and on a practical working level to do a variety of work to make ends meet. Charles Handy (1995) categorises this perception as a "portfolio life" which is not only now the norm but also one in which Etienne Wenger (2005) expands upon and develops into the signifiers for both a Community of Practice and a Community of Interest.

Students' expectations
At the beginning of the course students were asked to write about their writing experience to date and how this related to their choice of course. Students' writing experience varied enormously:

'Writing for a local paper'
'Writing short stories'
'Writing a short book of poetry, but mostly write plays and one novel'
'Never found it comfortable writing essays or stories at school'
'Written screenplays for two short films'
'Contributed to fanzines and music websites'
'Love storytelling in the form of lyrics and visuals'
'Want to write because I love to read and just escape everyday life'
'I have always kept a diary but I get very frustrated with writing because I always go blank.'

The reasons they chose the course could be summarized as follows:

'This will add to my main course'
'I want to use the skills I learn in the elective to learn to express myself more clearly.'

'I look forward to learning techniques, which will aid my quest to write poetry.'

'This will give me new ideas of how to explore creativity from a writer's point of view.'

'To exercise my skills through many different types of writing.'

'I've never tried poetry: needed to break away from comfort zone.'

'Hope to establish writing style.'

'This course is an opportunity to learn new ways of expressing myself using words as I have always been more of a visual person'.

'Chose this elective because I like to analyse text and find out what the underlying message is.'

'Chose course to rediscover the joy of writing.'

Student-writers' motivations reveal their goals and expectations of the course. According to Dweck & Legett 'the goals individuals are pursuing create the framework within which they interpret and react to events (Stark, Shaw & Malcolm, 1989, p.1). Our research suggests that students select goals they expect to achieve, and that these reflect their needs, motives and values. The next stage of the research was to discover the interaction of these factors within the 'in-between world'. The student-writers goals would be acting as mediators between the **learning** outcomes the professional writers' sought and those the student-writers actually achieved for themselves. (Stark, Shaw & Malcolm, 1989)

Stage Two

On the first day the lecturer's proposed the overall outcomes for the elective, and how the assignments related to these. One of the assignments was to write a short poem or piece of text to accompany an image they had seen in the **Black House Exhibition** - shown at the College in the early weeks of October 2007. The exhibition consisted of photographs taken by Colin Jones "The George Orwell of British photography" (The Sunday Times, 1973). Students who wanted to revisit the exhibition at any time could do so on the internet within *Second Life* where it had been recreated in a 3D Virtual Reality world. This also enabled students at other institutions such as Cape Town University, Barcelona University and VHS Frankfurt the ability to undertake the same task as our LCC student-writers.

The way in which the assignment was approached could be seen in the light of each student's particular perspective and their social and ethical codes. The variance amongst students in the way a problem was perceived, approached and resolved, suggests a multiplicity of learning experiences.

Feedback sessions allowed students to receive comments on their written work in a process which engaged both writers and students. During these sessions it became apparent that students had interpreted the images in many different ways. The interpretation of the image involved a constant movement between guessing and validating. The students made a guess about the meaning of a part and checked it against the whole and vice a versa. Then they guessed the relative importance of the several parts. (Riccoeur 2007)

In addition to viewing "The Black House" exhibition in *Second Life* student-writers could view the previous 'Impressions' exhibition with an earlier cohort of student-writers' poems. A number of lectures were also streamed live (audio only) to student-writers at the site in *Second Life*, and then saved as pod casts. Another facility was a simple (two-click) method of accessing these audio pod casts, both from ones linked with other Internet sites and the recordings made specifically for the Writers' Club. Finally, tutors 'post-boxes' were provided in *Second Life*, enabling LCC student-writers to submit work from within the same environment and to work iteratively - which is central to the writing process.

Learning occurred not only within the lecture theatre, as student discussions regarding their writing skills continued into the breaks and beyond.

> *Participation goes beyond direct engagement in specific activities with specific people. It places the negotiation of*

> *meaning in the context of our forms of membership in various communities. It is a constituent of our identities. As such, participation is not something we turn on and off. Writing is given meaning through social participation. (Wenger, 2005: .57)*

The act of writing a piece to accompany an image illustrated that students were projecting meaning into the world and then perceived this meaning as existing in the world, as if the work produced had a reality of its own.

According to Lave & Wenger (1991) learning within a community of practice takes the form of 'legitimate peripheral participation' (LPP) which is a type of apprenticeship model in which student-writers enter the writing community from the periphery and move toward the centre as they become more and more knowledgeable. At the centre of the community are the knowledgeable members and knowledge systems. Student-writers enter the writing community from the periphery moving over time more and more towards the centre through participating in the community.

> *A community of practice has many possible paths and many roles (identities) within it (e.g. leader, scribe, power user, visionary, and so forth) over time most members move toward the centre, and their knowledge becomes part of the foundation of the community's shared background.*

However, according to Tusting (2005) these ideas of communities of practice rarely intertwine with the power of discourse.

Learning in a community of practice such as the student-writers at LCC could be characterised as

> *learning within a single knowledge system, whereas learning in a community of interest is often a consequence of multiple knowledge systems. A community of interest has multiple centres of knowledge with each member considered to be knowledgeable in a particular aspect of the problem and perhaps not so knowledgeable in others. In informed*

> *participation the roles of expert or novice shift from person to person, depending on the current focus of attention. (Bomme, Hesse & Spade, 2005: 222)*

This is of particular importance when considering that the bulk of students engaged with creative writing were primarily engaged in the visual arts, as indeed were their counterparts in Cape Town, Frankfurt and Barcelona.

According to Bishop (Earnshaw, 2007) 'Classrooms need to encourage and reward risk taking and experimentation as here you learn to conform and break genre convention. Here, then is the possibility that composition and creative writing are versions of the same field.'

Stage three

Ten weeks after they had been asked the original question student-writers were asked what their writing experience had been during the course and if this tied into why they joined the elective in the first instance. The following could summarize the response:

> 'I've found it motivating as well as we've been pushed to write pieces within a fixed length of time.'

> 'There was a good creative atmosphere in the classroom, and the tutors were all extremely encouraging and sympathetic if you did not have too much faith in your skills as a poet or writer.'

> 'By sharing work I have gained more confidence in my work'

> 'Being able to access the exhibition online at any time I wanted was great.'

> 'I enjoyed looking at last year's exhibition in *second life* as I got the chance to see last year's students' poems and it gave me ideas of my own.'

> 'The writer's club pod casts were very helpful.'

> 'I can't wait to see my work in an exhibition and it's great to know that friends abroad can see it on second life.'

Students from LCC, Cape Peninsula University, University of Barcelona and VHS Frankfurt all submitted poems based on Black House.   Images of black youth in the inner city in the 1970s, either seen at the exhibition or on www.secondlife.com. In VHS Frankfurt an Anthology was produced containing poems submitted by students from Germany, Korea, Vietnam and Poland. The resulting experience of participating according to the creative writing tutor meant that

> *The students grasped how the "other" cannot be easily captured either in photography nor in poetry—such an attempt remains elusive, but the effort brings the beholder closer to comprehending the "other's" reality and allowed for a shifting of understanding. By the end of the project, the students had entered into the narrative space of the subjects of the photos. Indeed, many of the poems here represent a shift in the act of seeing itself.* (Preciado, 2008)

This community of interest will continue long after the elective course and exhibition has ended and as secondlife.com is updated. Students' found that the space could enhance their writing experience and in the freedom to view the exhibition at times of their choosing, the process itself was similarly enhanced.

Conclusions

The "in between" world is the world of transitions and like every transition between the formal and informal has a large territory of its own. It is often the place where we make sense of situations in the exposure to different identities and communities of interest. The use of *Second Life* brings a new dimension to the exploration of this "in between" world. This recognition has large implications, not only for all the creative writers of one cross college elective, but in general for all Personal and Professional Development programmes. It is the negotiation between formal and non-formal contexts and the transition between the myopic and the universal that gives greater resonance to a more experiential undergraduate curriculum trying to understand the implication of 'cultural capital'. This supports the assertion that using creative writing to engage the imagination of the student-writing *as* making - can enable art and design students to grasp the word confidently as part of their own practice.

References

Austin, R., Galvin, C. and Mullen, A. (2000) in 'Dissolving Boundaries: ICTS and Learning in the Information age': Proceedings of a conference held in Dublin (May 1999) National Centre for Technology in Education, Ireland.

Barton, David, Tusting, Karin (2005) *Beyond Communities of Practice: Language, Power, and Social Context*, Great Britain: Cambridge University Press.

Bordieu, P. (1998) *Practical Reason*, Stamford: Stamford University Press.

Brome, R., Hessle, F. W. and Spade, H. (eds) (2005) *Barrier and Biases in computed –mediated knowledge communication: and how they may be overcome,* Springer Science and Business Media Inc, USA.

Deleuze, G. (ed.) (2003) *Francis Bacon: Logic of Sensation,* London: Continuum.

Earnshaw, S. (ed.) (2007) *The handbook of creative writing,* Edinburgh University Press.

Handy, C. (1995) *The Age of Unreason,* London: Arrow.

Lave, J. and Wenger, E. (1991) *Situated learning: legitimate peripheral participation,* Cambridge: Cambridge University Press.

Leahy, A. (ed) (2005) *Power and identity in the creative writing classroom: The Authority project.* MPG Books Ltd, Great Britain.

Panesar J. and Wailey, T. (2004*) Migrant Women,* London: SoftNet Books.

Riccoeur P. (2000) *The Just,* Chicago: University of Chicago Press.

Smith, M. A. and Kollock, P. (eds) (2004) *Communities in Cyberspace*, London: Routledge.

Stark, J. Shaw, K. A., and Malcolm Lowther (1989), *Student Goals for College and Courses: A Missing Link in Assessing and Improving Academic Achievement.* ASHE-ERIC Education Report. No. 6. Washington D.C.: George Washington University, USA.

The Sunday Times Magazine (30th September, 1973) "On the edge of the ghetto".

VHS Creative writers (2008) English Creative writers' poetry anthology, Germany: Volkshochschule Frankfurt.

Wenger, E. (2005) *Communities of Practice,* Cambridge: Cambridge University Press.

Pathways Into Higher Education: Working With Disadvantaged Groups Including BME Learners

Dr Samar Al-Afandi, Fiona Chapel, University of Leeds, Lifelong Learning Centre

This paper examines two areas of work of the Communities and Partnerships team at the Lifelong Learning Centre, University of Leeds. The Aimhigher funded Realise project, which has been running since 2003, and the Islamic Studies programme which was initiated in 1997, both work with non-traditional learners from some of the most disadvantaged areas in West Yorkshire.

Both the Realise project and the Islamic Studies programme take a community development approach to working with 'hard to reach' adults. Both programmes aim to provide community-based pathways into higher education (HE) through a range of provision. The Realise Project works with adult learners at Level 2 and provides a programme of activities which aim to stimulate the demand for HE through raising aspirations and attainment. The Islamic studies programme provides an opportunity for adults to study a negotiated curriculum at Level 1 in accessible, community based venues. It aims to raise the awareness of Islam amongst both Muslims and non-Muslims and positively encourages the questioning of stereotypical views and promotes better relations in the wider community. The knowledge obtained and skills learned through such courses often act as a springboard into higher education.

This paper looks at the barriers faced by diverse groups of 'hard to reach' learners. It will outline the support embedded in the work which enables learners to overcome barriers to progression and, finally, explore how this work is recognised and embedded within the institution. The Islamic Studies programme will be used as a case study.

The University of Leeds and 'hard to reach' groups

There is an increasing awareness that higher education institutions do have a responsibility to their local communities. The Talloires Declaration set out the following exhortation:

> *Our institutions recognise that we do not exist in isolation from society, nor from the communities in which we are located. Instead, we carry a unique obligation to listen, understand and contribute to social transformation and development. Higher education must extend itself for the good of society to embrace communities near and far. In doing so, we will promote our core missions of teaching, research and service.*
> ('On the Civic Roles and Social Responsibilities of Higher education', The Talloires Declaration, 17 September 2005)

The University of Leeds has been involved in the delivery of adult learning with groups under-represented in higher education for over 25 years. The Communities and Partnerships section of the Lifelong Learning Centre is continuing this commitment, working with communities across the sub-region which are economically and /or socially deprived. We seek to ensure that our engagement is sustained and responds to the various community needs. In order to work with 'hard-to-reach' groups we have developed an array of partnerships, from strategic to community-based and involving various sectors including, education, regeneration, health, social services, work and pensions. The constituencies we work with include: minority ethnic groups, refugees and asylum seekers, lone parents and carers. We have also started working with the employers of small to medium-sized enterprises.

This is a critical moment in the continuance of funded adult education in England. Not only do we, like many other countries, have an instrumental focus on employability and basic skills, but a Labour government has put the mechanisms in place for two-tier provision. The poor can access basic skills, narrowly defined workforce skills and a modicum of personal development, whilst those that can pay have access to traditional evening class provision

– though this varies greatly in different local authority areas. According to the National Institute of Adult and Continuing Education (NIACE):

> *55,000 adult learners have been lost to publicly funded safeguarded adult learning in the last year. This now means that in just three years there has been a fall of 184,600 adult learners in programmes for personal fulfilment, civic participation and community development. This fall is on top of the 1.4 million adult learning places which have been lost from all publicly-funded adult learning over the last two years.* (Tuckett, 2008).

Loss of provision means not only loss of jobs and expertise but also loss of adult learners who might potentially progress onto higher education. (Fraser, 2008)

The Realise Project

The Realise Project (formerly 'Beyond GCSE?') was developed in 2002 based on the premise that in order to increase the numbers of adults from areas of socio–economic disadvantage participating in higher education, the sector needed to engage with these potential students whilst they are studying at Level 2. The project aims to do this through targeted outreach and development work and a programme of activities which aim to stimulate demand amongst community-based adult learners for progression to HE.

A flexible and responsive programme was developed with our project partners at Leeds Thomas Danby and Park Lane College, which include the following elements:

- Subject-specific study days held at the University, including study skills support
- 'Associate Student' events enabling learners to attend undergraduate lectures at the University
- University taster days for learners to sample aspects of university provision

- 'Top-up' sessions at college community bases taught by university subject specialists
- Group and individual IAG sessions, both on campus and the community.
- Consultation and staff development events to improve communication between the HE and FE sectors

We have learned that:

The more study days and visits to the University campus, the greater the knowledge and understanding of higher education and the increase in motivation to progress. The role of information, advice and guidance (IAG) is a key factor in raising HE awareness and this needs to be a pro-active service, engaging students throughout their programme and not waiting until students make an appointment. It can take a while for people to understand what IAG is and feel confident about making use of the service.

The sustained partnership with adult education colleagues in FE is another crucial component in the delivery of this project with both FE and HE deriving positive outcomes. Often the most important staff, in terms of community learners, are part-time tutors and we have undertaken formal and informal staff development so that they gain a greater awareness of progression routes and higher education opportunities in order that they can be influencers and signposters. Tutor and student feedback indicates that the staff involved with this project are now making links with HE that they have not done in the past.

What our learners say:

> 'I didn't come from a family where you'd go to University. I got lower grades at school than I should have done and I lost my confidence when I had my children. I started GCSEs because I wanted to know I could do it, and I wanted my kids to be proud of me. I thought university was just for rich people. This project took me out of my own reality; made me believe I can do more.'

'I never thought I'd go to University. I never thought I'd go to college. I want to do a degree for me because I want to set my own standards. I want to show that I can break the standards that my educational experiences have expected of me.'

What our FE partners say:

'I think most of the students I see wouldn't dream of enquiring about courses at Leeds University because they would be scared that they would be laughed at and they wouldn't know who to approach. So in those terms the project has been very valuable. There is a perception, true or not, that University is for middle class people and people from middle class areas so the project has helped to break down some of those ideas and that's very worthwhile'. (FE Centre Manager).

Islamic Studies Programme at the University of Leeds

The Islamic Studies Programme was established in 1997 in collaboration with the local Muslim communities and the university departments of Arabic & Middle Eastern Studies and Theology & Religious Studies. It was a new development of the Widening Provision project at the School of Continuing Education, University of Leeds, to meet the needs the local community.

Now in its eleventh year of delivery by the Lifelong Learning Centre, Islamic Studies is a Level 1 programme which aims to recruit a diverse student audience, in particular ethnic minority students with little or no post-16 education, in order to do the initial development work of bringing the learners back into education and introducing them into higher education. The Programme acts as an accessible pathway into higher education and raises aspirations.

The Learners

The Programme is attracting participants from all backgrounds. There is a wide range of learners according to age, gender, ethnicity and religion. The majority of the students are Asian Muslim women. However, the number of men is steadily increasing. Ages range between 18 and 71 with the majority falling into the age group 18-30 years.

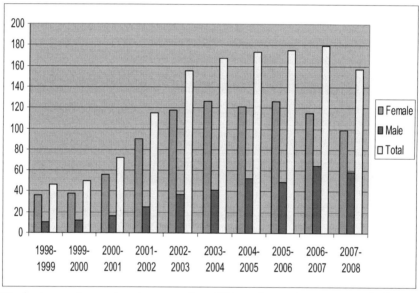

Student numbers showing gender (This chart does not include figures for semester two 2007-2008)

The Programme has also generated interest from the non-Muslim community, who are looking to gain a greater understanding of Islam. This may be in response to the increasingly multicultural society we are living in, in addition to recent international events.

One of our learners told us:

> 'My interest in doing the course was because I feel that we in Britain need to try to understand the profound changes

which the future will bring, especially in West Yorkshire as we move into a true multi-faith society.'

Another student described the course content:

'I really enjoyed the Islamic Law classes which were taught at very professional level. They allowed me to see the differences and the similarities between law in Arabic countries and this in western ones and I am happy that I have such a knowledge which not many English people have.'

Learner barriers

Culture/family
One major barrier for many students is the lack of family and, often, community encouragement to gain academic qualifications and further education, which often suppresses aspirations. This doesn't only apply to women; we have also found it a barrier to participation by men. Family restrictions also link with this, for example, caring for young children is usually seen by families as "women's work".

One of our female students told us about the broader benefits of studying:

'The Programme offers the gateway to all kinds of people, as this will enable individuals to build their own personal goals and objectives in their lives. The Lifelong Learning Centre has been invaluable to me in fulfilling my career aspirations.'

No previous experience of HE
Most of the Islamic Studies students have no previous experience of HE, often combined with a poor experience of schooling and a long absence from education. This leads to low self-esteem and limited expectations, as well as creating a sense of fear and resistance.

One of our learners told us:

'I felt throughout the years that I had lost my confidence within myself, being a wife as well as a mother of three. The staff have encouraged me and by giving me that motivation, I applied to the Arabic and Middle Eastern Studies Department to do an undergraduate degree, which has been successful.'

Learner motivations

Learners join the programme with different aims and objectives. It provides the opportunity to seek knowledge whilst gaining a qualification. However the knowledge is acquired in a familiar environment, without the formalities, processes and systems that can be daunting for them. Another important reason for undertaking such courses is the social aspect. The courses provide an opportunity to meet new people and make friends; in some cases the courses are used as a pretext for women who are isolated within their families and want an acceptable way of lessening that isolation. Siddiqui's report on Islamic Studies (2007) courses states that they act as a way of 'encouraging young Asian women to be involved in education, in order 'to rationalise and think through their gendered, ethnic, and religious identities'.

Overcoming Learner barriers

Every attempt is made to facilitate and overcome structural barriers from the start to the end of the course. At the start of the course, students are consulted on the timetabling of sessions in an attempt to accommodate their needs. Dedicated separate induction events are arranged to welcome the Programme's new students and to give them an insight into the University and to introduce the services/facilities available. This, in turn, makes the University more accessible emotionally as well as physically and encourages learners to make use of university resources.

During the course, study skills sessions are offered as one element of on-course support. In addition, all tutors are experienced in working with adults in the community and have a good understanding of the academic and pastoral support required. The programme provides pastoral care for all students, and most importantly, free childcare wherever possible.

Information, advice and guidance, in addition to an academic support tutor, are always available to students throughout the Programme on an appointment basis, or open drop-in sessions at the teaching location. University lecturers are invited to give one-off sessions in community venues, giving students the opportunity to find out about university study and to introduce the students to the research element. A library 'book box' is provided on the premises in line with the University's library support policy.

One of our students reported:

> 'I have gained a multitude of skills having done these modules: in essay writing, researching, increased confidence in public speaking while doing presentations for my peers and much more.'

Although a further three of our students, all young women, secured offers to enrol on the full-time degree, cultural and family issues prevented them from going to university. This suggests that community based learning is regarded as less threatening by families compared to university, campus-based, study.

The Curriculum

The Islamic Studies Programme is inter-disciplinary with 12 modules, and is increasing in response to community demand. Modules include: four levels of the Arabic Language, Islamic History, Islam in Western Societies, Islamic Art, Law and Religious Studies. These modules may be studied separately to fit the students' lifestyle and commitments, or as a package to build towards a certificate.

A student recently told us:

> 'My elder sister personally recommended this style of studying where I could choose from an array of subjects and only study modules that interested me. This reminded me of having toast without having to eat the crust, which is great!'

In addition, the Programme offers community students access to three elective undergraduate modules delivered on campus.

Delivery

The programme's primary objective is the provision of accessible courses to those at an educational disadvantage. Inner city, socially deprived areas are specifically targeted, in order to increase minority ethnic participation in higher education. The courses are delivered on and off-campus mainly in local community venues alongside Adult and Community Education programmes. These venues are more convenient for the potential students, especially for women who report that they feel safer and more at ease in their own area.

One female student told us:

> 'As well as studying these part time courses I am working full time, it has been hard work sometimes but life has been made much easier with the courses running within the community, local areas with venues, which are easily accessible.'

The success of this work is evidenced by its popularity. Having been delivered initially in one location in Leeds, Islamic Studies is now taught across West Yorkshire in Leeds, Bradford and Batley. Outreach work and community networks continue to be crucial to the recruitment of priority groups.

Retention

Over the years the Programme has gone from strength to strength, with the number of students steadily increasing, as well as maintaining a good rate of retention. Very few students have withdrawn from the courses; withdrawal is usually due to other commitments or gaining employment. Student evaluation forms indicate that the support and guidance provided by the programme plays a key role in sustaining retention. The chart below shows the retention rates 2000-2008. (The figures for 2007 – 2008 do not include semester two).

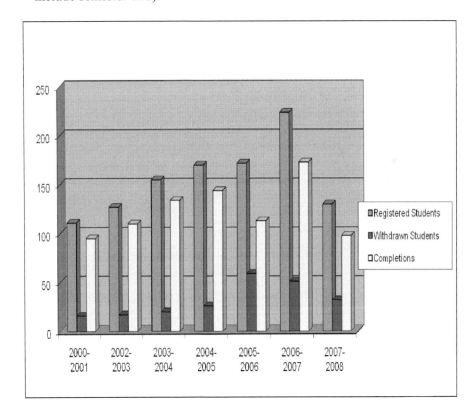

Progression and achievements

Our continued support and guidance has enabled 13 of our students to go onto higher education. Three of these students have now graduated and one is just completing his masters degree. The remainder are currently at different levels/years completing their Islamic Studies or Arabic language degree with the Arabic and Middle-Eastern Studies Department. The Programme provides access to study on a full-degree scheme in the subject area; we have an agreement with the Arabic and Middle-Eastern Studies department in place.

Our students are keen to encourage others to join the courses:

> 'I'd say "Go for it" to anyone who was thinking about University. I needed to feel that I'd achieved something in life – this makes me feel confident that I can move in a world which, at times, I felt was beyond reach. When I did small courses I thought college was beyond reach, you go higher and higher, to college then Uni.'

> 'I applied for the Arabic and Middle Eastern faculty, which has been successful. The Programme offers the gateway to all kinds of people, as this will enable individuals to build their own personal goals and objectives in their lives. The LLLC has been invaluable to me in fulfilling my career aspirations.'

Case Study

Asim 23, former Islamic Studies student now studying full-time on the Arabic & Islamic Studies degree

> 'I was always interested in learning the Arabic language at an academic level and attaining a deeper knowledge of Islam. Initially I enrolled for three modules on the Islamic Studies programme and successfully obtained the 60 credits required to enrol on the full-time Arabic & Islamic Studies degree.

I found these courses very flexible and they fitted in well with my full-time job. The courses were very interesting, taught in a very relaxed and professional manner and not too intense.

I was particularly impressed by the support offered by the University. I had plenty of guidance and support from my course tutors and even though we studied off campus, we had access to the same university resources, including the library, as other students. I found the support from the Guidance Officer invaluable when it came to completing my UCAS application for full-time study.

The courses were wonderful and without them, I would never have had the motivation to begin the full time study again. The courses have equipped me with all the skills required to study at degree level.'

Islamic Studies in the Wider Context

By most socio-economic measures Asian Muslims are amongst the most disadvantaged of the ethnic minorities in the UK. For example, over 60 per cent of Pakistani and Bangladeshi households are in poverty – compared to 20 per cent of Whites – and have the highest proportions of school leavers without any qualifications (Tariq Mahood, 2006). According to the Higher Education Funding Council for England (HEFCE), nearly half of students undertaking Islamic Studies programmes are from Asian/Black Asian backgrounds when compared to eight per cent across all programmes. This is consistent with the fact that many faith based programmes are studied by people of that faith (HEFCE November 2007) At Leeds we have used faith as a tool to engage hard-to-reach groups in higher education.

Studies reveal that for many young Asians, Islam is a source of educational aspirations and the motivation to improve oneself and lead a disciplined, responsible life. It is particularly used by girls to justify and negotiate educational and career opportunities with conservative parents, often of rural backgrounds with little knowledge of the scriptures. Islam encourages the pursuit of Islamic knowledge and other knowledge..

The HEFCE report highlights the need for Islamic Studies programmes that are responsive to the needs of Muslim communities as well as enhancing awareness and improving community relations.

A recent report 'Time for Change: Report on the future of the study of Islam and Muslims in Universities and Colleges in Multicultural Britain', led by academics at Dundee's Al-Maktoum Institute for Arabic and Islamic Studies concluded that a more multicultural and community based approach needed to be taken in the UK to Islamic Studies (Scott-Bauman).

Conclusion

The work with under-represented groups as described here has its roots in collaborations with communities over a long period of time. These activities have been developed as a response to needs identified by local communities and other providers.

We aim to progress under-represented groups into higher education, but we also act as a conduit between communities and the University. Islamic Studies is an example of how partnership working can support University requirements of widening participation as well as supporting a broader agenda of social cohesion. The developmental work of the Realise project builds relationships with community education at every level and links community-based and academic staff.

Finally, delivering programmes in the community has implications for resources both in terms of staffing and costs. The targeting of funding towards the 14 – 19 age group and employer engagement has clear implications regarding the future of community-based work. HEFCE has indicated that Islamic Studies programmes should be delivered to target groups in a responsive manner, but if resources are not forthcoming the good practice that we have developed in Leeds cannot be sustained and replicated elsewhere.

References

HEFCE (November 2007) *Islamic Studies: current status and future prospects*, Lion Court Conference Centre. http://www.hefce.ac.uk/aboutus/sis/islamic/seminarreportjan08.doc

Modood, Tariq (2006) Ethnicity, Muslims and higher education entry in Britain, *Teaching in Higher Education*, Journal Vol. 11, No.2, pp.247-250.

Scott-Baumann, Alison, *A Collaborative Partnerships as Sustainable Pedagogy: Working with British Muslims, a case study*. www.glos.ac.uk/shareddata/dms/FF071DBEBCD42A039FF8B1E4 A2EE4606.pdf.

Siddiqui, A. (2007) 'Teaching Islam in Universities' DSCF.

Tuckett, A. (2007) (ed.) *Participation and the pursuit of equality Essays in adult learning, widening participation and achievement*, Leicester: National Institute of Adult Continuing Education.

Tackling Regional Development through Lifelong Learning: *Amaze Yourself*, a case study

G. Miller, J. Irvine, University of Leeds

Introduction

This paper illustrates the key role that Higher Education Institutions can play in supporting regional development and regeneration through targeted interventions. The University of Leeds in partnership with seven other regional universities collaborated on an European Social Fund (ESF) project to provide enterprise training to the regions hardest to engage groups (see appendix A for details of partners and priority groups of learners). *Amaze Yourself* was designed as a major new initiative intended to encourage enterprise learning, improve employability, and promote enterprise development and business start up.   Focusing primarily on the business start up element to engage learners, an outstanding proportion of beneficiaries at the University of Leeds (75% by October 2007) were successfully supported into self-employment, employment, further study or other positive outcomes.

The *Amaze Yourself* delivery partnership covered black and minority ethnic groups, long-term unemployed people, older workers, women and young people.   However the focus of this paper is on the experience of the University of Leeds.   Our activities targeted people with a disability or long term health condition in Yorkshire and Humberside who were over 21 and had not been working for over six months. The aim of this paper is to highlight critical success factors of the programme, examine successful outcomes, set in context the current circumstances in relation to the target group and set out our forward plan. The paper incorporates both the destination data of the participants, including case studies and success stories and also refers to the independent evaluation carried out on the project.   Thus we describe participant and partner experience and autonomous opinion.

Background and Evidence of Demand

The project encompassed the Yorkshire and Humber region and ran from 1st January 2006 to 31st January 2008. The majority of individuals taking part in the training were in receipt of Incapacity Benefit (IB). It is known that the chances of returning to work rapidly diminish the longer an individual is claiming IB. After one year a person has only a one in five chance of returning to work, and more than half of IB claimants have been claiming for five years or more. The average length of time for making a return to work after one year on IB is currently between eight and ten years. Statistically, after two years on incapacity benefits, a person is more likely to die than to find a new job.

The wider partnership programme was launched in response to a number of regional and national strategies such as the Regional Development Agency's Economic Strategy, the Regional Economic Strategy (RES) and the Framework for Regional Employment and Skills Action (FRESA). These strategies drew on a number of economic and employment related indicators to demonstrate Yorkshire and Humberside's comparatively low levels of business start up, self employment and economic activity. In 2005 the University of Leeds target group (people with a disability or long term health condition in Yorkshire and Humberside) represented 7% of the working age population claiming IB in the UK. The University of Leeds identified a gap in higher level skills training for these individuals and tailored its established model of delivery for hard to engage groups to provide a flexible training package. By this means the project met the diverse needs of the learners in a higher education setting.

Evaluation for Leeds City Council: Eldwick Research Associates

Innovation
The Jobcentre Plus respondent explained that prior to Amaze there had 'never been targeted self-employment for people with disabilities' and they were not aware of any similar provision. The flexibility and responsiveness of the programme to client need was innovative and highly valued by participants and stakeholders.

Government Office stated, that 'there is a lot of provision out there, but this group has just been ignored'.

Some critical success factors

Partnership & engagement
The University has over six years of experience of working in the area of employability with hard to engage groups. Past award winning programmes have included working with older unemployed males (Grey Panthers), IB claimants (RISE) and with single parents and carers (OPTIMISE). Drawing on associations formed through these programmes influenced the *Amaze Yourself* partnership.   At the same time it was clear that establishing tailored contacts and support services was key to meeting the needs of this particular group of learners.

For recruitment, delivery and support services, strong relationships were developed with local entrepreneurs, Leeds City Council (Jobs & Skills), Business Link West Yorkshire, Job Centre Plus, Shaw Trust and West Yorkshire Social Enterprise Link amongst others who provided and received referrals as well as delivering information sessions to the learners. By involving a range of individuals from a broad spectrum of industries in teaching and mentoring, students were granted access to broader enterprise expertise and a comprehensive network of support.

The majority of learners reported that they had repeatedly experienced inappropriate referrals between organisations, which had led to many questioning the suitability of the training from the outset. By allowing the learners to experience 'co-creation' of the course and recognise that their involvement was on an individual support basis (rather than counting towards a specific predetermined outcome), trust was built which led to a high retention rate (87%). The project team was also assisted by the ESF payment structure which linked to engagement rather than outcomes.   Although output and outcome targets were set, the team had flexibility in delivery. To ensure support and training services were equipped and flexible enough to meet learner needs, staff in prominent employment and disability organisations were fully briefed about *Amaze Yourself*.

Evaluation for Leeds City Council: Eldwick Research Associates

Innovation in engagement
Embedding Amaze on the internal systems of Jobcentre Plus was essential to the access and engagement of programme participants and viewed as innovative and cutting-edge in terms of successful engagement.

Partnership working
Partnership working has been an important aspect of the Amaze programme. Key Partners such as Jobcentre Plus, Shaw Trust, and the West Leeds Family Learning Centre (WLFLC) valued the partnership and were keen to pursue this in the future if there were opportunities to do so. Shaw Trust described how 'the partnership delivered a support package to clients, which was 'complementary. It was a two way process and this was necessary to deliver the best support possible.' Amaze staff invited agencies to be involved in the programme, providing knowledge and understanding to participants on the further developmental opportunities that were available to them.

Course structure

The course was split into three elements, firstly the initial taught enterprise training at the University, follow up support, including 'ask the expert' sessions led by business professionals and finally mentoring on both a formal and informal basis. The course was delivered in a flexible way, tailoring the training and support to the requirements of the group. (See appendix B for course content).

Evaluation for Leeds City Council: Eldwick Research Associates

The Amaze team are a highly skilled and committed group of individuals and demonstrate excellence from project management to delivery of sessions and mentoring advice. Project staff are very accessible and tutors offer support beyond that required of them contractually. This was recognised and valued by participants and stakeholders. Tutors are highly skilled, fostering an interactive, participative approach, listening to clients and adapting programmes to individual and group needs.

Unique Aspects

Choice of destination
Unlike many programmes, the *Amaze Yourself* project at the University of Leeds offered learners the choice of being supported into work through one of three outcomes; self employment, employment or further study.

Experience suggests that many people with a health condition, and a prolonged period of unemployment, decide to make major changes and embark on a new direction in life. Receiving training and support helped to rebuild learners' confidence at this period in their lives assisting them to nurture ambitions and identify their most suitable forward plan.

Social inclusion
Primarily the central focus of the project was to support people through the programme to self-employment, employment or further study, but an additional significant result has been the atmosphere of social inclusion it has encouraged. For many learners, as a result of taking part in the training, have re-connected with mainstream services and activities such as volunteering, job searching and self improvement courses.

Choice of style
Teaching was delivered by tutors with experience of working with non-traditional students. From the start, learners were encouraged to take ownership of their own learning experience by guiding content and direction which ensured its relevance to the group's interests.

The association with a higher education institution proved a considerable attraction, learners reported a sense of status and pride. A unique learning experience, where academic tutors and business experts used their knowledge and expertise in a two-way exchange with learners, was created.

Evaluation for Leeds City Council: Eldwick Research Associates

How Amaze differs from other related initiatives
Respondents believed that the programme was innovative, as it was aimed at those with higher level skills. It was 'student led' and was 'developed and moulded around collective and individual needs. So, although there was group delivery and the 'collective decided what and how they wanted to learn within a broad framework,' there was also a one-to one element embedded in the programme.

Responding to learner needs
The Project Management Team are advocates of co-creation, where delivery is steered by participants. 'They are the experts. They [the beneficiaries] have the expertise you don't have and we value them and embed their skills and knowledge in the programme.' Participants on the programme were keen to develop social enterprises and 're-establish their lives'.

The Learners

Learners came to the training with a broad range of academic skills and life experiences. Many of the course participants were in receipt of IB. All learners who took part in the training had a disability, or long term health condition, including physical and sensory impairments and mental ill-health (both psychotic and neurotic conditions such as stress and anxiety).

Evaluation for Leeds City Council: Eldwick Research Associates

Participants were initially attracted by the idea of a relatively short programme. They were seeking the confidence to progress, and valued a programme that was delivered to people in similar circumstances, who empathised with their issues, barriers and limitations. 'A number of students wouldn't have taken part if they hadn't been with others with mental health and disability issues' (PMT). Enterprise was considered an ideal route back into work for individuals, whose ill health may result in periods when they would be unable to work or had limitations on hours of working. They would be in control and could work around their illness and/or disability.

Learner Outcomes

The project exceeded the original target of 22 beneficiaries, with a total of 82 learners taking part. The retention rate was particularly high for a hard to engage group with over 87% of beneficiaries completing the taught element of the course. Individuals progressed to take advantage of follow-up support offered to them in the form of mentoring, 'ask the experts' and 'business awareness' sessions which was followed by (to date) 32% of learners starting their own enterprise and overall, 67% progressing to a positive destination (self-employment, further study or other enterprise activity).

The project was available both to people who have a long-term health condition and those who have a disability. 74% of completers described themselves as having a disability. A slightly higher percentage (81%) of these individuals had been long-term unemployed or economically inactive (12 months or more). 62% of this group reached positive destinations, with over 32% starting their own business.

In a short space of time the learners have made astounding progress; of the beneficiaries who did start their own enterprises over 78% had previously been long-term unemployed or economically inactive as were over 82% of those who went on to pursue accredited study or further training. 63% of learners who gained either part, full-time or voluntary employment had also been long-term unemployed or economically inactive before joining the *Amaze Yourself* Project. Beyond statistical detail of these outcomes are the life changes the individuals have seen – from joining the project as someone who was unemployed with a long-term health condition or disability to leaving reconnected to mainstream services and activities such as job searching and volunteering.

Evaluation for Leeds City Council: Eldwick Research Associates

Interview respondents described how they 'didn't expect to come this far.' They valued being guided to 'where to go next,' 'I can see where I am going,' 'the course gave me focus,' 'I felt valued as a person, not just an output target,' 'it gave me courage,' and 'consolidated my ideas.' 'In May I was in hospital and in July I was standing up in front of a group of people presenting a new model at Leeds University. There was no other way I could have done that except through Amaze.'

A number of Stakeholders emphasised the difficulties faced by the Amaze client group and the enormous distance that some needed to travel. The OR [Osmondthorpe Resource Centre; see case study] explained that their group 'have developed their skills so much they may not need our support soon.' The group had 'ownership of the project and had set up a stall at Mosaic, a Sunday market, and had started selling their products.' 'If you would have said at the beginning of the programme, that you will be running your own market stall in the middle of Leeds they would have run a mile, but this is the ultimate in success.'

Current circumstances

In Britain there are currently 2.64 million people claiming Incapacity Benefit (IB) at a cost of £12.5bn in 2006-07 (DWP 2007). The most common health issues cited by people claiming IB are depression, stress and anxiety and musculo-skeletal conditions. According to a recent study, IB claimants were twice as likely as the general population to have no academic or vocational qualifications. (DWP 2007).

Long-term claimants face the greatest barriers to employment. In a survey conducted by the Chartered Institute of Personnel and

Development in 2005 it was revealed that one in three employers deliberately exclude people with a history of long-term sickness or incapacity when recruiting staff. (CIPD 2006).

However, Government Ministers estimate that a million claimants would like to work given sufficient help and support and that nine out of ten people coming on to IB expect to get back to work quickly. (The Secretary of State for Work and Pensions (Alan Johnson): Hansard, 2 Feb 2005: Column 842).

The issue of welfare reform is a politically sensitive one, however the current Government is undertaking significant reforms to the system, including IB. The aim is to achieve an 80 % employment rate for people of working age including reducing the number of IB claimants by one million (DWP 2006). The previously piloted Pathways to Work programme, with its mandatory work focused interviews and programmes to support people in preparing to work, will be rolled out across the country by April 2008.

Moreover, the Welfare Reform Act 2007 creates a new Employment and Support Allowance which will replace IB and income support paid due to incapacity from October 2008, initially for new claimants but this will apply to existing claimants in the coming years.

At the same time a new eligibility test, the Work Capability Assessment, will also be applied to those claiming the new allowance. Unlike the old assessment, the Work Capability Assessment focuses on what an individual can do rather what they cannot do. It is estimated that 50% of those who take the assessment will not pass it, meaning 20,000 people a year will not enter the sickness benefits system (DWP press release 19/11/07) and will require assistance and support to determine and achieve their ambitions.

Impact of the *Amaze Yourself* project

Learners with health conditions in the region have been successfully supported to move to employment, self-employment, further study and social inclusion, but the success of the model is not exclusive to the beneficiary group, higher level skills training or regional setting. The model of delivery has demonstrated a flexibility which could be transferred to other groups facing multiple disadvantages in the labour market. It is adaptable for learners who require lower level skills training, or for those who have additional requirements (see the ORC case study in appendix C).

Equally important is the distance travelled of those learners who have been inspired to reconnect with society through becoming involved in mainstream services and who have achieved social inclusion. By using aspiration raising and confidence building techniques, the model is an effective tool in re-engaging with individuals distant from the labour market.

Evaluation for Leeds City Council: Eldwick Research Associates

Impact and achievement
Partners such as Jobcentre Plus, Shawtrust, Leeds City Council Jobs and Skills 'relied on the programme, as there was nothing else like it,' and it has become an important option in terms of the effectiveness of their activities for clients.

Forward Plan

The *Amaze Yourself* project at the University of Leeds ended with the cessation of funding. As is often the case with short-term funding, partnerships and projects are lost. Whilst the support of people with long term health conditions, IB support and enterprise remain amongst the highest on the Government's agenda, this does not necessarily translate into continuation ESF funding.

The greatest hurdle to long term sustainability is the lack of coordinated funding across organisations who have their own short term priorities and outputs. There is a clear economic business case for the project in that it has successfully moved large numbers of people from IB to self-employment and consequently reduced the benefits burden on the state as well as generating tax income from new enterprises. Unfortunately no single agency has a remit or responsibility for both benefit reduction and tax generation and therefore the long-term sustainability is lost between two different priority areas. Only with long-term planning and integrated agency working can projects such as this clearly deliver this collective benefit. Short-term outputs of partner agencies make longer term planning a secondary concern.

The University of Leeds therefore continues to seek external funding to try and embed this programme as best practice in economic regeneration, as well as skills development, reducing worklessness and raising aspirations.

Evaluation for Leeds City Council: Eldwick Research Associates

Partners were unanimous that Amaze fills a niche in the market and there is no suitable alternative and this programme should at the very least be funded in its current form, but has significant transferability potential and could be applied to other target groups and programmes cross city.

Appendix A

Partnership Profile
The project was delivered by a partnership of six universities and one further education college and included:
 The University of Bradford (lead partner).
 The University of Huddersfield.
 The University of Hull.
 Joseph Priestley College.
 Leeds Metropolitan University.
 The University of Leeds.
 The University of York.

Partnership Target Group
 Unemployed.
 Economically inactive.
 Working or in education/training for less than 16 hours a week.

Priority Groups Across the Partnership

Long-term unemployed.
Young people.
Women.
Older workers 50+.
Inner city communities.
Rural residents.
Ethnic minority communities.

Appendix B

Course Delivery

Course structure
Adaptability in delivery methods has been a feature of our work to ensure that the beneficiaries are supported in the most appropriate ways. The training package is comprised of the following main components:

Taught course
The first part of the package delivered training at the University of Leeds using workshops and seminars for a group of around ten to fifteen people. Teaching days involved both group working and individual learning elements. Both university staff and external business professionals delivered modules such as market research, marketing and promotion, networking, business planning, presentation skills, using information technology, direction finding and personal skills development.

Teaching was generally three days per week over two weeks. The course was free of charge and included a complementary lunch. Travel expenses were also reimbursed and course materials provided.   On completion of the course learners were entitled to apply for a small grant (up to £250) to assist them in setting up their business, accessing further study or finding employment.

Business experience
The second part of the package provided business update, or 'ask the experts' days, organised for people to communicate with external business professionals from a broad range of occupations. These two way sessions informed learners of recent business developments and helped to bring skills and knowledge up to date through a two way exchange of knowledge and personal experiences between learner and business professionals.

Mentoring
The third part of the package, mentoring, was offered on a regular basis. Both group and individual mentoring sessions were available, which helped learners to maintain their enthusiasm and direction on completion of the course.

Appendix C
Case Studies

Philip
Philip was referred to the *Amaze Yourself* Project by Shaw Trust and Job Centre Plus in March 2007; prior to this he had been unemployed for over 16 months. Philip was keen to be his own boss as he wanted to be independent from benefits, but did not feel able to return to his previous occupation. He had considered setting up a business before and joined the course in order to pursue this goal and to gain more skills. He found the CV workshop particularly useful as he had had no need to market his skills for 7 years. The course helped to sharpen his ideas about his business plan and showed him how to market his business.

Philip used the mentoring available to the students to discuss the direction his business should take. As a result he decided to register for test trading with Job Centre Plus to see if his business idea was viable without affecting his benefit.

Since the course Philip has set up his own coaching and training enterprise; he offers courses in conflict management and negotiation skills which he has already presented in schools, to voluntary sector organisations and private sector companies. This utilises skills gained in his previous work experience of 20 years as a mental health manager and consultant.

Philip recently presented one of only ten new business ideas in Leeds to win a place on Enterprise Island, (a national enterprise competition) and is currently involved in several projects aiming to promote entrepreneurialism in economically deprived parts of Leeds; he is also currently undertaking an MSc in Regeneration at Bradford University.

He has put his skills to good use by deciding to jointly set up and support (on a voluntary basis) a new peer support network for others who took part in the *Amaze Yourself* partnership training. Conscious that learning and being with others in a similar situation was the experience that motivated him to develop his business idea and help his progression, the network will provide the same support to others. Targeting over 200 learners initially, the network will provide a platform for others who want to go on to set up their own business, go on to further study or go in to employment.

Osmondthorpe Resource Centre 'Ozzie Wooden Tops'
An outstanding example of beneficiary achievement came through partnership working with Osmondthorpe Resource Centre (ORC), Leeds; ORC predominantly provides care and support to people with acquired head injuries and aims to support them back to a life of independence from the centre. Service users on a beginner's woodwork course run by the Workers Educational Association accepted the proposal from the *Amaze Yourself* project of bespoke enterprise training built around their current skills development.

The result of this partnership has seen a group of 11 service users gain skills, confidence and aspirations at a rate not seen with any previous programmes. The woodwork group (Ozzie Wooden Tops) created their own business and marketing plan, and have secured further funding to move towards becoming sustainable as a small social enterprise, diversifying their garden range and selling their products at a regular arts market.

The individuals in the group have grown in confidence, skills, awareness of their strengths and capabilities, motivation and direction, all as a result of the programme. The project has brought opportunity of choice to the group and supported them to find their own direction. The group have recently won a national award for their lifelong learning.

It is not just the students who have taken part in the *Amaze Yourself* project who have benefited at the Centre; Stuart Simmons, Manager of Osmondthorpe Resource Centre, reported 'The ethos of the whole place is changing. We're thinking about shifting the way we deliver all of our support as a Centre to have more of an enterprise based approach leading to increased service user independence. Moving away from 'doing for the sake of it' to doing for a purpose has motivated our eleven service users and developed them in their rehabilitation amazingly'.

References

Department for Work & Pensions Quarterly Statistical Summary, November 2007; *Work is good for you: new medical test to assess work capability - Hain*, DWP press release 19/11/07.

Kemp, Peter A., and Davidson, Jacqueline (2007) *Routes onto Incapacity Benefit: Findings from a survey of recent claimants*. DWP Research Report No 469.

Incapacity Benefit Reform: Why it is Needed and How to Engage Employers, (2006) CIPD.

A new deal for welfare: Empowering people to work, (2006) DWP.

Towards an Inclusive Higher Education: Crossing the Boundaries of Research Traditions in Widening Participation and Student Diversity

Jenny Shaw, Yorkshire & Humber East Lifelong Learning Network

Introduction

Widening participation (WP) in the UK and student diversity in the US appear to be running on parallel tracks despite having the same broad ends. In this paper I explore literature from both countries to highlight the similarities and differences, concluding with a number of lessons that may be learned by the UK from experiences, research and practice in the US. At a fundamental level, the problem may be framed as one of privilege, tradition and hierarchy in terms both of the reproduction of patterns of privilege, and conceptions of 'legitimate' or 'valid' culture and knowledge. In seeking to challenge this status quo, I argue, ideas around diversity and difference drawn from postmodernist philosophies seem likely to bring about more profound and effective change than current WP approaches which appear to be modernist in their origin.

The UK: WP and the skills agenda

Educational policy in the UK is currently dominated by a discourse around 'skills', which increasingly presents the concept of a future crisis in the UK economy from a combination of an aging population, competition from emerging economies and the relatively poor educational performance of the UK in comparison with other developed nations (DfES, 2003b, 2005; Leitch, 2006; DIUS, 2007). More recently there has been a shift in emphasis towards 'high level skills', a level of development, training and/or education covered by the higher education sector (DIUS 2007, 2008). Features of this discourse include an emphasis on lifelong learning, the social and financial benefits to individuals and the need, therefore, for individuals and their employers to 'invest' in such 'skills training'. All of this is being proposed in the name of the 'twin goals of social justice and economic success' (DfES, 2005:1), goals which are also asserted as the rationale behind WP policy (DfES, 2003a, 2003c) For the UK, widening access to the benefits that higher education brings is worth the investment (of the Government, industry and individuals) because knowledge is a commodity and *increasing* the numbers of people able to participate in the knowledge economy has benefits from the individual to the national level. This appears to be a fulfilment of Lyotard's statement that, in the postmodern era, higher education's role is to:

> *Create skills, and no longer ideas...to supply the players capable of acceptably fulfilling their roles at the pragmatic posts required by its institutions* (Lyotard, 1979: 48).

However, flowing from this policy discourse has arisen a set of distinctly modernist responses resting, I would suggest, on a 'metanarrative' of the HE institution as a guardian of legitimate knowledge and culture:

1. 'Raising aspirations' of those who would traditionally 'exclude themselves' from higher education. This rests on an 'academic' model (Shaw et al, 2007; Jones and Thomas, 2005) in which academically selected participants are expected to assimilate within the existing system and adapt to its current norms and practices.

2. Broadening the HE offer through a range of new provision thought to be particularly suited to those currently under-represented in the system. This includes the vocationally oriented Foundation Degrees (England, Wales and Northern Ireland), often offered through Further Education Colleges. This 'differential provision' model (Shaw et al, 2007) effectively allows HE institutions to widen and increase participation with minimal impact on their offer for 'traditional' students.

3.   Review of admissions procedures and practices to ensure that a range of professional, vocational and work based qualifications, and professional experience, are considered as appropriate pre-requisites for degree level study.

Across these interventions, the notion of a nation divided on lines of social class permeates and the relatively low levels of participation among those from lower socio-economic groups is considered to be the most urgent issue.

In parallel with these developments, a body of literature from the academic community in the UK critiques the status quo within higher education from a range of post-structuralist and/or feminist approaches, making explicit the hidden power relations within the existing system.   For the most part this work concentrates on the implications of the current higher education system in terms of the lived experiences of 'non-traditional' participants, frustrated participants and non-participants (West, 1996; Archer and Hutchings, 2000; Reay, 2001; Ball et al, 2002a, 2002b; Archer et al, 2003; Bowl, 2003; Leathwood and O'Connell, 2003; Forsyth and Furlong, 2003; Quinn, 2004; Reay et al, 2005). However with few exceptions (e.g. Thomas, 2002a, 2002b, Gorard et al, 2007) these studies stop short of proposing solutions to the problems they identify.

The US: inclusive higher education

The US drive for inclusivity in higher education and diversification of the student body has strong roots in the civil rights movement (Rudenstein, 2001; Atherton and Adibi, 2008) and race, rather than class, is the dominant issue. Because of the history of racial segregation and the challenges that the US has faced in creating a multicultural society, there are very strong imperatives for embedding multiculturalism and inclusivity across all of society's institution, HE included.   Responses have included affirmative action, and one spin-off of this policy has been a drive to defend and protect affirmative action measures within HE by demonstrating through research that student diversity is not detrimental but in fact positively beneficial to HE's aims and values (Hu and Kuh, 2003; Gurin et al, 2002; Hurtado, 2001; Chang, 2001; Smith and Schonfeld, 2000) . Moreover, this literature seeks not only positive evidence but also useful pedagogic approaches and tools in order to work constructively with the diversity of the student base (Ghere et al, 2007; Aragon and Kose, 2007; Higbee et al, 2007; Higbee et al, 2005, Miksch et al, 2003) . It should be recognised that these are by no means universally adopted and championed, nonetheless where they are they may be said to represent a 'transformative' approach (Shaw et al, 2007; Jones and Thomas, 2005) to managing student diversity in which the mainstream of HE is adapted to meet the requirements of all its current and potential students, in contrast to the 'academic' and 'differential provision' models noted above.

Campus climate

Campus climate is a term that has often been used in the US to refer to the attitudes and beliefs within a HE institution that define it, and that deeply affect the experiences of its different participants. As a theoretical tool by which to gain insight into social issues of actual inclusion and exclusion in the HE system it offers two advantages; firstly that it largely avoids deficit-thinking in relation to groups traditionally experiencing exclusion, and secondly that it concentrates on aspects over which HE institutions have some measure of control. This second aspect contrasts with much of the UK-based policy literature which tends to concentrate on issues of access, thus intensifying largely unhelpful debates about meritocracy and, at times, leading to the conclusion that problems of exclusion and inclusion are located outside the control of HE institutions (see Gorard et al, 2007).

Sylvia Hurtado and her colleagues in a seminal study synthesised all relevant US-based literature to identify four key and interlinked aspects of campus climate. These are:
- Historical legacy of inclusion/exclusion
- Structural diversity
- Psychological climate
- Behavioural climate
    (Hurtado et al 1998, 1999; Milem 2001)

A comparable theoretical framework is absent from the UK literature, though the UK is struggling with issues of class-determined participation in many of the same ways that the US is struggling with ethnic/racial participation. Furthermore the lack of direct evidence of success of UK-based WP programmes is causing significant concern (Guardian, 12th June 2007; Times Higher Education, 28th July 2006). It may be argued that given the huge cultural differences between these two societies, and between the structures of HE in both countries, it is neither possible nor desirable to attempt to import this framework for application to the diversity issues faced by HE institutions in the UK. Nonetheless, a look below the surface of the Hurtado model reveals similarities, in terms of the issues identified, with a number of UK based studies. Therefore I propose that a cautious attempt to map UK research findings to the model will reveal previously neglected aspects of the student experience, and the institution's impact upon it, which may lead to further theoretical and practical insights. This, I contend, is particularly important for the UK given the over-emphasis on access and the instances of deficit-thinking outlined above.

Structural diversity

This is perhaps the most easily dealt with aspect of the campus climate as it refers to the actual diversity of students and staff. In both the US and the UK, this differs considerably between institutions, often linked to historical and/or geographical factors. The three remaining aspects, discussed below, undoubtedly have a strong impact on the structural diversity of an institution, but this interplay works in both directions. It is clear from the US literature that while educational benefits are derived from a diverse student body (Baron et al, 2007; Gurin et al, 2002; Hurtado, 2001; Chang, 2001), structural diversity alone is insufficient to achieve these benefits (Ghere et al, 2007; Higbee et al, 2007; Smith and Schonfeld, 2000). Rather, the psychological and particularly behavioural climate are key not only to achieving a diverse student body but also to maintaining it.

Historical legacy of inclusion/exclusion

This aspect focuses on the historical track record of an institution in relation to inclusion and exclusion and, associated with this, its mission and its policies. Within the US this has clear links to 'resistance to desegregation' (Hurtado et al, 1999) and therefore the reputations of institutions as being hostile towards or welcoming of 'students of color'. In the UK, and elsewhere, it may be applied more broadly to the widely acknowledged stratification of the HE sector (for example Reay et al, 2005; Bowl, 2003; Hutchings and Archer, 2001). In part this may be linked to strongly held conceptions of meritocracy, both within HE institutions and more broadly in certain parts of society. Meritocrats 'suggest that university should be open to all those of a certain perceived ability, irrespective of their social background' (Sheeran et al, 2007: 252). This notion, as Harland Bloland has argued, is a profoundly modernist idea in a world that is becoming postmodern (Bloland, 1995). As Liz Thomas has argued, 'meritocracy largely fails to deliver equality in education, because it does not take account of the underlying causes of educational success and underachievement' (Thomas, 2002:76). A stark example of this was uncovered by Sheila Riddell and her colleagues who found that within some 'old' (i.e. traditionally 'high ranking') institutions in the UK, many academics believed that additional support for students with disabilities 'contravened the fundamental values of the university, which was to distribute rewards on the basis of merit' (Riddell et al, 2004:24). As this illustrates, meritocratic (or 'academic') approaches to selection, curriculum offer and learner support are by and large associated with the older, more prestigious institutions (also noted by Sheeran et al, 2007; Thomas, 2002). Recent work in the UK has pointed to a potential though complex link between an institution's history, mission and self-identity, and its success in mainstreaming diversity approaches (Shaw et al, 2007) and there are clear links between public perceptions of HE hierarchy, and class-based patterns of application (Reay et al, 2005; Forsyth and Furlong, 2003; Ball et al, 2002a; 2002b). Thus it may be said that the way in which the institution is socially constructed, both by those within and those without, conspires to maintain perceptions of inclusion or exclusion, and therefore to the decreased likelihood of those from traditionally excluded groups applying, gaining entry to and thriving in any particular institution.

Psychological climate

One clear message from the US literature is that perceptions of racial tension and discrimination differ strongly between different groups (Hurtado, 1999). Thus within an institution there may be different, though equally valid, interpretations of the same reality. This may be intensely challenging to HE institutions since 'the modernist idea of community…emphasises that which unites people, smoothes over disruption, and places limits on the depth and intensity of differences' (Bloland, 1995:529). This effect has been identified in numerous studies in the UK. For example work by Diane Reay demonstrates that the experience of HE can threaten the identity of working class mature students, leading to 'a combination of achieving educationally and still being able to be themselves that stops short of transformation' (Reay, 2001:339). This suggests that a working class and an academic identity are to some degree incompatible and that this contradiction must be borne by the individual rather than the institution. Marion Bowl found that even on courses in which challenging discrimination was an explicit curriculum element, such as social and community work, 'black students on these courses reported that their attempts to raise issues of discrimination were either sabotaged or silenced by white students' (Bowl, 2003: 137), linking this to the findings of Michael Apple who contends that 'ideological consensus' is assumed within the US school curriculum (Apple, 1990). This evidence is suggestive of a psychological climate in which difference is tolerated only up to a limited point, and some level of assimilation - or dissimulation - is required.

The psychological climate of an institution, therefore, may be experienced as oppressive by traditionally excluded and minority groups both in the US and the UK. However at present only the US seems willing to make explicit and re-politicise this issue, particularly on racial/ethnic grounds (Apple, 1990). In the UK, despite the studies cited above, this aspect of 'campus climate' has received virtually no policy attention which has undoubtedly had an effect on the behavioural aspects covered below. Furthermore, stereotyping, prejudice and discrimination on the grounds of social class is still socially acceptable in many sections of society and in the popular media. Why are we, then, surprised that progress in ensuring equitable participation in HE for those in lower socio-economic groups has stalled?

Behavioural climate

In addressing the behavioural climate of a HE institution, scholars in the US have sought to answer the question 'what practical measures can be taken to ensure success for a diverse range of students'. Important factors include both social interaction of students (Hu and Kuh, 2003; Gurin et al, 2002; Chang, 2001; Hurtado et al, 1999) and positive measures to address and utilise difference in the classroom (Higbee et al, 2005; Maruyama and Moreno, 2000). This has led to approaches such as Universal Instructional Design, an approach to pedagogy that seeks to take into account the potential needs of all possible students. On the social front, while it acknowledged that there are limits to the influence that can be exerted upon students' leisure hours, nonetheless various measures have been proposed to increase interaction across racial and cultural boundaries. These include constructing diverse study or project groups, increasing the number of diversity-focused social events, organising student housing to encourage interactions among diverse peers, and explicitly including diversity issues in the curriculum. George Kuh and colleagues propose an overarching concept of the 'involving college' which involves itself in and promotes positive social interactions among students, while maintaining high expectations of all students and promoting multiculturalism (Kuh et al, 1991).

Within the UK widening participation literature some attention has been given to the 'adaptations' that may need to be made to curriculum in order to enable a more diverse student body to succeed (Parker et al, 2005; Warren, 2002; Powney, 2002). There is a sense of reactivity here, that has been noted elsewhere (Shaw et al, 2007), in that UK HE institutions are tending to address issues of diversity within the curriculum only when they are required to do so by the structural diversity of their actual student body - and sometimes only when the status quo results in financially punishing lowering of retention rates. Furthermore, this strategy is often not adopted centrally within the institution, but rather at the departmental level or even by individual staff.

On the social front, it is a noted phenomenon in the UK system that while the 'traditional' middle-class 18-21 year old student has previously been able to devote him - or herself full time to study and immersion in a student-centred social experience, this model is now largely a thing of the past. A large proportion of students now study at a local institution, and those from lower socio-economic groups tend to be significantly over-represented (Holdsworth, 2006). Moreover, the majority of UK students now undertake some paid work during term time (Moreau and Leathwood, 2006; Curtis and Shani, 2002, Callander and Kemp, 2000), and unsurprisingly the amount of the paid work undertaken tends to be linked to socio-economic status. Many of these studies note the difficulties faced by students in feeling 'involved' with their institution because of these factors, and the impact this may have on academic performance.

Within this UK literature the emphasis appears to be on the role of the student in 'being involved' rather than on the institutions as 'involving', though adaptations may be made to the curriculum in a reactive way in order to support student success. Evidence from the US, however, supports the assertion that planned and centralised approaches to supporting diversity within the curriculum, and to establishing an 'involving' culture, can result in benefits for all students. These benefits may take a number of forms, including enhanced learning and teaching outcomes (e.g. critical thinking skills), employability skills and, perhaps most importantly, helping students to prepare for work in a diverse society.

Campus Climate and Widening Participation

In comparing the two literatures what can we point to as useful lessons in the effort to widen participation, particularly for the UK?

Firstly it seems likely that simply increasing the diversity of the student body is insufficient to widen participation in its fullest sense of allowing a wider demographic of individuals to succeed in higher education. Although this is widely recognised within the UK, particularly in practice, there is still an emphasis on compensatory activities designed to make up for the perceived deficits of individuals from particular groups or backgrounds. Thus an 'academic' model prevails and the concept of change within the higher education system remains a fairly marginal debate (see for example Taylor and Bedford, 2004:390). A stronger emphasis on the psychological and behavioural aspects of diversity within UK HEIs may help to address some of the difficulties currently faced in encouraging applicants from a more diverse social group, and to ensuring their success within HE. Work in the US suggests that a wider range of tools and techniques may be available than are currently being used in the UK and it would seem a useful way forward to evaluate these for use (with suitable adaptation) in the UK HE system.

Secondly, the concept of using and building on the diversity of the student body in a positive way appears only weakly recognised in the UK. Research from the US suggests that this may represent a missed opportunity for the academic and future professional development of all students who may benefit from a more proactive approach to managed diversity both within and outside of the curriculum. Again, putting this into practice is likely to draw on a number of techniques and approaches not widely used in the UK, and careful research would be needed in order to gauge the effectiveness of such approaches on a variety of outcomes in the UK context. However there is some cause to believe that there would be strong gains to be made in preparing students for employment in a diverse society in a way that would help to meet the wider goals of UK society (Jones and Thomas, 2005; Langlands, 2005). Furthermore the US literature suggests strongly that academic outcomes such as enhanced critical thinking skills may also result from such an approach.

Finally, we may say that history and tradition matter, though in ways that may seem to be counter-intuitive. As Ted Nunan and his colleagues have pointed out, commonly held perception of 'excellence' in higher education can lead to the conclusion that diversity is threatening to 'high standards', something to be avoided or mitigated (Nunan et al, 2000). For higher education, excellence is traditionally based on exclusivity and tight controls on what constitutes valid knowledge.

HEIs in the UK outside of the recognised 'elite' have an opportunity to propose and market their own definition of excellence, which often draws on their history of inclusion (Shaw et al, 2007), and may incorporate aspects such as approachability, supporting student success, a welcoming environment and so on that are core to a diversity management approach. Moreover institutions may choose to enhance their distinctive market niche by specialising in subject areas considered to be associated with less privileged groups in society. These may range from women's studies and black studies to media and popular culture, and 'lower status' vocational programmes such as construction or retail.

Although this is currently linked to the stratification of the UK HE system, there are signs that such distinctions may be beginning to break down. The whole concept of legitimate or privileged knowledge is being seriously challenged on a broader basis by postmodernist approaches particularly those driven by societal shifts such as a move to globalisation. In a global society it is much more difficult to point to a single 'truth' or 'standard' and as working with multiple truths and realities becomes more entrenched in daily life so it is likely to affect societies institutions, including HE. This is surely good news for those who support the principles of WP and diversity which at heart are fundamentally postmodern projects. The only problem appears to be that, in the UK at least, they are currently being addressed by broadly modernist approaches which if left unchecked are likely to limit their effectiveness.

References

Apple, M. (1990) *Ideology and Curriculum.* London: Routledge

Archer, L., Hutchings, M., and Ross, A. (2003) *Higher education and Social Class: Issues of exclusion and inclusion.* London: Routledge/Falmer.

Archer, L., and Hutchings, M. (2000) 'Bettering Yourself? Discourses of risk, cost and benefit in ethnically diverse, young working-class non-participants' constructions of higher education'. *British Journal of Sociology of Education* 21 (4) pp.555-74.

Atherton G. and S. Adibi (2008) 'The politics of access: comparing national widening access strategies in the UK and USA'. Paper presented at 'Neither a Moment nor a Mind to Waste' Conference, 6-8 April, Toronto, Canada.

Ball, S. J., Davies J., David, M., and Reay D. (2002a) 'Classification and Judgement: social class and the cognitive structures of choice of Higher Education'. *British Journal of Sociology of Education* 23 (1) pp.51-72.

Ball, S. J., Reay, D., and David, M. (2002b) 'Ethnic choosing: minority ethnic students, social class and higher education choice'. *Race, Ethnicity and Education* 5: pp.333-57.

Barron, R., Pieper, J., Lee T., Nantharath, P., Higbee, J.L., and Schultz J. (2007) 'Diversity and the Postsecondary Experience: Students Give Voice to Their Perspectives'. In Higbee, J.L., Lundell, D.B., and Duranczyk, I.M. (eds) *Diversity and the Postsecondary Experience,* pp. 37-48. Minnesota : Centre for Research on Developmental Education and Urban Literacy.

Bowl, M. (2003) *Non-traditional entrants to higher education: 'They talk about people like me'* .Stoke on Trent: Trentham Books

Bloland, H. G. (2005) 'Whatever happened to postmodernism in higher education: No requiem for the new millennium'. *Journal of Higher Education* 76 (2) pp.121-50.

Bloland, H. G. (1995) 'Postmodernism and Higher Education'. *Journal of Higher Education* 66 (5) pp.521-59.

Callender, C., and Kemp, M. (2000) *Changing student finances: income, expenditure and the take-up of student loans among full - and part-time higher education students in 1998/1999.* London: Department for Education and Employment.

Chang M. L.(2001) 'The Positive Educational Effects of Racial Diversity on Campus'. In Orfield, G. (ed.) *Diversity Challenged: Evidence on the Impact of Affirmative Action,* pp.175-86. Cambridge, MA: Harvard Educational Publishing Group.

Curtis, S. and Shani, N. (2002) 'The effect of taking paid employment during term time on students' academic studies'. *Journal of Further and Higher Education* 26 (1) pp.129-38.

Department for Education and Skills (2003a) *The Future of Higher Education.* London: The Stationery Office.

Department for Education and Skills (2003b) *21ˢᵗ Century Skills: Realising our potential.* London: The Stationery Office.

Department for Education and Skills (2003c) *Widening Participation in Higher Education.* London: The Stationery Office.

Department for Education and Skills (2005) *Skills: Getting on in business, getting on at work.* London: The Stationery Office.

Department for Innovation, Universities and Skills (2008) *Higher Education at Work - high skills: high value.* Online http://www.dius.gov.uk/consultations/documents/Higher_Education_at_Work.pdf. Accessed 30 April 2008.

Department for Innovation, Universities and Skills (2007) *World Class Skills: Implementing the Leitch review of skills in England.* London: The Stationery Office.

Forsyth, A. and Furlong, A. (2003) 'Access to Higher Education and Disadvantaged Young People'. *British Educational Research Journal* 29 (2) pp.205-25.

Ghere, D. L., Kampsen, A., Duranczyk, I.M., and Christensen, L.L. (2007) 'Adopting and Integrating Multiculturalism: A Closing Assessment of General College'. In, Higbee, J.L., Lundell, D.B., and Duranczyk, I.M. (eds) *Diversity and the Postsecondary Experience.* pp.25-36. Minnesota: Centre for Research on Developmental Education and Urban Literacy.

Gurin, P., Dey, E.L., Hurtado, S., and Gurin, G. (2002) 'Diversity and Higher Education: Theory and Impact on Educational Outcomes'. *Harvard Educational Review* 72, no.3. pp.330-66.

Gorard, S., with Adnett, N., May, H., Slack, K., Smith, E., and Thomas, L. (2007) *Overcoming the barriers to higher education.* Stoke on Trent: Trentham Books.

Higbee, J., Chung, C., and Hsu, L. (2005) 'Enhancing the inclusiveness of first year courses through Universal Instructional Design'. In Duranczyk, I., Higbee, J., and Lundell, D. (eds). *Best Practices of Access and Retention in Higher Education,* pp.13-26. Minnesota: Centre for Research on Developmental Education and Urban Literacy.

Holdsworth, C. (2006) 'Don't you think you're missing out, living at home?': Student experiences and residential transitions. *The Sociological Review* 54 (3) pp. 495-519.

Hu S., and Kuh, G. D. (2003) 'Diversity Experiences and College Student Learning & Personal Development'. *Journal of College Student Development* 44 (3) pp.320-34.

Hurtado, S. (2001) 'Linking Diversity and Educational Purpose: How Diversity Affects the Classroom Environment and Student Development'. In Orfield, G. (ed) *Diversity Challenged: Evidence on the Impact of Affirmative Action.* pp.187-204. Cambridge, MA: Harvard Education Publishing Group.

Hurtado, S, Milem, J, Clayton-Pedersen, A. and Allen, W. (1999) *Enacting Diverse Learning Environments: Improving the Climate for Racial/Ethnic Diversity in Higher Education.* ASHE-ERIC Higher Education Report Vol. 26, No 8. Washington DC: The George Washington University.

Hurtado, S, Milem, J F, Clayton-Pedersen, A. R. & Allen, W. R. (1998) 'Enhancing campus climates for racial/ethnic diversity: Educational policy and practice' *Review of Higher Education* 21 (3) pp.279-302.

Jones, R., and Thomas, L. (2005) 'The 2003 UK Government Higher Education White Paper: a critical assessment of the implications for the access and widening participation agenda'. *Journal of Education Policy* 20 (5) pp.615-30.

Kuh, G. D., Schuh, J. H., Whitt, E. J., and Associates. (1991). *Involving colleges: Successful approaches to fostering student learning and development outside the classroom.* San Francisco, CA: Jossey-Bass.

Langlands, A. (2005). *The Gateways to the Professions Report.* London: DfES.

Leathwood, C., and O'Connell, P. (2003) "'It's a struggle': the construction of the 'new student' in higher education." *Journal of Education Policy* 18, no.6. pp.597-615.

Leitch S. (2006) *Prosperity for all in the global economy: world class skills* London: HM Treasury/The Stationery Office.

Lyotard, J-F. (1979/1984) *The Postmodern Condition: A Report on Knowledge* Manchester: Manchester University Press.

Hutchings, M., and Archer, L. (2001) "'Higher than Einstein': constructions of going to university among working class non-participants". *Research Papers in Education* 16 (1) pp.69-91.

Maher, F., and Tetreault, M. (2007) *Privilege and Diversity in the Academy.* New York/London: Routledge.

Maruyama, G., and Moreno, J. F. (2000) 'University faculty views about the value of diversity of campus and in the classroom' In American Council on Education and American Association of University Professors *Does Diversity Make a Difference? Three Research Studies on Diversity in College Classrooms.* Washington DC: ACE and AAUP.

Metcalf, H. (2003) 'Increasing Inequality in Higher Education: The Role of Term-Time Working' *Oxford Review of Education* 29 (3) pp.315-29.

Milem, J. F (2001) 'Increasing Diversity Benefits: How Campus Climate and Teaching Methods Affect Student Outcomes'. In Orfield G. (ed.) *Diversity Challenged: Evidence on the Impact of Affirmative Action.* Cambridge, MA: Harvard Education Publishing Group.

Moreau, M-P., and Leathwood, C. (2006) 'Balancing paid work and studies: working (-class) students in higher education'. *Studies in Higher Education* 31 (1) pp.23-42.

Parker, S., Naylor P., and Warmington, P. (2005) 'Widening participation in higher education: what can we learn from the ideologies and practices of committed practitioners?' *Journal of Access Policy and Practice* 2 (2) pp.140-60.

Powney, J. (ed.) (2002) *Successful student diversity. Case studies of practice in learning and teaching and widening participation.* HEFCE: 2002/48.

Quinn, J. (2004) 'Understanding working-class "drop-out" from higher education through a sociocultural lens: cultural narratives and local contexts' *International Studies in Sociology of Education* 14 (1) pp.57-74.

Reay, D. (2001) 'Finding or losing yourself?: working-class relationships to education'. *Journal of Education Policy* 16 (4) pp.333-46.

Reay, D., David, M. E., and Ball, S. (2005) *Degrees of Choice: social class, race and gender in higher education.* Stoke on Trent: Trentham Books.

Riddell, S., Tinklin, T., and Wilson, A. (2004) *Disabled students and multiple policy innovations in higher education*, final report to the Economic and Social Research Council. Online www.ces.ed.ac.uk/PDF%20Files/Disability_Report.pdf. Accessed 27 June 2006.

Rudenstein, N. L. (2001) Student Diversity and Higher Learning. In Orfield, G. (ed.) *Diversity Challenged: Evidence on the Impact of Affirmative Action.* pp.31-48. Cambridge, MA: Harvard Educational Publishing Group.

Sheeran, Y., Brown, B.J., and Baker, S. (2007) 'Conflicting philosophies of inclusion: the contestation of knowledge in widening participation'. *London Review of Education* 5 (3) pp.249-63.

Shaw, J., Brain K., Bridger, K., Foreman, J., and Reid I. (2007) *Embedding Widening Participation and Promoting Student Diversity: what can be learned from a business case approach?* York: Higher Education Academy.

Smith, D.G., and Schonfeld, N.B. (2000) 'The benefits of diversity: what the research tells us'. *About Campus* 5, no.5. pp.16-23.

Taylor, J. A., and Bedford, T. (2004) 'Staff perceptions of factors related to non-completion in higher education'. *Studies in Higher Education* 29 (3) pp. 375-94.

The Guardian (2007) '*Aim, shoot...miss again.*' 12th June 2007
Thomas, L. (2002a) 'Student retention in higher education: the role
of institutional habitus'. *Journal of Education Policy* 17 (4) pp.423-
42.

Thomas, L. (2002b) *Widening participation in post-compulsory
education.* London: Continuum.

Times Higher Education (2006) *Tories: £2bn access drive is a
'failure'.* 26th July 2006.

Warren, D. (2002) 'Curriculum Design in a Context of Widening
Participation in Higher Education'. *Arts and Humanities in Higher
Education* 1 (1) pp.85-99.

West, L. (1996) *Beyond fragments: adults, motivation and higher
education, a biographical analysis.* London: Taylor & Francis.

Section Two

Work related learning

Maximising Options: Perceived Meaning And Value Of Vocational Learning

Jim Tate and Arthur Baxter, University of the West of England.

There are perhaps two general ways in which a widening participation activity might be classified as addressing the 'vocational'. One is where the *learners* are identified as vocational learners because they are studying for a qualification which is recognised as being vocational in character, for example BTEC students. The other is where the *activity itself* is identified as being vocational in that it relates specifically to an area of employment, for example an engineering summer school. Interventions targeting vocational *learners* which focus upon a vocational *activity* are mutually complementary and can be readily combined.

However, there are interesting variations in terminology amongst widening participation practitioners. For example, the "vocational" can be understood as being *distinct from* as well as *inclusive of* the "work-based", or the vocational may be limited to studies that qualify the learner in an occupation, as demonstrated in the following quotes from two different practitioners.

> 'The people who are actually employed, like apprentices . . . I would term work-based learners, but I also deal with people in FE Colleges doing BTEC National Diplomas and I would call them vocational learners.'

> '[The new Diplomas] aren't vocational because the thing about a vocational qualification, if they're work-based or work-related, is you can then go and do a job in it. You can go and get a Level 3 National Diploma and then go and be a hairdresser . . . an engineer . . . a business administrator. You couldn't get a Level 3 Diploma and then go and do any of those things . . . you would have lots of information that

would help you on your way but you wouldn't actually be qualified to do that.'

Even where education professionals may feel that they have conceptual clarity in the idea of vocational learning, what do learners understand by the term? How is it that from a group of students on a summer school those taking a 'vocational' BTEC and those taking A-Levels can both think of their progression routes as being vocational, both believe that their choice of route maximises their vocational options, *and both are right*?

Vocational learning is now a prominent part of the education agenda. In its response to the Tomlinson Working Party Report (2004) the Government declared that vocational learning was the main problem inside the English education and training system. Since then pedagogic innovation has repeatedly built a pronounced vocational element into policy change, as with vocational GCSEs, vocational A-Levels, and Foundation Degrees which had input from employers from the design stage.

But what are the learners themselves to make of all this? In the multi-layered contemporary pedagogic world of the vocational, the work-based, the work-related, and exchange-value education-as-commodity, it is worth pausing to consider what learners themselves understand the 'vocational' to be. In this paper we will address this question and the type of value learners place upon vocational study.

Aimhigher Southwest – the Healthcare Summer School

This paper is based primarily on a study conducted with Year 12 students at a four-day, health and social care summer school in July 2007 organised by the Aimhigher Healthcare strand. Quantitative data was derived from 31 questionnaires (16 A-Level students and 15 BTEC students) and qualitative data from 18 interviews conducted in six groups of students, divided by the type of qualification of their current study. Three groups (10 students) were studying for BTEC National diplomas, and three groups (8 students) were taking A-Levels. Quotes below are identified as coming from learners in one of the BTEC groups (B1, B2, B3) or one of the A-Level groups (A1, A2, A3).

The purpose of the study was to compare students who were taking BTEC National diplomas with students who were taking A-Levels. Two themes emerged: (1) How the term 'vocational' may be understood differently by different groups of learners; (2) How students respond differently to the perceived values of vocational learning.

This material has been augmented by interviews conducted with Aimhigher practitioners who are the co-ordinators of 'vocational' strands of Aimhigher activity.

The vocational character of study

It would be wrong to assume that the BTEC students interviewed saw their current course of study as being vocational and that the A-Level students did not. Both career-orientation and higher education (HE) aspiration (84 per cent wanting to go to HE) were common to both groups. We are a long way here from the traditional distinction between education and training (Williams 1961). A-Level students could be very definite about the vocational nature of their choice of courses.

> 'I want to be a midwife so that's where Biology, Psychology and Health and Social Care comes from.' (A2)

> 'I want to be a Physio, and I like doing a lot of sport and knowing what goes on in people's minds and why they do things so that's why I am doing Psychology.'(A2)

> 'A Midwife . . . . I always wanted to do that.' (A1)

In deciding how to progress towards a career in medicine these students had moved from GCSE to A-Levels apparently without considering other options such as BTEC. They suggest the reason for this is that the school had a 'normal' path set out for them (Ball et. al. 2002).

> 'Well, my school goes, sort of, straight into 6th form and A-Levels and so it was the path to follow.' (A3)

> 'And I'm on the same lines really.' (A3)

These students, therefore, might be thought to represent a fairly traditional A-Level student, being aware in general terms of what sort of occupation they might want to go into and how this relates to available university courses and course entry-requirements. They have chosen their A-Levels studies with this in mind.

They also value the way in which A-Levels can leave their progression pathways open, in that it permits them a measure of choice to change their mind at a later date. This appeared to be true even for two students who were taking the AVCE (vocational A-Level). Both of these students were undecided between a job in healthcare and a job in social work.

> 'I definitely wanted to be a Midwife when I came out and I'm now debating between social work and midwifery.' (A1)

> 'And me, so I don't know.' (A1)

It may, therefore, be significant that these students saw the AVCE very much as an A-Level rather than as a vocational course. They had chosen the course for its vocational content, yet denied that it was organised in any way differently from the other A-Levels they were studying.

> *How is it different from the other A-Levels you are doing?*

> 'I did not know it was?' (A1)

> 'I don't think it is.' (A1)

The perceived virtue of the A-Level in keeping the learner's options open can be very marked. One student had a range of A-Levels mostly unrelated to healthcare (German, English, Biology and PE) and her interest in a career in the health professions was more speculative. Her attendance at the summer school was intended to help make up her mind, and it had done so:

> 'I was not sure and I wanted to come to see if I really did want to do it, but I want to be a Science teacher now, because I did the, like, biomedical science workshop today and I found the science behind more interesting than the actual working with the patients, that kind of side of it.' (A1)

In the considerations present in their choice of their course of study the A-Level students can be seen to be making a vocationally informed choice. They choose the subjects which will enable them to move to the next stage, university, on the way to achieving their career-goals.

But courses of study can be vocational in more than one sense. Whereas the vocational aspect for the A-Level students seemed to be understood more in terms of acquiring the qualifications that will enable them to progress one step closer to their subsequent career, the BTEC students understood the vocational aspect of their study in more immediate terms of hands-on work-experience through – for example - placements. They wanted courses which are vocational in a deeper sense of being directly work-related, offering them contact with the work environment throughout the course.

As a result, the students taking the BTEC National Diploma generally displayed very positive attitudes to their courses. Not only was their general preference for assessment by coursework rather than the more traditional academic exam, but they viewed the BTEC as superior to the A-Level in meeting their career-progression needs.

> 'I thought doing a BTEC is, like, more relevant to what we want to do than A-Levels.' (B3)

> 'It had work placement, like, every week so you could get out of college. It's not all, like, theory and you know, so you can actually get out and practice there and then.' (B2)

> 'It is kind of both; you kind of get to do practical experience and the written experience . . . .' (B1)

Their preference for hands-on vocational experience was more than merely a matter of personal learning styles. They expressly perceived it as being a desirable asset for the future so that having a variety of work placements was seen as a strong advantage of the BTEC.

> 'It is better than doing A-Levels because you actually get vocational experience as well and, like on, when you apply for University they like to know you have had experience working with people as well as doing that written documents.' (B1)

As these comments suggest, the BTEC students had much more to say about the vocational character of their courses than did the A-Level students. They were much more interested in how their course prepared them directly for a particular job or choice of jobs and in contrast to the A-Level students they tended to be more firmly decided and narrowly focused in the range of their employment ambitions. When they spoke of career-choice they meant the availability of jobs within that more narrowly-focused area of employment.

> 'It is better, the BTEC, because there is so many opportunities.' (B1)

> 'The course that we do allows us to go into loads of different areas of childcare.' (B3)

On this view, whilst A-level students might be looking for the opportunity to pursue a career in childcare or to change their mind and choose something entirely different, the BTEC students are looking to promote the maximum of opportunities available within the range of health and childcare related employment. In this way they saw the BTEC as being the course of study that kept their future opportunities open because they thought it provided a greater availability of employment choices. For this reason, they spoke explicitly of the BTEC in terms of its superiority over A-Levels.

> 'Yeah, well, my friend's doing A-Level but she has got a limited choice on what she can go on to because, like, our field covers all types of health and social care whereas she is fixing on childcare. So she, it means that she can't go into nursing or social work and . . . .' (B1)

In arguing for the superiority of BTEC the student is applying criteria of value which are to do with the vocational relevance of the course. If the A-Level student does not pursue childcare, then she will have no other healthcare-related options (although, of course, she will have more options outside of healthcare-related careers). This is symptomatic of the way in which the two sets of students seem to understand the term 'vocational' differently.

Interestingly, this means that *both* groups, A-Level and BTEC, felt that *their* choice of qualification was the one that maximises their subsequent options. The perception seems to be that A-Levels involve study of a wider more diverse range of subjects (thereby touching upon a wider range of future study/employment options) whereas the BTEC focuses in more breadth upon a range of study/experience within one vocational area (thereby offering a wider range of future study/employment options within that vocational area).

Use-value and Exchange-value

This argument suggests that A-Level students will be more likely to see their qualification as a credential which is an acknowledgement of transferable skills that may open doors to a variety of jobs. Consequently, they are less concerned as to how closely the specific content of their courses will map onto their future employment. BTEC students, on the other hand, appear to target a more narrowly defined range of occupations and so have a greater concern with the specific content of their courses and how far the content is directly relevant to their target range of occupations. To explore this further we will draw upon the work of Williams (2000) who employs a distinction between the use-value and exchange-value of courses. This is derived from the earlier work of Saunders (Saunders 1993) although, of course, the use of these terms goes back at least as far as Marx. When writing about the development of GNVQ, Williams argues that it was designed;

> . . . *both for its 'exchange' value, the value which is attributed to it in terms of what it can 'buy' the student in the way of entry to higher education institutions (HEIs), and for its 'use' value, the skills and knowledge which employers want and can use.* Williams (2000: 350).

Although they do not use the actual jargon, BTEC interviewees spoke about their courses in a way that we might identify as its use-value. They frequently commented on how relevant or useful aspects of the course are to the needs of specific jobs. They were also aware of the exchange-value of the courses. The value of the BTEC as a qualification for entry into HE does matter to them as the quotes have shown, but it is less to the fore in their comments than is the case with the A-Level students.

Since Williams' concept of use-value is understood here merely in terms of *use to employers*, the use-value is reduced to that which generates the exchange-value that buys a person's way into a job. By contrast, in Marx's original formulation use-value depicted the non-commodified aspects of objects and when we speak of BTEC students' concern that their studies have use-value as well as exchange-value, it is not just in Williams' entirely commodified form of the term. The BTEC students were concerned that their studies have a future *use to themselves* as well as to their future employers; that their experience of study should help them to get ahead in the actual work they must do in their future career.

This reinforces a result found earlier in the Aimhigher Southwest tracking study where some students revealed an instrumental attitude to study at level 4. As one interviewee said:

> *I'd rather have a degree in something . . . that's going to help me in my job, not just a degree that's going to get me a job.* (Tate, J. Hatt, S and Baxter, A. 2006)

The distinction revealed here between use-value to the person herself ('help me in my job') and exchange-value ('get me a job') was similarly apparent in the interviews with the BTEC healthcare students. Whilst this is not a strictly Marxist reading of use-value it is certainly something more than Williams' commodified version. Further, this does not mean, as Williams contends in relation to the development of GNVQ, that utility is not about what education can do for the student but what use it might be to a future employer. Whilst the attitude quoted above is not an endorsement of education for education's sake, there is a definite concern with its *use and benefit to oneself* when in employment, not solely with its use to employers.

Valuing different courses

The BTEC students interviewed emphasised that they had actively and positively chosen the BTEC as opposed to A-Levels. It may be that this is the reason why the BTEC interviewees were more inclined to contrast their courses with A-Levels in order to demonstrate the vocational superiority of their chosen study. The A-Level students did not make such contrasts. The BTEC students had made a choice contrary to the traditional route of GCSE to A-Level to University and perhaps have thereby had to think more about the choices they were making. Moreover, they may have made their choice within a context where their course is thought of as being of lower status than the A-Level, and so they have a desire to justify their choices. Be that as it may, they expressed firm opinions as to the BTEC having greater value to them personally as a qualification than the A-Level, which contrasts with the wider academic context where there is concern about the relative lower status of vocational courses in relation to the traditional A-Level (Connor et. al. 2006).

The interviewees were not unaware of this. It was mentioned in two of the interview groups, once by an A-Level student, once by a BTEC student.

> *'Why do you think you didn't [do BTEC] ?'*

> 'Because, I don't know, but this might sound a bit horrible, but I feel that they are not so intelligent, people who go to college, whereas the intelligent people stay on. I don't know if that's just a view I have but so, I always knew that I was going to go and I thought for me that was the best possible route to get to University.' (A-Level student)

> 'I was thinking about doing A-Levels just because, I find that people like, that if you say you are doing a BTEC, they don't, they look down on you a bit compared with A-Levels. But I believe that if we go to University and we do a childcare course, we have got more experience because we have done it already.' (BTEC student)

It is notable that this student's response to the perception of the low status of BTEC is to offer a reason for its superiority in terms of the advantage she expects to have when studying at university. Another group of BTEC students responded to the question about parity of esteem by pointing out that there were different levels of study within BTEC; implying that this perception of lower esteem might be true of other levels of BTEC but not of their own. They refer to their own course as the highest level which you need "good grades" to get on to. So they are arguing against the view that BTEC is in some way inferior by pointing out the error of treating all BTEC levels as being the same.

> *'What impression do you get about how those qualifications are perceived?'*

'It depends on what, like, GCSEs you get and what sort of level you get on. Because we are on the Level 3 which is, like, the highest one because we got good GCSEs, so I had a choice.' (B2)

This raises one point which is significant to the conclusions of this paper overall, namely that as BTEC students who are sufficiently HE-oriented to be attending an HE summer school, these interviewees are not typical of BTEC students in general. The interviewees themselves pointed this out and observed that many other students on their courses have dropped out:

'But some of them are going to go off and do other things next year, like, probably half our class have quit haven't they?'

'As many as half?'

'Yeah, probably. We did have a big class, though.' [Laughter]

'Now it's, like, just us.' [Laughter]

'. . . they like the practice but they just don't like the writing; they just find it too horrible, too much.'

The fact that these students are, so to speak, the survivors on their course; the ones who have coped with its academic aspects because they got the good GCSE grades and could have chosen to do A-Levels had they wished; the ones who are still interested in university study; may mean that in regard of these particular BTEC students and A-Level students it is not surprising that the similarities between them may be more marked than the differences. Both sets of students share an aspiration to HE that is linked to career-orientation and they made numerous comments which showed that they share common concerns about finance, the competition for university places, and the availability of jobs when they graduate. In this way, our sample of BTEC students may have more in common with our sample of A-Level students than they have with their fellow

BTEC students who are studying at a lower level of BTEC or with those where "half our class have quit". None the less, in regard to the questions that concern this paper as to the meaning of vocational learning, its character and its value, the differences between the two groups of learners provides plenty of food for thought.

References

Ball, S., Davies, J., David, M., and Reay, D. (2002) 'Classification and Judgement: Social Class and the Cognitive Structures of Choice in Higher Education'. *British Journal of Sociology of Education, Vol. 23, No. 1.*

Connor, H., Sinclaire, E., and Banerji, N. (2006) 'Progressing to Higher Education; Vocational Qualifications and Admissions'. *Action on Access: Ormskirk.*

Hatt, S. (2007) *South West Summer Schools Review.* Aimhigher South West.

Saunders, M. (1993) 'TVEI and the National Curriculum: Culture Clash Between Use and Exchange Value', *Evaluation and Research in Education*, 7 (2), pp. 107-115.

Tate, J., Hatt, S., and Baxter, A. (2006) 'You Can't Ask a Leaflet a Question: Relevant Information about HE for Under-Represented Social Groups'. *Journal of Access Policy and Practice* Vol. 3, No. 2. pp.103-118

Williams, S. (2000) 'The Paradox of Assessment: the effectiveness of the GNVQ as a preparation for higher education', *Journal of Education and Work*, Vol.13, No. 3, pp. 349-65.

Williams, R. (1961) *The Long Revolution.* Chatto and Windus.

WhoseSpace? Employer Engagement and Inclusive Education: Are They Unnatural Bedfellows?

Cate Thomas, Kingston University

Introduction

This paper details an initiative at Kingston University to engage Small and Medium Size Enterprise (SME) employers, by providing online work based learning opportunities. The constituency of learners who will be reached are adults with few qualifications, but a wealth of work experience. The Kingston Project uses social constructivist pedagogies and a web 2.0 social networking platform to empower participants to become independent learners who learn partly by engaging in varied Communities of Practice.

The Context

The current UK Government Employer Engagement agenda, as outlined in the Higher Education Funding Council (HEFCE 2006) strategy document, and the inclusion of educationally marginalised learners may not, at first sight, seem natural bedfellows. However in a HEFCE Strategic Development Fund backed Employer Engagement Project, led by Kingston University, the potential for including 'hard to reach' adult returners to Higher Education is being teased out of the agenda. Indeed, if Higher Education is going to tackle the issues raised in the Treasury Report, the *Leitch Review of Skills* (2006), and meet the Leitch review target of 40 % of adults being qualified to level 4 and above by 2020, educationally marginalised learners are an important target group. The review states that more than 70% of the 2020 workforce were, in 2006, already over the age of 16. Therefore, the new Higher Education students of the future, will need to come partly from this constituency.

The Kingston Project

The Kingston initiative is called KUBIS (Kingston University Business Integration with Small and Medium Size Enterprises) and aims to provide learning opportunities at level 4 and above for employees in SMEs. It plans to promote business improvements in participating companies by the education of staff in areas that are highly relevant to SMEs, and in particular manufacturing SMEs. At the same time, it is attractive to adult learners who, although they may not have many formal qualifications, have rich and complex areas of expertise which they have developed through their jobs. Such a programme gives them the tools to validate this expertise, to build on it, and learn new skills.

Much of the educational opportunity will be in accordance with a 'learning through work' model, where learning agreements based on work projects which the learners are undertaking, will be used as a basis for formal learning and accreditation. Learners will not need to take regular chunks of time off from work to travel to the University and attend lectures or tutorials, but instead will be provided with access to tutors and their fellow students via a personalised learning portal.

The learning portal, KubiSpace, forms a vital plank of the pedagogy of the KUBIS project, as discussed in more detail below, under the *WhoseSpace? KubiSpace* sub-heading. In short, it provides a way for learners to have contact with mentors, tutors, other learners in the programme, and with their wider communities of practice. It enables them to find, evaluate and share information, and it provides a structure for the programme of study for everything from preparing the learning contract, to creating online groups of colleagues, to building an online portfolio, to submitting work for assessment and getting feedback, and many other activities in between.

> In the first instance KUBIS will offer qualifications up to Foundation Degree, with a third year exit route for learners wishing to progress to degree level study. Kingston already has a comprehensive workbased learning Masters programme in place, to which learners may progress.

Additionally, early discussion with SME employers supports the findings of the BECTA Literature Review of 2004, that providers should ensure that 'the learning meets specific needs and is not necessarily qualification led', so possible credit bearing stopping off points below the Fd level are also built into the programme.

The Role of Employers

SMEs currently provide 60% of all employment in the UK. This has increased significantly since 2000 with the decline in number and size of large corporations, and indications are that this increase is continuing. However, SMEs typically find that Higher Education Institutions (HEIs) are geared more to working with, and producing graduates for, larger companies both in the practicalities of how courses are delivered, and the typical subject matter of such courses. KUBIS aims to specifically build learning opportunities designed for smaller organisations.

In the early stages of KUBIS, interviews with employers and representative organisations have indicated specific needs. SME employers typically want a number of things from an employee training or education programme: they want it to bring benefit to the company to ensure the employee is more effective in their job role; they need it to be flexible in terms of delivery (as it is difficult for small organisation to lose a member of staff for one day a week over a number of years to attend a University course); and they need it to be relevant to employees' work:

High-quality content that is linked closely to an employee's work tasks and can be accessed when the learner wants are important. (BECTA 2004 : 5).

Cost is more likely to be an issue for smaller companies, so near term benefit for the organisation is important. However, employers are also likely to see providing staff with educational development opportunities as a way of ensuring retention, growing their own managers, with an eye to succession planning. Employers are expected to contribute to student fees, and to provide in kind contribution to the learning. This may be the provision of mentors and facilities for the work.

The role of the mentor is important in the KUBIS model, and is seen as a development opportunity for the mentor, with the option available of following a credit bearing work-based learning mentorship module. The mentor helps the learner by providing advice and information relating to the workplace and sector, and helps to open doors to contacts or information sources which might be helpful. Mentors will have their own online network on KubiSpace where they can share their experience of mentoring, and provide support and information to their mentor peers. This is seen as a valuable professional networking opportunity for mentoring staff. Where companies are too small to provide mentors, organisations such as the Manufacturing Advisory Service (MAS) may be able to enrich the mentoring mix in the online network.

The Learners

Students will be enrolled on this programme for a Spring 2009 start. Early indications are that learners will typically be mature adults with little formal education but significant work experience. Such learners are likely to have financial responsibilities with respect to families and housing, as well as carer responsibilities, which mean that taking time out of work to be a full time student (and accumulating the kind of debt that this implies) is not an option for them. Such learners need to be able to build on the specific expertise they have gained in the workplace to gain academic credit for demonstrating and articulating that expertise in a way that can be demonstrated in terms of an awards framework (Boud, 2001).

The Student Journey

Typically, a learner will start off with a face-to-face taught session where they will meet other learners and their tutors and learn to use the KubiSpace environment. They will then work remotely on taught online elements which are designed to prepare learners without recent experience of formal education, and no experience of online or workbased education, for this programme. They will learn how to locate, evaluate and utilise information from a range of sources, (including the web) how to participate in online communities, and how to design their own learning contract projects. They also look at how their company works, within a broader context, and at their role within that company. When they are sufficiently prepared, and have planned their projects, they then embark on them sequentially. Learners may also choose to follow a range of taught online modules, as part of their overall learning agreement. With the support of their tutor they each design their own programme of study, within a given framework, and review it regularly. Throughout the programme, they may step back and look at their own learning experience and how it affects and relates to their company. This involves keeping a reflective log, the completion of which forms their final piece of work for a Foundation Degree award.

WhoseSpace? KubiSpace

KUBIS has harnessed freely available Web 2.0 technologies (namely Elgg and Drupal) to enable learners to be supported by an online environment that decreases the isolation of being a workbased distance learner. It is this environment that we have called KubiSpace.

Web 2.0 technologies are, broadly speaking, about maximising the potential of the web to allow users to network with others, and to create, share, locate and collaborate on content, rather than being merely consumers of web information. Typical types of technology that are described as 'web 2.0' are wikis, which permit the collaborative construction of webpages, web logs or blogs. Readers can add comments to entries, share peer to peer files (such as Napster) as well as video and photo environments (such as YouTube and Flickr) and last but most famously engage in social networking environments such as MySpace.

Web 2.0 technologies are not yet widely used in Higher Education. They tend to be seen as the 'territory' of children and teenagers, and it has been suggested that university staff, although seeing the potential of such environments for educational use, feel that they are not 'OurSpace' but an arena belonging to the young (Thomas, 2008). However, the potential for using such technologies to support pedagogies which are broadly social constructivist in their approach is enormous. KUBIS has already made inroads in making KubiSpace a site where web 2.0 technologies can be claimed as legitimate home ground by both academic staff and mature adult returners to education.

KubiSpace is designed to be a learner centred environment, with a personalised portal for all learners. Learners have a high degree of control over the look and feel of their portal, can make choices about what's available in it, can create, modify and share content with others, and can choose who has access to any of their content. The various aspects of KubiSpace are outlined below.

Personal Profile
All users have a personal profile, which is what another user will see if they click on that person's name. In their personal profile they post a photo of themselves and any other information that they want to make available to tutors, mentors and fellow learners. This means that, whilst they rarely meet each other, learners have a sense of other people in KubiSpace existing in a 'human' way, as they can see a photo of them, find out what their interests are, and interact with them socially, outside any course related discussions. This 'humanising' of the environment decreases the isolation that can be experience by distance learners and encourages social networking which in turn supports the learners' work on the programme.

The personal profile is also the locus of the learner's portfolio. The portfolio is an area where a learner can keep all their coursework, and anything else they deem relevant. They can organise it as they wish, to ensure they can easily find elements of their work, and can make elements of their portfolio available to whichever audiences they choose. So, for example, a learner might make chosen, finished pieces of work available to their tutor, and work in progress available to peers for comment. Importantly, learners can opt to publish pages of their portfolio to people outside KubiSpace, and so can create a community with those with similar interests who are not connected with the course – and these can be anywhere in the world.

Social Networking
KubiSpace is essentially a social networking environment. Users can choose who their contacts are, and connect to these contacts. For a student, these would be fellow learners, tutors and mentors. They can create shared areas where they can build webpages with colleagues, or share found or created content with others; they can have online discussions using noticeboards or chatrooms, they can send each other private messages or post public messages (they can choose how public) for individuals to see and respond to. This encourages what Bosley and Young (2006) describe as the 'soft underpinning'; the social and affective elements which support a workbased, online programme of study at a distance.

In some of the formal structured learning ,students carry out exercises where they work together and learn from each other, but the social networking aspect of the environment encourages this to continue into the individual learning contract projects which form a substantial part of the programme. Boud's point that collaborative learning can be further consolidated if the 'environment of mutual help…continues over time and beyond the classroom' (Boud, 2001 : 11) is one that very much applies to the pedagogy behind KubiSpace.

Creating Communities of Practice (CoPs)
Lave and Wenger's early work in 1991 on CoPs was based largely on studies of how people learned in workplaces, according to an apprenticeship approach, which they call legitimate peripheral participation. This describes the process by which newcomers to the work group learn more about the work and gradually develop expertise, and then, themselves help to develop newcomers. Educational technology theorists have become interested in CoPs over the last ten years or so, as it describes the ideal situation where students might learn from each other in online environments. However, it is particularly a key concept for KubiSpace, as learners

are in the workplace, learning from colleagues, peers on the programme who work for other companies, and the wider online community. And it is the third area that is a particularly significant addition to the learners' CoP.

Learners on a workbased/distance learning programme, where much of the learning is individually tailored, are not exactly a cohort of one. Rather, they are having a more individualised learning experience than similar learners on a more traditional externally structured and taught distance learning course. They will be carrying out similar activities and preparing similar assignments as their fellow more traditional learners. Many of the kinds of areas that learners will be working on in their projects will be very specific and specialist. The KubiSpace environment, however, offers them tools and skills development to enable them to locate and appropriately utilise sources of information available to them on the web. Importantly, these tools also enable them to make contacts with others who are interested in the same areas. The 'long tail' often referred to in discussion of web 2.0 culture means that there will be online communities available for any area of interest, however specific. For example, a student may work in Basingstoke and be a specialist in a particular method of designing and making sash windows. Whilst there might be only one or two other people in their home town who work in this area, there might be twenty or thirty in the UK and hundreds or thousands in the world. And some of these people will have already created an online CoP, in which the learner can participate.

Structured taught elements
KubiSpace has an area designed for structured taught online distance learning elements, such as the Personal Development Module, where learners start their studies. This has been designed to make it very easy for academic staff to publish content for modules. Staff can create their own content web pages as easily as they can create a wordprocessor document (indeed they can prepare it in a wordprocessor document and paste it into the webpage if they wish). They can easily provide links to discussion areas, where they may have asked learners to debate specific topics, wikis, where they may have set up a space for learners to collaborate, and to other

resources, external or internal to KubiSpace. Staff can also easily change and manipulate the structure of the websites they are creating, all without any technical knowledge. Making it possible for people who do not possess technical skills to become contributors to the web is one of the fundamental principles of web 2.0, and this should apply to university staff as much as it applies to students.

Conclusion

The KUBIS project is carrying out experimental and ground breaking working in providing workbased learning opportunities for adult returners to education, who work in SMEs and will be using social networking software to form local, national and international learning communities. It has become a truism in the educational technology community that when a new online course is set up, learners never use it in exactly the way the creators expected them to. They often do totally unexpected and interesting things that were never anticipated. It remains to be seen how learners will make the KUBIS opportunities their own, and what exactly they will do with them. Given the opportunity and the skills needed to become highly networked independent learners, the possibilities are indeed exciting.

References

BECTA. (2004) *Research into the use of ICT and e-learning for work-based learning in the skills sector.* Coventry, UK: BECTA.

Bosley, S., and Young, D. (2006) 'On-line Learning Dialogues in Learning through Work.' *Journal of Workplace Learning*, Vol. 18, No. 6, pp. 355-66.

Boud, D. (2001) 'Introduction: Making the Move to Peer Learning'. In Boud, D., Cohen, R. and Sampson, J. (eds). *Peer Learning in Higher Education: Learning From and With Each Other*. pp.1–17. London: Kogan Page.

HEFCE (2006) 'HEFCE strategy to support links between higher education and employers on skills and lifelong learning.' Online http://www.hefce.ac.uk/learning/employer/strat/

Lave, J., and Wenger, E. (1991) *Situated Learning: Legitimate Peripheral Participation.* Cambridge: Cambridge University Press, 1991.

Leitch, S. (2006) *Prosperity for all in the Global Economy - world class skills* http://www.hmtreasury.gov.uk./media/6/4/leitch_finalreport051206. pdf

Thomas, C. (2008) 'Cyberacademics or Sidelined Guides? What roles does the educational use of web 2.0 technologies offer to academic staff?' In Graham, D. (ed.) *'e' Teaching and Learning 2008.* Workshop Proceedings, London: University of Greenwich.

The Step-In To HE Project: A report on project activity from September 2007 to July 2008

Suzanne Leech, Step-In to HE Project Leader, Aimhigher Greater Manchester

Introduction

The Step-In to HE Project is an innovative project from Aimhigher Greater Manchester and Greater Manchester Strategic Alliance (GMSA). Aimhigher is a national initiative, organised in sub-regions, to encourage more people primarily from socio-economic groups (NS-SEC) 4-8 to progress to HE. (Groups 4-7 cover small employers and own account workers, lower supervisory and technical occupations, semi-routine occupations and routine occupations and the unemployed). The Greater Manchester Aimhigher has a special strand of activity aimed at promoting progression to HE among work-based and vocational learners. GMSA is the Lifelong Learning Network for Greater Manchester and also aims to encourage more work-based and vocational learners to progress to HE.

During 2007, Aimhigher Greater Manchester and GMSA agreed to work in partnership to develop a new course, later entitled the 'Step-In Module' (SIM), to build the confidence of Advanced Apprentices and other work-based and vocational learners in their ability to progress to HE. The aims of the course were designated as follows:

- To help Advanced Apprentices develop and demonstrate the transferable higher level skills needed for the successful completion of a HE qualification
- To help employers to "grow their own" staff by encouraging more Advanced Apprentices to progress to HE and take vocationally relevant courses, including Foundation Degrees
- To enable Advanced Apprentices to develop their careers and progress within their companies

- To raise the status of vocational learning and to encourage more able young people to take vocational progression routes in future.

In 2006-2007 there were approximately 3,000 Advanced Apprentices in Greater Manchester. Data from the Greater Manchester Learning Provider Network, to which the majority of providers of Advanced Apprenticeships belong, shows that only around 100 Advanced Apprentices are known to have gone on to HE immediately after their Apprenticeship - a progression rate of approximately 3 per cent. Therefore, Aimhigher Greater Manchester and GMSA agreed that Advanced Apprentices should be the first group targeted to benefit from the SIM. It was further agreed that the course should be at Level 4, worth ten credits, delivered over seven weeks and would be validated by the University of Bolton.

The first deliveries of the course were highly successful in bringing about a rate of progression to HE far in excess of the estimated rate referred to above. However the experience also highlighted a need to improve the collection of data on progression to HE by Advanced Apprentices and other groups of work-based and vocational learners.

Delivery centres and course development

Four centres were engaged to deliver the Step-In Module: Bury College, Skills Solutions, Stockport College, and Wigan and Leigh College. All centres have substantial experience of working with Advanced Apprentices and significant experience of delivering at Level 4 and above. Skills Solutions is a work-based learning provider based in central Manchester and the other three partners are Further Education Colleges with some HE provision.

It was agreed, after extensive consultations with Aimhigher Greater Manchester's partner HEIs and SIM delivery centre representatives, that the course should focus on three key skills areas identified as critical for success in HE: research skills, personal development planning and writing techniques relevant to HE study. The two assessment tasks agreed for the course were a personal development log to be completed throughout the course, and a portfolio incorporating a variety of smaller assessment tasks carried out in the classroom or in learners' own time, and ranging across the three skills areas within the course.

In preparation for validation, delivery centre representatives agreed a shared scheme of work, contributed to a common bank of course materials and the Project Leader appointed by Aimhigher Greater Manchester developed course procedures with accompanying documentation.

Project funds were set aside to offer a grant of £100 to those sponsoring Advanced Apprentices to take the Step-In Module, payable on an Apprentice's successful completion of the course: sponsors could be employers or Apprentices themselves. The aim of offering the grants was to act as an added incentive for learners to take and complete the course, thus establishing it as a successful model for progression to HE. However, the course was kept deliberately short not only to avoid study fatigue for learners who may still be completing or have just completed long Apprenticeships, but also to keep the course fee low at £115. Therefore, the relatively low cost of the course and the short time commitment needed to complete it may help the course to become self-sustaining without the grants after the pilot phase of the first two years.

The Project Leader developed detailed data capture pro-formas for the project. Extensive data capture and analysis is central to the Step-In to HE Project, not only to evaluate the effectiveness of the Step-In Module in achieving its aims and reaching the designated target group, but also to offset the lack of available progression data for Advanced Apprentices.

Outcomes and Analysis

Data on starters
From the information submitted by learners in response to the Step-In to HE Advanced Apprentice Starter Questionnaire completed by

all starters on the Step-In Module on the first runs of the course, the following can be identified as significant characteristics of the cohort.

- Of the 36 starters, 20 were male and 16 were female
- 5 of the 36 were aged over 25
- 20 had no immediate family members who went to university
- 12 had finished their Apprenticeships, 19 had Apprenticeships still ongoing and 5 gave no information about this
- Learners had completed or were completing a wide range of Apprenticeships including Administration, Management, Engineering, Customer Service, IT, Motor Vehicle Mechanics, Childcare, Health and Social Care, Hairdressing, Electrical Installation, Heating, Plumbing and Housing
- 13 learners (36 per cent) had their course fees paid by employer.

The male to female ratio of the cohort is more balanced than is typical among Advanced Apprentices: DIUS's recent report "World Class Apprenticeships: Unlocking Talent, Building Skills for All", states that 70 per cent of Advanced Apprentices are male. The report also notes that certain sectors of employment tend to be primarily female and any Apprenticeships associated with them tend also to be mainly female (2008: 46). The occupations of the female learners in the cohort bore this out with female job roles being confined to Administration, Management, Customer Service, Childcare, Health and Social Care, Hairdressing and Housing.

Learners in the cohort were typically aged 20-24. Of the learners who were still completing their Apprenticeships, several had only a matter of months until their frameworks were completed. The proportion of learners who had their course fees paid by their employers was rather higher than expected for this first cohort bearing in mind the difficulties often reported with regard to gaining a commitment to paying fees by employers. However, 8 of the 13 learners concerned were employed by the delivery centre where they were studying, so this may account for this early success in encouraging the payment of fees by employers.

Reasons for participation

Fig 1 Please rate how important the following considerations were to you in deciding to take the Step-In module

Respondents Saying consideration was Important or Very Important

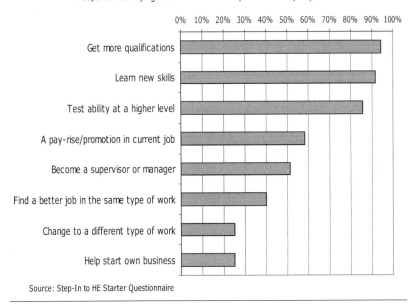

Source: Step-In to HE Starter Questionnaire

At the beginning of the course from among the 36 starters:

- 50 per cent of learners rated becoming a supervisor or manager as very important or important (Fig 1)
- 58 per cent of learners rated getting promotion as very important or important (Fig 1)
- 83 per cent of learners rated the opportunity of testing their ability at higher level as very important or important (Fig 1)

- 92 per cent of learners rated both getting more qualifications and learning new skills as very important or important (Fig 1).
- 31 per cent strongly agreed or agreed that they had always planned to go on to HE (Fig 2)
- 80 per cent knew nothing or a little of the range of HE courses, of career opportunities open to them after HE, of costs, of courses most useful to job or of the support available (Fig 3)

Fig 2 Agreement with the Statement: I always Planned to Go to HE...

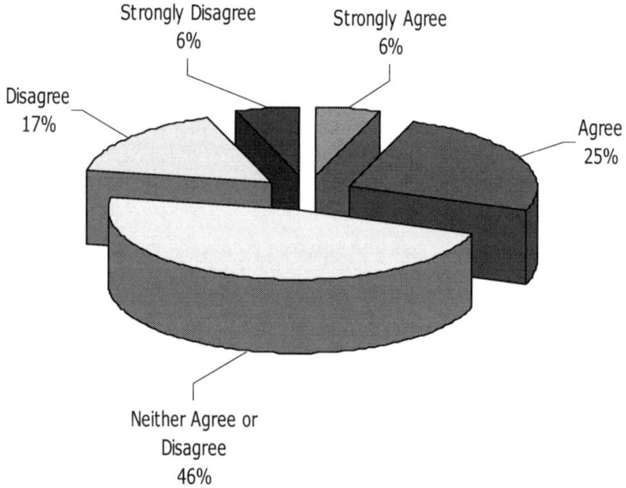

Source: Step-In to HE Starters Questionnaire

The proportion of learners who strongly agreed or agreed that they had always planned to go on to HE was higher than might be expected for Advanced Apprentices as actual progression to HE for this group appears markedly low (see above). However, it may be that the percentage of learners who had always planned to go on to HE illustrates the gap between Advanced Apprentices' aspirations and the level of practical encouragement they usually receive to progress to HE. The percentages of learners who strongly agreed or agreed that getting more qualifications, learning new skills and testing their ability at a higher level is important also suggests that, given the opportunity, many Advanced Apprentices demonstrate a strong level of interest in progression to HE.

Fig 3 What do you currently know about the following...

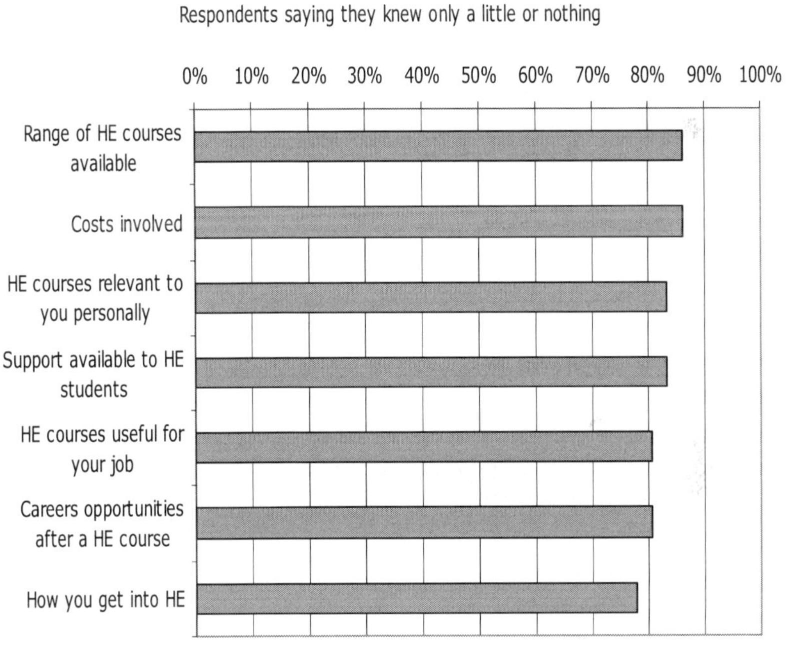

Respondents saying they knew only a little or nothing

Source: Step-In to HE Starter Questionnaire

Data on completers

Of the 36 learners who started the Step-In Module in April-May 2008, 32 completed the course successfully and had their course outcomes confirmed at the first Assessment Board for the Step-In Module at the University of Bolton in July 2008. Therefore, the level, content and modes of delivery and assessment appear to have been well suited to the target group. All of the 32 learners who had completed the course successfully by July 2008 completed the Step-

In to HE Completers' Questionnaire from which the following data is derived.

Fig 4 Which of the following do you agree with...

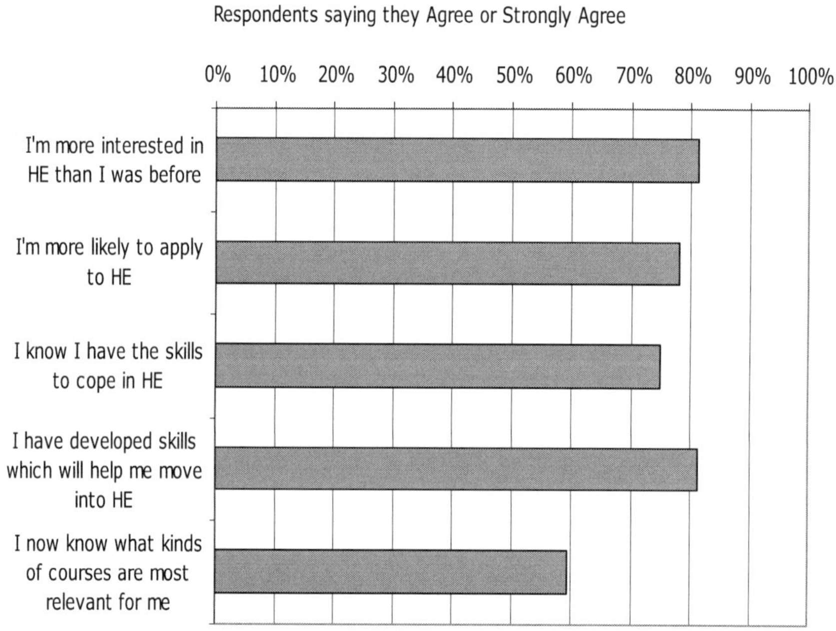

Respondents saying they Agree or Strongly Agree

Source: Step-In to HE Completers Questionnaire

At the end of the course from among the 32 completers –

- 75 per cent of learners strongly agreed or agreed that they had developed skills to cope successfully with HE study (Fig 4)
- 78 per cent of learners strongly agreed or agreed that they were more likely to apply to HE than before (Fig 4)
- 81 per cent of learners strongly agreed or agreed that they were more interested in HE than before (Fig 4)

- 78 per cent of learners strongly agreed or agreed that they knew more about HE could be useful for their careers (Fig 5)
- 75 per cent of learners were very or quite confident that they would be accepted into HE if they applied (Fig 6)

Fig 5 Agreement with Statements about HE

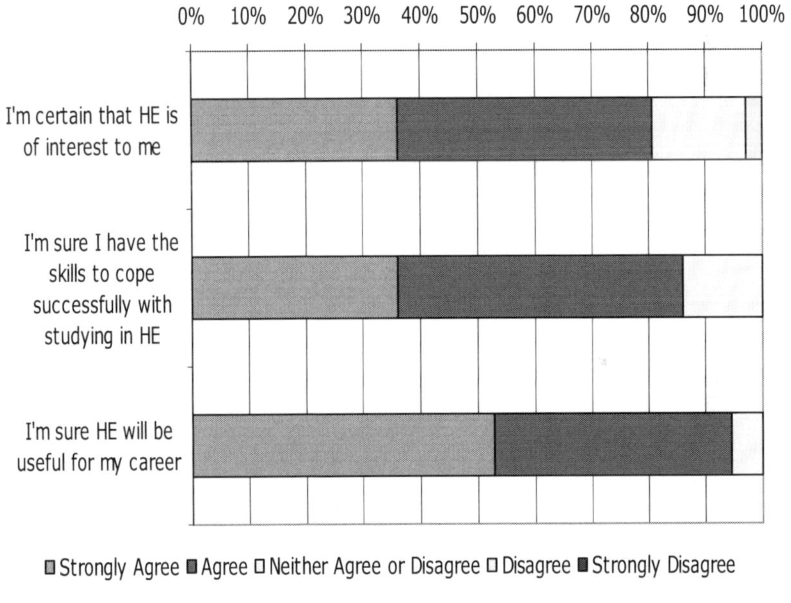

Source: Step-In to HE Starters Questionnaire

The deficit of knowledge concerning HE among the cohort which is noted above appears to have been addressed with a considerable measure of success by the end of the course. Some 75 per cent of learners rated their knowledge of how to get into HE as very good or good, and 78 per cent strongly agreed or agreed that they knew more about how HE could be useful for their careers than at the beginning of the course. The level of confidence learners showed in the likelihood that they would be accepted into HE if they applied therefore appears to be justified and supported by practical skills for coping with HE successfully.

Fig 6 How confident are you that if you apply to HE you will be accepted?

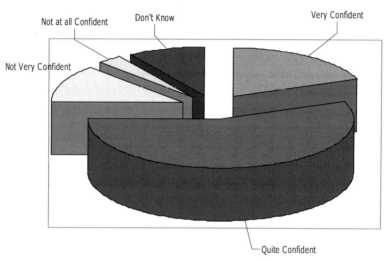

Source: Step-In to HE Completers Questionnaire

Progression to HE

12 of the 32 learners who completed the course expressed the intention to progress to HE immediately and their intended destinations for September 2008 were as follows.

No of learners	Course/s	Institution/s
1	HND in Business	Bury College
1	HNC/HND (subject not stated)	Bury College
1	Cert Ed	Stockport College
1	HNC (subject not stated)	Stockport College
1	FD in Early Years	Skills Solutions
1	CPD (Leadership and Management)	Skills Solutions

1	Management	Skills Solutions/University of Derby
1	HNC in Mechanical Engineering	Wigan and Leigh College
1	HNC in Electrical Engineering	Wigan and Leigh College
1	Executive Diploma in Management	Wigan and Leigh College
1	HNC in Electrical/Electronic Engineering	Wigan and Leigh College or St Helen's College
1	FD in Business and IT	MMU

The above destinations include:

- 11 applications for HE courses at Step-In Module delivery centres
- one application for a course elsewhere in Greater Manchester
- one application for a course outside Greater Manchester.

Thus 38 per cent of learners who completed the course intend to progress to HE immediately. One learner is interested in progressing to a full time course but all other learners are interested in part-time study.

A further 13 learners who completed the course expressed the intention to progress to HE within the next 1-2 years and their intended destinations are as follows.

No of learners	Course/s	Institution/s
1	HNC/HND Business	Bury College or MMU or University of Bolton
1	HNC (subject not stated)	University of Bolton
1	HNC/HND (subject not stated)	MMU or University of Bolton
1	HNC or FD in Construction/Property	Stockport College or University of Salford
1	Motor Mechanics	University of Sheffield
1	Surveying	Undecided
1	CPD or FD in Management	Skills Solutions or other HEI
1	FD in Management	Skills Solutions
5	Undecided	Undecided

The above destinations include:

- four potential applications for HE courses at Step-In Module delivery centres
- five potential applications for courses elsewhere in Greater Manchester
- one potential application for a course outside Greater Manchester.

Consequently, 41 per cent of learners who completed the course intend to progress to HE within the next one to two years, meaning that 79 per cent of all completers expressed the intention to progress to HE either immediately or within the next one to two years. This rate of progression compares very favourably with other data available on Advanced Apprentices' rate of progression to HE as described in the Introduction. Where learners cited a specific reason for applying to HE, the most popular reason was to improve prospects (cited by 16 learners). There is, therefore, a significant link between progression to HE and improved career and earning potential in the perceptions of Advanced Apprentices.

The remaining seven learners who completed the course stated that they will probably not apply to HE in the near future. Where learners cited specific reasons preventing them from applying to HE, the most common reasons were the cost of further study and lack of time, either because of home and personal commitments, or because employers are unwilling to give time away from work for study. These reasons underline the difficulties faced by part-time, work-based learners trying to juggle work, study and home commitments, particularly where employers are unwilling or unable to contribute to the costs of work-related study or allow time away from work for study.

Successes and lessons learnt from the first course delivery

Delivery centre representatives completed the Step-In to HE Provider Questionnaire to evaluate their first course runs. There were many successes noted in these evaluations, but also some issues to follow up and lessons to be learned. Successes included:

- The scheme of work was found to be useful by all tutors
- The common bank of materials was found to be useful by all tutors
- The identification of a theme or goal around which to base course activity was found to be very helpful where applied
- A general introduction to HE early in the course, including types of courses available and finance for part-time learners, was found to be useful

Overall, the partnership established between the delivery centres was key to the project's success in developing the course, validating it and recruiting to it within the short timescale of seven months. The partnership approach helped enormously in finding solutions to practical problems as they arose. The partnership has also been very helpful in developing a standardised approach to the course aided by the common course materials

Lessons learned from the first course delivery included:

- Building in more guidance for learners on the development of reflective practice to be included in their personal development logs
- Agreeing speedier procedures for registration at the University of Bolton
- Incorporating a visit to the University of Bolton in the course
- Establishing procedures for referring potential Step-In learners from work-based learning teams to HE teams within delivery centres.

The next phase of development

Plans for the further development of the Step-In to HE Project from August 2008 - July 2009 encompass a significant increase in the number of Advanced Apprentices taking the Step-In Module; the expansion of the targeting of the project to include other specified groups of work-based and vocational learners; and plans to widen the scope of recruitment to all Greater Manchester boroughs.

Numbers targeted during 2008-2009 will be 200 Advanced Apprentices and 100 adults. Adult learners will include work-based learners identified via employer engagement, vocational learners taking Level 3 qualifications and trade union learners.   The project will prioritise learners from occupational areas where there are currently little progression to HE or issues associated with progressing to HE: Child Care; Adult Care; Hair and Beauty; Food and Drink; Manufacturing; Financial; Customer Care; Retail and Logistics; Hospitality; Engineering and Construction Trades; Automotive Engineering and Health. Target numbers will be split equally between the four delivery centres but, once identified, learners will have a choice about which delivery centre they attend.

Recruitment from 2008-2009 onwards will be supported by the Aimhigher Greater Manchester Strategic Progression Framework. The Progression Framework will be a menu of activities aimed at increasing progression to HE among Apprentices and other work-based learners and will provide a coherent sequence of developmental opportunities from Year 10 through to adult learners. The Progression Framework will be based on a new partnership of work-based learning providers across Greater Manchester. Work-based learning provider partners will be identified in each borough and they will identify most Progression Framework cohorts so that as time goes on, the numbers of learners who have taken part in activities at the various levels will increase and thus delivery centres will benefit from the development of a pool of learners ready to take the Step-In Module and to progress to HE.

Conclusion and Recommendations

One of the most important issues for demonstrating the efficacy of the project is to find reliable progression data on Advanced Apprentices so that the success of the project may be judged relative to the numbers of Advanced Apprentices progressing to HE without having taken the course.

It is not a requirement of UCAS, HEFCE or HESA that learners who have completed Apprenticeships should be identified upon entry to HE or tracked thereafter. Those who have carried out national research on the progression of Advanced Apprentices have encountered problems because of the lack of data. Vic Seddon in his 2005 report for UVAC, 'An Analysis of the progression of Advanced Apprentices into HE in England', notes 'The most obvious finding has been the shortage of data on Apprentices' progression' (Seddon p.5). He goes on to consider a variety of sources of incomplete data and concludes: 'All of the evidence points to a progression rate of between 2-4 per cent of Apprentices' (p.32); this concurs with the best estimate of the rate of progression to HE by Advanced Apprentices in Greater Manchester in 2006-2007 (see Introduction).

Recommendations to improve the range and quality of data available on rates of progression to HE by Advanced Apprentices (and other work-based and vocational learners who may participate in the project in future) are that Aimhigher Greater Manchester should:

- work with the LSC to amass specific data on the numbers of Advanced Apprentices and other relevant work-based learners completing their qualifications successfully, broken down to the second tier of QCA sector classifications
- influence partner HEIs to collect data on the types of qualifications with which part-time learners enter work-related HE courses, both for learners entering courses delivered on campus and for learners entering courses delivered at partner institutions
- encourage the tracking of a sample of Advanced Apprentices and other relevant work-based learners on their journeys through HE

It is very important that data collection methods do not assume that progression to HE from Advanced Apprenticeships or other work-based qualifications will be immediate upon completion of the Level 3 qualification/s as many learners may progress several years later. Adding to this the time taken to complete part-time HE qualifications, many learners' journeys into and through HE could be completed up to 10 years after the completion of the Level 3 qualification/s

The high level of interest in progression to HE generated by the first runs of the course indicates that the course is a very successful model for promoting progression among Advanced Apprentices. Next academic year, testing the model further with larger numbers of learners, including other target groups of work-based and vocational learners, and tracking learners' progression into HE will provide further important data on the needs of a group currently very under-represented in HE.

References

National Statistics Socio-Economic Classifications (NS-SEC)

World Class Apprenticeships: Unlocking Talent, Building Skills for All (2008) Report published by DIUS

Seddon, Vic (2005) *An Analysis of the progression of Advanced Apprentices into HE in England*, Report published by UVAC

New Route To Recognition: A Work Based Learning Model To Remove Barriers To Professional Registration In Engineering.

D. R. Edmonsone, W. Glew, Kingston University; I. S. Lidberg, University of East London

Introduction

The Langlands Report *Gateways to the Professions* (Department for Education and Skills, 2005) highlighted the need for the professions to provide clear, accessible gateways to individuals who may not otherwise pursue professional qualification. The age for professional qualification in engineering tends to be later than in other professions at around 30 years. In addition, the total number of registered engineers has fallen by 21,500 or eight per cent in the last decade and the percentage of chartered engineers over 65 has risen from around 30 percent to 40 percent during the last ten years (Engineering and Technology Board, 2007). One of the reasons for this decline in registrations could be that graduates from 2002 onwards with an accredited bachelor's degree are required to undertake further learning at Master's level to be eligible for Chartered Engineer registration, possibly resulting in increased student debt. This is in addition to the required demonstration of generic competences to achieve professional registration that were essentially unchanged during this period (UK-SPEC, 2005).

The Government response to the Langlands Report was to instigate the 'Gateways Development Fund'. The Engineering Council was invited to develop a project to bid for this funding. Kingston University is the lead university partner in this work to develop models of flexible pathways into and through HE towards professional registration. There are now four HEI partners (Kingston, Hertfordshire, Northumbria and Stafford) and three of the Professional Engineering Institutions (PEIs) (Institute of Mechanical Engineering, Institute of Engineering & Technology and Royal

Aeronautical Society) working with the project team to accredit the programmes. The aim of the project is to provide routes that integrate education with supervised work-based professional development. Successful participants would achieve an academic qualification and be able to apply for a professional review, possibly leading to registration, without having to spend a significant period of time away from work. It is also hoped that the project will help graduate engineers achieve professional registration earlier in their careers and enable the professional institutions to maintain contact with them.

This paper describes the results of a survey conducted at the four partner HEIs aimed at assessing the attitude of recently qualified engineering graduates to professional registration. It also examines how the Work-Based Learning Model, developed during the project, will help to remove the barriers to registration.

Survey of Engineering Graduates

The aim of the baseline project was to identify the engineering graduate's reasons for not pursuing chartered and / or incorporated engineering registration, as well as to find out the general attitudes to professional registration.

A questionnaire was designed to measure engineering graduate's attitudes to professional registration. In order to assist in obtaining a reasonable response rate, the questionnaire was limited to four sides of A4 and a total of 26 questions. Slightly less than half of the questions established factual details about the respondents. The rest of the questions were in two groups. The first group of questions attempted to examine the attitude of both the respondent and their employer to professional registration. The second group of questions sought to establish reasons why recent graduates were *not* pursuing professional registration. Respondents were asked to examine a series of fourteen statements and indicate their agreement / disagreement. An example statement would be '*Lack of opportunity at my place of employment*'.

A cover letter was included with the questionnaire to inform the graduate of the purpose of the research and explaining the benefits of finding out the graduate's attitudes to professional registration.

Survey Results

Sample
A total of 2845 questionnaires were sent out to recent engineering graduates with accredited BEng degrees from the four participating HEIs. The overall response rate was 8.4 per cent, giving a total of 239 respondents. Kingston University (1000) and University of Hertfordshire (1397) mailed out around 85 per cent of the questionnaires and provided 76 per cent of the participants. The mean age of graduates was 31.82, and the percentage of male to female graduates was 93 per cent male and seven per cent female. The participation rate for females in Engineering and Technology is around 15 per cent (Engineering Training Board 2007). Thus, this sample appears to under-represent females. The main nationality (80%) was British.   The next largest groups were Asian/Asian British, Sri Lankan, and South African.

More than 75 per cent of the participants work in the engineering sector though around 7 per cent are not employed in engineering and have no wish to be.   Fourteen per cent of participants are not employed in engineering but would like to be. Given the perceived shortage of engineers in the UK, this is a little surprising.

Attitudes to Registration
Around half of the relevant participants considered that their employer valued their staff being registered as professional engineers. However, more than 23 per cent of participants did not know their employer's views on this topic.   A small majority of participants indicated that attaining CEng status was very important or important to them, though around 15 per cent regarded it as not important.   Maillardet et al (2005) obtained a very similar result, using an identical question, from a much smaller sample of graduate engineers in the early stages of their career. In contrast, more than 60 per cent of participants viewed IEng status as only fairly

important or not important. Participants considered the greatest benefit of professional registration to be better promotional prospects, with 64 per cent indicating this as an advantage. Around 13 per cent believed there were no advantages to being registered as a professional engineer.

The survey does show that the attitude of the employer was a very strong influence on the pursuit of professional registration. Of the 65 respondents who were pursuing professional registration, 51 (79%) had employers who valued it. Only 14 respondents whose employers valued professional registration were *not* pursuing professional registration.

Reasons for NOT pursuing professional registration
Although 47 per cent of respondents are members of a PEI, only 29 per cent are actively pursuing registration (23 per cent CEng and six per cent IEng). This is in stark contrast to the sample of engineers surveyed by Maillardet et al (2005) where 28 out of 32 engineers had enrolled or were going to enrol on the registration programme. A ranking list for the reasons why recent graduates are *not* pursuing professional registration was constructed from responses, ranging from strongly agree to strongly disagree, to a number of statements. These are shown below.

- Insufficient advice/support to progress through to UK-SPEC competences
- Have not completed the necessary further learning and am unclear about UK-SPEC
- Have completed the necessary further learning but am unclear about UK-SPEC
- Cannot take time away from work to meet further learning requirement
- Not pursuing a career in Engineering
- The prospect of further debt to complete a taught programme
- Lack of opportunity at my place of employment
- It is still too early in my career
- Family commitments and responsibilities

- I am not career minded
- The work environment is gender biased and it does not suit my expectations
- Don't know how to go about it
- Not interested
- I do not believe that I have an equal opportunity of becoming a professional engineer

Overall the two top reasons for not pursuing professional registration from the combined data were:

> 'Insufficient advice/support to progress through to UK-SPEC competences'
> 'Do not know how to go about it'

On inspection of the ranking lists constructed from the data for the four individual universities, it was found that in every case the above two reasons appeared within the top three.

Virtually all of our respondents were career minded. However, many recent graduate engineers were not pursuing professional registration as they do not know how to go about it and feel that they are offered insufficient advice and support. In some ways, a lack of understanding about the way in which to go about professional registration is surprising. Engineers are very computer literate and information on this topic is readily available on any PEI website. (The Institution of Engineering and Technology: Professional Registration [Online], 2008). The majority indicate that opportunities at work for professional registration are limited and there is a lack of understanding of the precise requirement for further learning. Those who are concerned about the cost of pursuing professional registration only just outnumber those who are not. In view of the other responses, it may be that potential registrants are not aware of the precise financial implications. However, the fact that 43 per cent of all respondents had no student debt at the completion of their undergraduate qualification tends to back up this finding. It is interesting to note that though 35 per cent of respondents had student debt in excess of £10,000 on completion of their undergraduate qualification, *"Financial"* only ranked at number seven as a reason for not pursuing professional registration. No doubt these students are balanced by those (43 per cent) who managed to emerge debt free from their undergraduate studies.

Overall lessons from the survey
For engineering graduates completing an accredited BEng/BSc award in 2002 or later, further learning has been a requirement to obtain professional registration. This has no doubt contributed to the lack of understanding of the way to engage with this process. It is apparent that potential candidates for registration require more information on the process and would like more guidance as they acquire and record the competences leading to professional registration.

Impact assessment
In approximately three years time, there will be a requirement to undertake an impact assessment of the programme. As with all programmes of this type it will be necessary to establish the direct, indirect and intermediate impact of the project. It is likely that the direct impact of the programme will be measured by the number of students enrolling on the MSc Professional Engineering. One measure of indirect impact would be engineering graduate students' awareness of this new route to registration.

A WBL Model for Professional Registration

The normal basis for the vast majority of WBL / negotiated learning programmes is a three-way collaboration between the student, the university and the employer (Coldstream, 1994). In this case, the added partner will be the PEI. It is vitally important that at the end of the programme the candidate not only acquires an academic qualification but also is fully prepared for professional registration.

> *In order to be registered as a Chartered Engineer (CEng) a candidate needs to demonstrate within a Professional Review, undertaken by a PEI, that the UK-SPEC (2005) threshold standards of competence and commitment have been substantially met. Those who, on initial paper review,*

> *meet these UK-SPEC requirements are asked to attend a Professional Review and Interview (PRI) with trained, registered engineering professionals. Successful candidates are registered as CEng.*
>
> *Under UK-SPEC, successful demonstration of competence and commitment is the sole criterion for registration. The development of competence and commitment requires the acquisition of skill sets and experience for which underpinning knowledge and understanding has to be acquired. Education and Professional Development are the two key activities which facilitate this.* (Engineering Council UK, 2008)

The model adopted will need to both meet university academic standards for Level seven (Masters) learning and demonstrate that threshold standards of competence have been met.

The Model in Detail

After enrolling, all participants undertake a Professional Development Audit (PDA) to define the scope of their own work based Learning Agreement. The Professional Development Audit is a reflective assessment of their education, qualifications, experience and competences achieved to date. The PDA is then matched against the UK-SPEC requirements to meet three objectives:

> 1) to determine the gap between current competences and those required by the PEI / UK-SPEC;
> 2) as an aid to writing the remaining MSc Learning Contract goals; and
> 3) as a plan of how the candidate intends to meet the required *competences*.

If the expectation is that completion of the resulting Learning Contract will fall short of meeting UK-SPEC competence requirements, the candidate, who remains registered with the University, may transfer to a normal work-based learning MSc in Technology. Thus, the aim at the outset is to achieve a convergence between gaining an academic qualification and being prepared for professional registration.

While undertaking the PDA, full engagement is maintained with the employer via an industrial mentor. The output of the PDA is a reflective CV that identifies and evidences UK-SPEC competences which will accompany the delivery of a learning contract which aims to meet the needs of all stakeholders. The reflective CV will identify a candidate's shortfalls against the requirements of UK-SPEC. It is then necessary for the candidate to evaluate work-based opportunities to generate a series of strategically important learning goals that will fill the competence gap.

Example of a Learning Contract
Goal A – Professional Development Audit (PDA)
Goal B - Research and evaluate the current Telematics marketplace.
Goal C - Build a database of current suppliers and their technologies
Goal D - Develop a Telematics products project proposal and project plan
Goal E - Produce a data modelling system for the analysis and interpretation of Telematics data.
Goal F - Develop a business case for the exploitation of a technical market opportunity.
Goal G - Construct a hardware design brief, technical specification and a manufacturing specification for the production of the hardware.
Goal H - Prepare an academic paper of publishable quality.
Goal I - Prepare final summary, presentation and undertake viva examination.

In the example given above, Goal A, the PDA defines the work based learning element. It has resulted in six learning goals. The final two learning goals, Goals H and I in this case, are standard assignments for every candidate. Thus Goals A, H and I (highlighted grey) represent the "shell" Learning Agreement that is filled as a result of the PDA. The complete Learning Agreement is scrutinised by the relevant PEI to establish if the candidate, on successful completion of the programme, would be in a position to undertake a

Professional Registration Interview, possibly leading to registration as a Chartered Engineer.

It can be seen that the process of developing the Learning Agreement and the subsequent execution of the programme emphasises "the pivotal position of the candidate as the principal agent of control of a programme situated within critical and demanding academic and professional contexts." (Stephenson et al, 2006).

Project Progress
The project started in November 2006 and will be completed in March 2011. For Chartered Engineer registration, a detailed guide has been produced. The award has proved to be popular and in academic year 2007/2008, twenty-four candidates have been enrolled at Kingston University, seven candidates at Staffordshire University and a further three at the University of Hertfordshire. It is interesting to note that the model has proved to be attractive to engineers in both large and small companies / organisations. The next phase of the project will involve rolling out the concept to more universities and additional PEIs. This activity is already underway with a number of universities and PEIs already examining the model developed.

The results from the survey have influenced the way in which the programme has been designed and marketed. Much less emphasis has been placed on cost and cost benefits and more on the "guided" nature of the programme.

It is also a major aim of the programme to obtain support from employers. Those employers approached so far have been very enthusiastic about the project. In addition, WBL routes leading to Incorporated Engineer (IEng) and Engineering Technician (EngTech) registration are under development.

Conclusions

The survey of recent graduates has revealed that a lack of knowledge and understanding of the process involved in achieving professional registration, combined with a perceived lack of support in participating in the process were the main reasons for not pursuing professional registration. A key finding is that unless employers value professional registration, graduate engineers are much less likely to pursue it.

At the outset of the project it was anticipated that the financial penalties for undertaking a taught Master's degree would be a barrier to many candidates. The survey reveals that this is not a major issue. However, none of the respondents would have completed a course where tuition fees of £3000 / annum were required. This has influenced the way in which the programme has been designed and marketed. Student support and guidance has been emphasised at the expense of cost benefits.

The WBL model being used has two features not commonly found within WBL models used at other HE institutions. These are the involvement of a professional institution in scrutinising a learning agreement prior to HE approval and the mapping of a learning agreement against a competence framework. It is likely that this model can be utilised in sectors other than engineering.

The project has made excellent progress in establishing a framework within which both HE institutions and PEIs are happy to operate. Pilot cohorts of students have been recruited at three of the four HEI partners. An impact assessment will be completed towards the end of the project in March 2011.

References

Coldstream, P. (1994) 'Training minds for tomorrow: a shared responsibility.' *Higher Education Quarterly* 48 (3), pp. 159-68.

Department for Education and Skills (2005) *The Gateways to the Professions Report (Sir Alan Langlands)* GPR1, Nottingham: DfES

Engineering Council UK (2005) *UK Standard for Professional Engineering Competence: Chartered Engineer and Incorporated Engineer Standard,* London: Engineering Council UK

Engineering Council UK (2008) *Guide to the MSc Professional Engineering*   Available at: http://www.engc.org.uk/registration/registration_process.aspx Accessed 10th May 2008

Maillardet, F., Ali, M. and Steadman, S. (2005) *Learning During the First Three Years of Postgraduate Employment – the LiNEA project – Interim Report for Engineering,* Brighton: University of Brighton

Stephenson, J., Malloch, M. and Cairns, L. (2006) 'Managing their own programme: a case study of first graduates of a new kind of doctorate in professional practice', *Studies in Continuing Education,* 28(1), pp. 17 – 32

The Engineering and technology Board (2007) *Engineering UK 2007*, London, ETB

The Institution of Engineering and Technology, *Professional Registration* Available at < http://www.theiet.org/careers/profreg/index.cfm> Accessed 10th May 2008

Geographically Dispersed Work Based Learners – A Pedagogical Support Programme

Mike Goodwin, Senior Development Officer, University of Wolverhampton, UK, Alec Forsyth, H A Forsyth Consultancy

Work-based learning requires the individual learner to take a greater degree of responsibility for their learning whilst working outside the HE institution remote from tutors and other course members. Cohorts of work-based learners, in addition to being geographically dispersed, frequently encompass people with differing ages, previous academic attainment and industrial experiences. Unlike more traditional modes of learning this creates additional student needs: it is therefore important that all learners feel that they are valued, fully involved and their needs integrated into a learning framework that enables them to attain their learning goals.

Work-based learning makes significantly different demands on both tutor and student from those made by traditional academic learning (Forsyth and Goodwin, 2005, Gray, 2001; Goodwin and Forsyth 2005b). The tutor is no longer the possessor of a body of knowledge that he imparts to the learner (Goodwin and Forsyth 2004a); his role is to facilitate the learner within a context with which the learner, not the tutor, is more familiar. The tutor's function is to enable learning, not to teach what he already knows. He has to do this within a range of contexts and to widely differing individual learners; his expertise must shift from his subject to facilitating learning wherever and however it occurs, while enabling the learner to become increasingly effective and efficient (Goodwin and Forsyth 2003, 2004a, 2005b).

Learners are required to play a far more responsible role in their own learning. They have to plan, manage, monitor and review their own learning with the support of their tutor. They have to evaluate their progress and use this to improve (Forsyth and Goodwin 2006, 2007; Goodwin and Forsyth, 2005a, 2005b, 2007). Both tutor and learner have to develop the confidence and self-belief to move from a pedagogical to an andragogical model of learning, and to develop a much more equal partnership than usually found in traditional programmes of study.

It follows, therefore, that, to succeed and retain learners, work-based learning programmes must be fully collaborative experiences, where partners fully understand the concepts, relationships and processes involved. This in turn, requires the development of:

- a common language;
- clearly defined relationships;
- confidence and security in all participants, tutors and learners, so that they can cope with the changes inherent in effective learning;
- transparency of process;
- tutor support based on emerging learner needs, not on tutor pre-prepared structures;
- flexibility to accommodate the changing needs of students and the work place;
- independence in that learners must explicitly understand and own their learning, and the tools by which they learn, so that they can transfer these across to any working environments in which they may find themselves.

To equip the learner with the necessary skills, knowledge and understanding to meet the challenges of work based learning detailed above, a support programme has been developed and implemented. It delivers the following objectives:

- To accommodate participants with a wide range of different experience and academic background with the necessary learning tools for successful work based learning.
- To create a shared understanding, among tutors and participants, of the nature, scope, academic levels and performance required for a given academic attainment.

- To develop the appropriate hard and soft skills to gain employer credibility.
- To develop and sustain a safe learning environment.
- To support successful progression.

This paper describes the support programme which is in three integrated sections. The sections were developed to equip the learner, at the outset, with tools that to develop the confidence and methodologies needed to achieve; and to provide a common understanding of the terminology, processes, functions and academic levels embedded within the work-based learning framework. The three programme sections are:

- How to measure success
- Managing your learning
- How to evidence learning

Section 1: How to Measure Success

The first workshop is designed to build learners' confidence in their ability to use the descriptors, and to explore how their experiences might be evaluated in the context of level, thus starting the process of bridging the gap between the world of work and academe. It demonstrates that the learning they will gain in the work place is as rigorous and valid as that found in traditional programmes, because it will be measured (assessed) against criteria that are as demanding as those used for judging the outcomes of traditionally taught modules. So whilst it is equivalent to traditional taught learning, it differs from it because it draws on a wider range of learning resources than are usually encountered in other forms of academic learning.

The aim of this session is to clarify the process of assessment so that at the end of the session the learner will:

- know what the assessment criteria look like
- understand how they are used

- be able to decide that what they have done/can do to meet the assessment criteria
- be able to monitor what they do against the criteria, so they should always have a clear picture of how far they are succeeding and can evaluate the effectiveness of their learning.

Description of the first workshop activities

1. Copies of the Northern Ireland Credit Accumulation and Transfer level descriptors (the assessment criteria) are issued to the learners. It is explained that they articulate the key knowledge, understanding and skills, which are generic to all taught courses and modules, although they are usually expressed there in terms relevant to that subject. A detailed description of what each element covers together with notes and guidance on how each element should be interpreted is included with the descriptors.

2. The structure and content of the level descriptors are explored and some of the progression markers within and across levels / descriptors are demonstrated.

3. A group workshop asks learners to explore the demands of level descriptors and compare / contrast different levels. To help with this, they are provided with a breakdown of the level descriptors where the constructs have been further sub divided into strands covering:

- Intellectual skills and attributes
    - Acquisition and application of knowledge
    - skills
    - problem solving
    - information management
- Processes
    - Content
    - Process
    - role and function
- Accountability
    - Autonomy

        o   Output
        o   Quality

4.   This enables them to see how each strand progresses by level.

5.   Groups discuss the following questions:

- What is the difference between acquiring and application of knowledge in HE Level 1 and HE Level 3?
- What is the difference between HE Level 1 and HE Level 3 in terms of accountability?
- How do HE Level 2 processes differ from HE Level 3 processes?
- What do HE Level 4 (Masters level) demand which earlier levels do not?
- Can they illustrate any of these differences by giving examples from their own professional area?

6.   A plenary discussion, tutor-led, is used to develop common agreement about the key differences and the key words which signal the differences between the levels.

The linked exercises provide the learner with some insight into the assessment criteria and their use. It is explained to learners that they are at the start of a learning curve and that the interpretation and use of academic levels is related to a common understanding by both tutor and learner of the application of the assessment criteria. Learners are led to an understanding of how the criteria allow them to offer for assessment those professional activities - which are most useful to them in their job – not just a series of academic assignments. This leads into the second session:

Section 2: Managing your learning

The aim here is to equip learners with the necessary knowledge, skills and understanding to enable them to take greater responsibility for managing their learning.

Objectives

- To understand clearly how their current work / future projects can be used as the basis for learning
- To use the level descriptors as a planning tool for their own learning and professional development.
- To understand clearly the difference between activities and the learning arising from these.
- To be able to use the level descriptors to recognise, plan and evaluate their own learning in any work-based context

In this workshop the learners are taken through an example of a planned, individual, work- based learning programme devised by someone working in the textile industry. Deliberately, the context is outside their work area because it is easier to see the process when not distracted by the complexities of their professional knowledge and current practice.

Activity 1.
Learners are asked to refer to the level descriptors to determine at what level the actions detailed below would sit. No common agreement is ever reached, demonstrating neatly that actions alone are not level specific.

Company Project - List of Actions from an individual work-based learning programme devised by someone working within the textile industry:

- Complete comparison trials of 3 proposed new polymers for inclusion in new, stronger, more flexible yarn.
- Summarise the outcomes: comparative strengths and weaknesses of each.
- Establish and compare production costs of each: for initial set–up, and for production run of three years.
- Submit findings to Board for evaluation and final selection.
- Liase with marketing department to supply information to support initial marketing.

Activity 2.

In order to help them distinguish between learning activities and learning outcomes, learners are asked to determine what they would learn from undertaking the actions listed above, using the level descriptors.

Activity 3.

Then, each group is provided with a range of learning outcome statements derived from the list of actions above. These are at HE Level 4 and HE Level 6, but learners are not told this. In groups, learners match each learning outcome statement to the appropriate activity and level by referring to the level descriptors. In this way the learners start to develop a common understanding of how activities within a work related context (Goodwin and Forsyth, 2007) can lead to rigorous learning, and the difference between work activity and the learning arising from it.

Learners are advised when writing learning outcomes to:

- always preface with "On completion of this, I will be able to…..
- include a statement of what is being learned / skill gained
- incorporate key words from the appropriate level descriptor and / or use short phrases which create a link with the appropriate level descriptors
- make sure each learning outcome contains a verb to do with learning e.g. evaluate, synthesize (each learner is provide with a schedule of action verbs linked to cognitive skills for use in drafting learning outcomes)
- remember that Learning Outcomes are the measurable results of learning activities
- write in the future tense and make all learning outcomes Specific, Measurable, Achievable, Realistic and Timely (SMART)
- divide the targets into those practical skills required to do their job and personal skills required in any workplace.

Now that the learners are clear about the differences between actions and learning outcomes, the next activity helps them to plan suitable activities to enable them to meet specific learning outcomes within a work context.

Activity 4

Learners are taken through part of the textile workers Individual Learning Plan, showing how she expanded an initial broad action into a series of detailed steps by using the learning outcomes to focus her professional knowledge into areas of specific assessable learning (see Figure 1 below).

Figure 1

Activities	1. Conduct needs analysis to establish characteristics required in new yarn within context of firm's current yarn profile marketing base; 2. Research and review previous comparison trails to establish strengths and weaknesses; 3. Establish precise criteria for effective comparisons; 4. Build comparative models of possible trial methodologies, indicating benefits and drawbacks of each; 5. Prioritise the above and determine more effective procedure; 6. Publish protocols and time frames for trials; 7. Brief section leaders.
Learning Outcomes	Establish appropriate criteria, methodology, resources and management structures for valid and reliable comparison trials of 3 proposed new polymers employing a range of specialised skills within company guidelines for such trials.

The next stage is to prove that the learning has taken place. In groups, students give examples of evidence that could be submitted as a result of these actions to show that the learning has taken place. Their results and ideas are discussed and compared with Figure 2.

Figure 2

Activities	8. Conduct needs analysis to establish characteristics required in new yarn within context of firm's current yarn profile marketing base; 9. Research and review previous comparison trails to establish strengths and weaknesses; 10. Establish precise criteria for effective comparisons; 11. Build comparative models of possible trial methodologies, indicating benefits and drawbacks of each; 12. Prioritise the above and determine more effective procedure; 13. Publish protocols and time frames for trials; 14. Brief section leaders.
Learning Outcomes	Establish appropriate criteria, methodology, resources and management structures for valid and reliable comparison trials of 3 proposed new polymers employing a range of specialised skills within company guidelines for such trials.
Evidence	Publish outcomes Report / comparative model Minutes of discussions. Copies of criteria from other trials used as basis for discussion - Publish criteria Report Published chosen model Published protocols Briefing notes and minutes of discussion

Two vital points arise: firstly the evidence must prove that learning has taken place, not simply that the actions have been completed. Secondly, where possible, evidence should be things which the learner would need to produce anyway to do the job properly.   Note the need for reflective review (topic of next session) to provide the non-concrete evidence of learning not embodied in the concrete work-based evidence.

In small groups learners take a second learning outcome from the textile student (see activity 3) and map possible actions in more detail plus identify appropriate evidence. The example outcome is then used as a comparison with the learners' own examples:

Figure 3

Activities	Organise briefing meetings of all involved Identify resource requirements Establish systems for resource provision Organise periodic review meetings of progress Monitor resource provision Establish quality control mechanisms
Learning Outcomes	Supervise and manage completion of above trials
Evidence	Briefing notes Resources schedules Agenda for periodic review meetings Minutes of review meetings

In order to summarise the workshop the following points are made:

- Use level descriptors to guide what you need to do because they tell you what you should be learning.
- As many of these actions and as much of the evidence as possible should be done/produced as part of your normal work on this area, not extra purely for the award.
- Evidence is of what has been learned (not what has been done).

- Planned learning can be modified at any point if the need arises.
- Learning plans will usually contain more than one learning outcome. It is therefore important when drafting to ensure that what the learner plans to learn is cross referenced to actions and actions to evidence. It is not the tutor's role to guess the relationships between actions, learning and evidence.

Session 3: How to evidence learning

In work related learning the reflective process is key to successful progressive learning (Barnet, 1995; Chernis and Goleman, 1998; Smith and Hughes, 2003; Forsyth and Goodwin 2006, 2007; Goodwin and Forsyth, 2005a, 2005b, 2007). Reflection upon the attainment and application of technical skills is more readily undertaken as they are more easily measured and denote technical expertise. Reflection upon the proficiency and attainment of soft transferable skills is more difficult, but of major importance as they significantly affect the ability of the participant to reach their learning and career potential within the work place. Such soft skills are encompassed within the "ought to know" activities often acquired through work and operational experience. The concentration by higher education and employers on the "need to know" aspects of the core curriculum at the expense of the "ought to know" knowledge and skills frequently affects the perceived capability by employers. Consequently "ought to know" is often acquired through unplanned and informal learning, which can make a major impact on a person's employability (Dale and Bell, 1999) and major contributions to their continuous improvement cycle (Goodwin and Forsyth, 2005a). The value of this can be greatly improved by learning through the workplace. This should be recognised and incorporated into work related learning frameworks. Work related learning frameworks tend to place a greater emphasis on the participant to provide and evidence the learning activities and outcomes undertaken (Gray, 2001; Goodwin and Forsyth, 2004a) and therefore provide the opportunity to identify, develop and apply "ought to know" knowledge and skills, so improving the perceived capabilities and employability of learners. This encourages the formation of a "can do" attitude to learning aimed at growing the talent of the participant.

The aim here is to explore the process of reflection as a means of learning from experience.

On completion of this section learners will understand the concept of reflection, and be familiar with the process of reflection.

Description of the workshop activities

In this session the learners are reminded:

- That a key feature of work based learning is the need to provide appropriate and valid <u>evidence of learning</u>, since it is against this which credit is awarded and NOT the completion of activities.
- That a significant part of their evidence of learning (which they will have identified in their plan) will arise as part of their work - reports, minutes of meetings, drawings/plans, artifacts etc.
- That some of what they learn will not be concrete - not captured and recorded in any way. Consequently, they will need, as part of their evidence, to <u>reflect</u> on what they have done and present the results of this reflection in writing.
- Of Boyd and Fales (1983) who defined reflective learning as: '*The essential difference between whether a person repeats the same experience several times becoming highly proficient at one behaviour or learns from experience so that the learner is cognitively and effectively challenged.*'

Boyd and Fales' definition is used to emphasise the difference between repeating practice to increase efficiency and learning from practice to increase effectiveness so enabling the learner to conclude that reflective learning is not just about describing what happened, rather it is about analysing actions critically to determine what worked and why, about what could be improved, and how.   The emphasis is on learning from our experiences.

It is explained that reflection is a two stage process: the first stage – review what has gone on so far and the issues arising;   the second stage - analyse this critically to increase effectiveness.   For learners both stages are a process of asking questions of themselves, their practice and their experiences so that they can move forward.   The next step is to suggest the sorts of questions which will be useful, and to give learners the opportunity to begin to practice using them during the session

Learners are reminded that the example questions are not sequential, not all the possible questions, and that they should select from/add to as appropriate.

Example questions:

Reviewing the issues	Improving practice
How do/did you see the situation at the beginning?	What are the implications of what was done, for you, your colleagues, the workplace?
Do you see it differently now? Why?	What would you keep unchanged in future in dealing with a similar issue/ situation? Why? What might you do differently? Why?
What were the effects of what you did/ didn't do/experience?	What information and/or assistance do you need to effect the changes you see as necessary?
In what way was the situation successful/of benefit?	What do you need in order to make good the deficiencies in your current understanding / practice?
What (if any) were its difficulties/ disadvantages?	What can you do to effect short-/ long-term improvement?
Were your experiences of the situation similar to your colleagues? If not, why not?	

The session is concluded with the learners undertaking the following activity:

> **Reflective exercise and Re-enforcement of learning**
>
> Consider today. Take 10 minutes, using any of these questions which are useful to you and any others you like, to jot brief notes on your experiences today, focussing on:
> What you have learned?
> What helped you to learn?
> Where your learning was not enabled by the day and what caused this?
> What you can do to improve the situation? a) for yourself and b) for others who might come on this module
> What feedback you would give to the session leader to improve the learning opportunities for participants?

Feedback received from learners on completion of the pilot monitoring phase provided evidence of the effectiveness and relevance of the support programme (Goodwin and Forsyth, 2005b). The programme has now been handed over to University departments for them to use.

The support programme encompassing the three integrated sections ensures that learning can be captured and assessed. Once learners are independent and autonomous, able to recognise their own learning and build upon it using rigorous criteria that capture the nature and scope of work based learning, then learning wherever and however it occurs can be attained. This approach provides the learner with the tools to implement a cycle of continuous learning improvement via effective planning, evaluating, review and subsequent development so initiating progressive cycles. It has received very positive feedback from participants and is of proven value both in enabling more effective independent learners, and in improving learner retention.

References

Barnet, B. (1995) 'Developing reflection and expertise: can mentors make the difference?' *Journal of Educational Administration*, Vol.33, No 5, pp. 45-59 MCB University Press.

Cherniss, C. and Goleman, D. (1998) 'Bringing Emotional Intelligence to the Workplace'. In *A Technical Report issued by the Consortium for Research on Emotional Intelligence in Organisations.* Pub. Graduate School of Applied and Professional Psychology, Rutgers University, USA.

Dale, M., and Bell, J. (1999) *Informal Learning in the Work Place.* Research Report (RR134) Pub. Department of Education and Employment, London, UK.

Evers, F.T., Rush, J.C. and Berdrow, I. (1998) *The Bases of Competence: skills for lifelong learning and employability.* Jossey-Bass.

Forsyth, H.A. (1980) 'Towards a "total catering concept"'. In Race P., and Brook D (eds). *Perspectives on Academic Gaming and Simulation 5.* pp.66-76 Kogan Page, London..

Forsyth, H.A. (1986) Simulations for management capability within the Hotel &Catering Industry. In *Perspectives on Academic Gaming and Simulation 11.* Craig D & Martin A (ed.). Society for the Advancement of Games and Simulations, (SAGSET), UK. pp. 114-126.

Forsyth, H.A. (1999) The National Innkeeping Business Game (1989-1997); Professional Development on a National Scale. In *The International Simulation and Gaming Research Yearbook, vol. 7. Simulations and Games for Strategy & Policy Planning.* Saunder D & Severn J (ed.) London: Kogan Page, pp. 108-119.

Forsyth, H.A. (2000) The Role of Benchmarked, pre computed National Catering Business Games (NCBG) in encouraging effective business decisions and lifelong learning. In *The International*

Simulation and Gaming Research Yearbook, vol. 8. Simulations and Games for Simulation and Change. Saunders, D. and Smalley, N. (eds) London: Kogan Page, pp. 176-186.

Forsyth, H.A. (2002a) 'The contribution bespoke National Catering Business Games (N.C.B.G.) offer to study at undergraduate and postgraduate levels via Negotiated Work Based Learning (NWBL)' in *The International Simulation and Gaming Research Yearbook Vol.10, Employability: the role of Games, Simulations and Case Studies.* Maggie Boyle and Yvonne Smith, (eds) Society for the Advancement of Games and Simulations in Education and Training, Napier University, Edinburgh. pp. 209-216.

Forsyth, H.A. (2002b) 'A role for the National Catering Business Games (NCBGS) to offer parity of experiential learning for Graduate Apprentices (G.As) in hospitality' in *The International Simulation and Gaming Research Year Book Vol.10, Employability: the role of Games, Simulations and Case Studies.* Maggie Boyle and Yvonne Smith, (eds) Society for the Advancement of Games and Simulations in Education and Training, Napier University, Edinburgh. pp. 202-208.

Forsyth, H.A. and Goodwin M.G. (2002) Games and Simulations; Their added value to Negotiated Work-based Learning (NWBL) and Emotional Competence Development. *Knowledge Work and Learning, Conference Proceedings of the Work Based Learning Network of the Universities Association for Continuing Education.* National Centre for Work Based Learning Partnerships, Middlesex University, London. pp. 74-89.

Forsyth, H.A. and Goodwin M.G. (2004) Higher Education – Does it meet employer's needs? A response. *International Conference on innovation, good practice and research in Engineering Education.* University of Wolverhampton, June 2004. University of Wolverhampton, Vol. 2, pp. 213-218.

Forsyth, H.A. and Goodwin M.G. (2005). Should a University be involved in work-based learning? - A UK perspective. *Challenges for Integrating Work and Learning, Conference Proceedings of the*

4ᵗʰ International Conference of Researching Work and Learning.
University of Technology Sydney, Australia
www.oval.uts.edu.au/ and click onto (RWL 4 papers)

Forsyth, H.A. and Goodwin M.G. (2006) The University Alumni- a
force for making a difference to lifelong learning through the
workplace. *Proceedings of the The International Conference on
Innovation, Good Practice and Research in Engineering Education
2006.* University of Liverpool July 2006. The Higher Education
Academy Subject Centres for Materials and Engineering. UK. pp.
110-114.

Forsyth, H.A. and Goodwin, M.G (2007) Widening Access and the
Transition to Higher Education: A Catalyst for Development.
*Transformation, Progression and Hope: What ever happened to
lifelong learning?* International Conference Proceedings, July 2006,
University of Swansea. Forum for Access and Continuing
Education, UK, pp.135-143.

Forsyth, H.A. and Goodwin, M.G (2008a)) The Development of
Employability and Capability for Sustained Workforce Development
through Vocational Higher Education. *Social Justice and Lifelong
Learning: Diversity, Globalisation & Transformation.* International
Conference Proceedings, July 2007, University of East London,
Forum for Access and Continuing Education, UK.

Forsyth, H.A. and Goodwin M.G (2008b) Quality Assurance for
Learning Brokers of HE – an Outline Proposal. *Social Justice and
Lifelong Learning: Diversity, Globalisation & Transformation.*
International Conference Proceedings, July 2007, University of East
London, Forum for Access and Continuing Education, UK.

Goodwin, M.G. and Forsyth, H.A. (2003a) Negotiated Work-based
Learning (NWBL) as a mode of learning designed to contribute to
sustainable economic development (An UK model) *Work and
Lifelong Learning in Different Contexts, Conference Proceedings of
the 3ʳᵈ International Conference of Researching Work and Learning.*
Department of Education, University of Tampere, Finland.
Proceedings Book II, pp 51-58.

Goodwin, M.G. and Forsyth, H.A. (2003b) Enhancing Negotiated Work-based Learning (NWBL) by utilising third party private providers – a model. *Work-Based learning opportunities for Lifelong Learning. Conference proceedings November 2003 of the Work Based Learning Network of the Universities Association for Continuing Education and Intercollege, Nicosia, Cyprus.* National Centre for Work Based Learning Partnerships and Intercollege, Cyprus, pp. 43-51.

Goodwin, M.G. and Forsyth, H.A. (2004a) The impact of a work-based learning framework on University external relationships and internal structures. *Learning Transformations - Changing learners, organisations and communities* International conference proceedings July 2003, University of Stirling. Forum for the Advancement of Continuing Education, UK, pp. 206-214.

Goodwin, M.G. and Forsyth, H.A. (2004b) A work-related Foundation Degree framework – its concepts, nature and scope. *International Conference on innovation, good practice and research in Engineering Education.* University of Wolverhampton, June 2004. University of Wolverhampton, Vol. 2, pp. 29-33.

Goodwin, M.G. and Forsyth, H.A. (2005a) The role of reflection in supporting a continuous improvement cycle – A University Model for work related learning. *Access, Retention and Employability: Transforming Higher Education* International conference proceedings July 2004, University of Portsmouth,   Forum for the Advancement of Continuing Education, UK. pp.39-45.

Goodwin, M.G. and Forsyth, H.A. (2005b) Preparing the worker for work based learning - A successful approach. *Challenges for Integrating Work and Learning, Conference Proceedings of the 4th International Conference of Researching Work and Learning.* University of Technology Sydney, Australia www.oval.uts.edu.au/ Click on (RWL 4 papers)

Goodwin M.G. and Forsyth, H.A (2007) Work Place Learning: Building a sustainable framework. *Transformation, Progression and Hope: What ever happened to lifelong learning?* International Conference Proceedings, July 2006, University of Swansea. Forum for Access and Continuing Education, UK, pp.154-163.

Gray, D. (2001) *A Briefing on Work-based Learning.* Assessment Series No.11. Learning and Teaching Support Network (LTSN). York, UK.

Harvey, L. Locke, W. and Morey, A. (2002) *Enhancing Employability – Making links between higher education and the world of work* A report prepared by Universities UK and the Higher Education Careers Service Unit (CSU) Universities UK, London.

Smith, V. and Hughes, H. (2003) *'Making the difference' Provider support for learner retention and achievement in work based learning.* London: Learning and Skills Development Agency.

Quinn, J., Slack, K., Casey, L., Thexton, W., & Noble, J. (2005). *From life crisis to lifelong learning. Rethinking working-class "drop out" from higher education.* York: Joseph Rowntree Foundation.

HE and the needs of voluntary sector work based learning in Wales: Case Studies from the Voluntary Sector

K. J. Addicott, Dr. R. R. Payne and Prof. D. M. Saunders. University of Glamorgan Centre for Lifelong Learning

Introduction

This report is based on research which was undertaken on behalf of the Higher Education Funding Council for Wales as part of the *'Strategic development of high level learning for the workforce in Wales'* a collaborative feasibility study co-ordinated by the University of Wales Institute Cardiff, entitled *Scoping project S2: work based learning and the potential of recognizing prior learning within the public and voluntary sectors in Wales* undertaken by the University of Glamorgan.

The research included 5 case studies investigating work-based learning and the potential for recognising prior learning within a sample of voluntary sector workforces.

Data were collected through one or more of the following

- Desk study of relevant organisational documents
- Face to face interviews
- Telephone interviews/discussions

Semi-structured interviews, using open-ended questions, were undertaken with a sample of voluntary organisations that were diverse in terms of size, geographical area of operation, and targeted beneficiaries. Key areas of research enquiry were as follows:

- Organisational context and profile
- Interpretations of work-based learning

- Content and accreditation of higher level learning and development (current and future)
- Assessment and evaluation of provision
- Accreditation, certification and potential for recognition of prior learning.

All case study data were systematically recorded through note taking and key information and/or matters of interpretation were clarified during the interview process. Draft case studies were returned to individuals within their organizations for validation in order to ensure accuracy.

Case Study 1
Wales Council for Voluntary Action

Organisational Profile
Wales Council for Voluntary Action (WCVA) is a long and well established infrastructure organisation providing support for the voluntary sector across Wales. First registered as a charity in 1963, it represents supports and campaigns for voluntary organizations, volunteers and communities in Wales. The mission of WCVA is to strengthen voluntary and community action at the heart of a civic society in Wales. It does this through a wide range of funding, training, information, advice, research and policy activities. Some of WCVA's main sources of funding include Welsh Assembly Government, Charities Aid Foundation (CAF), Education and Learning Wales, European Structural Funds, Countryside Council for Wales, Workforce Development, Wales Co-operative Centre, and Welsh Language Board. WCVA is managed by a volunteer Board of Trustees elected from its membership organisations and employs approximately 120 paid staff.

WCVA does not have a collective union agreement, but does have staff who are members of a trade union and have union representatives in North and South Wales. They have a learning and development strategy and a programme of staff development opportunities throughout the year. This is linked into the Investors in People standard and a declared internal ethos for creating a learning environment for staff and Board members.

WCVA is leading for Wales on the 'Voluntary and Community Sector Workforce Development Hub', a partnership, involving other voluntary sector infrastructure organisations, for example, National Council of Voluntary Organisations in England, Northern Ireland Council for Voluntary Associations, and Scottish Council for Voluntary Organisations, to create strategies to address skills needs across the UK . It should be noted that the hub is not a Sector Skill Council in its own right; instead it feeds into a number of sector skills councils in order to represent and lobby for the interests of voluntary sector workforces. Initial funding for the work of the hub came from the Sector Skills Development Agency (SSDA). However, this funding has now ceased and WCVA, along with its sister councils, is currently in discussion with DIUS (Department of Innovation, Universities and Skills) and the Office of the Third Sector at UK level, and with devolved administrations, to secure long-term support for voluntary and community workforce development.

Content and accreditation of existing higher level learning

Overview of WCVA provision
Apart from its own staff, attendees on WCVA training (as with its other services) are mainly staff or volunteers from its member organisations and other voluntary communities in Wales, although some participants are from the public and private sector. In 2007/08 WCVA delivered 106 courses attended by 1,658 people.

WCVA, County Voluntary Services (CVS) and Welsh Assembly Government currently have a 5 year partnership agreement. This involves clear guidelines for services provided by the Voluntary Sector infrastructure in Wales. Part of this involves a new national training programme "Courses for Communities Cymru", involving 54 core courses, set mainly at Levels 2 and 3. The final version of this programme is due to run from April 08 - May 09. WCVA and the CVSs provide this kind of infrastructure training throughout Wales.

WCVA infrastructure provision for the voluntary sector
WCVA delivery of training to the voluntary sector in Wales takes the form of an annual training programme on a range of subjects. Topics include:

- Personal and Organisational Development training - for example, train the trainer, equality and diversity;
- European Training
- Sustainable Funding Cymru training – for example, business and strategic planning
- Grants – for example Fit for Funding
- Participation Cymru training - such as Community Engagement – tools, techniques and strategies
- Participatory project management
- Methods for involving young people.

All these are delivered face to face, at venues around Wales, and range in duration from three hours through one or two day non-accredited courses to nine day accredited programmes. Where provided, accreditation is usually through external providers. For example, funding advisor training is OCN accredited for 2-day and 4-day courses; and a 9-day leadership development programme is ILM endorsed.

Provision for WCVA staff
The organisation provides an internal staff development programme for WCVA employees. This programme includes but is not restricted to the topics covered in the annual infrastructure staff training programme for WCVA outlined previously. In line with Investors in People requirements WCVA is refocusing its internal provision to focus on staff skills and strategic competencies. To this end the internal staff training strategy and programme includes topics such as:

- customer service
- administrative staff development
- communication & influencing
- presentation skills
- representing your organisation/sector
- grant giving /funding
- line managing
- team leaders
- management skills.

Accreditation

The majority of WCVA courses are non-accredited and of those that are accredited most are delivered by WCVA staff with the remainder involving outside consultant trainers. Many of the non-accredited courses are equivalent to level 3 outcomes (with potential for working up to level 4). They offer one course accredited by OCN Level 3 'training the trainer' which is delivered over three days. Other courses are endorsed by credit making bodies and are in the pipeline for accreditation. Examples include a six day ILM endorsed higher level project management course (70/80 hours learning, tailored and developed for the voluntary sector); and a volunteer management 4 day course, to be accredited in 2008/09.This latter programme will be based on NVQ standards created by the Voluntary and Community Sector Workforce Development Hub.

Scope for accrediting existing and future training

There is potential for accrediting a number of WCVA's courses, including those which could be termed community development, personal skills and management skills. WCVA do not currently engage in APL or APEL, but would be interested in exploring this in the future. WCVA is increasingly involved in reviewing and developing the quality, appropriateness and nature of their courses as well as those provided by other voluntary sector organisations and would be an important and influential strategic partner in any future development of accreditation processes for the voluntary sector in Wales.

Case Study 2
Voluntary Action Cardiff

Organisational Profile
Voluntary Action Cardiff (VAC) is a well established infrastructure organisation providing support for the voluntary sector in Cardiff. It was founded in 1997 as one of the County Voluntary Councils which exist independently in each local authority area. VAC's main funders are Cardiff Council, Welsh Assembly Government (through WCVA) and Cardiff Local Health Board. VAC is managed by a volunteer Board of trustees elected from its membership organisations, and employs twenty one paid staff.

VAC's mission is to promote social justice by supporting the development of a vibrant and flourishing voluntary and community sector in Cardiff. Its declared aims are to:

> *promote social justice through community action that challenges powerlessness, prejudice, discrimination and deprivation; support the development of a more effective and efficient voluntary and community sector in Cardiff through the delivery of a range of support and capacity building services including information, advice, and training; support the development of a more influential and cohesive voluntary and community sector in Cardiff by facilitating networking and partnership within the sector, and between it and the public and private sectors.*

VAC has a development and training strategy which is reviewed annually and which highlights the core training that all staff have to undertake as well as specific training relevant to their roles within the organisation. VAC also encourages staff to identify their own learning and development needs. Both core and individual learning processes are supported by line managers through the supervision and appraisal system.

Content and accreditation of existing higher level learning

Overview of provision
VAC is one of the 22 CVSs in Wales and has a five year partnership agreement with Welsh Assembly Government. This includes clear guidelines on the infrastructure services to be provided to the voluntary sector in Wales in that period. A number of the courses VAC offers are part of the new national infrastructure training framework which has been developed under this agreement. VAC's training provision is developed on the basis of regular training needs analysis (TNA) of its members' needs, providing ongoing feedback and evaluation of provision. These courses are intended to have the equivalent of Level 2 or 3 outcomes.

In 06/07 VAC delivered 35 courses, attended by 339 people, of which 5 courses were accredited. In 07/08 VAC plans to deliver 43 courses. Attendees on VAC training (as with its other services) are mainly staff or volunteers from its member organisations and other voluntary groups in Cardiff.

VAC delivers training on a range of subjects including:

- Management committee roles
- Funding applications
- Financial management
- Planning and reviewing
- Employment law and procedures
- Partnership working
- Teaching and training
- Protection of vulnerable adults (POVA)
- Child protection awareness
- Community development
- Presentation skills.

All are delivered face to face, either at VAC's own training room or other accessible venues in Cardiff, and are either half or full day courses. Approximately one fifth of these are delivered by trainers from outside partnership agencies, for example: Worker Education

Association (WEA), Wales Co-operative Centre, Cardiff and the Vale Coalition of Disabled People or freelance private sector trainers.

Accreditation

The majority of courses are non-accredited, and delivered by VAC staff. All these staff are qualified or working towards a teaching qualification. Some courses provided by VAC are considered to be at level 3 with potential for working up to level 4 and others deemed to be at level 2. Training staff felt that there is differentiated learning within groups on courses, so that some learning may be at level 2, whilst others may be at level 3.

There were a few accredited courses on offer, which are delivered in partnership with other organisations that provide the accreditation processes. The following examples illustrate this

- Certificate in Delivering Learning: An Introduction (City and Guilds 7302, Level 3). This is a 15 week course conducted one evening per week with two additional compulsory sessions of one day (usually held on a Saturday).

- Contemporary Practice of Community Regeneration (provided by University of Glamorgan, Centre for Lifelong Learning) HE Level 1, 20 credits) 48 hours duration. This programme has been agreed but not yet commenced.

- Skills for Community work (HE Level 1, 10 credits) (provided by University of Glamorgan, Centre for Lifelong Learning) – 24 hours. This programme has been agreed but not yet commenced.

In addition to the above, VAC has also previously developed and delivered 'Managing in the Voluntary Sector' 20 credits at Level 1 in partnership with Cardiff University

Accreditation of prior learning
VAC does not currently carry out APL or APEL but would be interested in doing so and felt there was potential for staff tutors to participate in these processes with appropriate training. However, additional resources would be needed as there is no current capacity to undertake this additional work.

Scope for accrediting existing and future programmes/learning
There appeared to be significant potential to accredit programmes through partner organisations.

Case Study 3
Black Voluntary Sector Network Wales

Organisational profile
Black Voluntary Sector Network Wales (BVSNW) is an umbrella organisation that actively represents supports and promotes the interests of the Black and Minority Ethnic (BME) communities and the BME voluntary sector in Wales. Black Voluntary Sector Network Wales was officially constituted and launched in1997. Its objectives are:

- raising awareness of the needs of the Black Voluntary Sector communities
- building the capacity of the Black Voluntary Sector
- developing the membership of the organization
- represent, support and campaign for Wales' BME voluntary organizations, community groups, volunteers and communities in Wales
- playing a strategic role to incorporate the needs of BME communities within policy and strategy.

BVSNW does this through a range of activities such as partnership working (in particular with Communities First Support Network); consultancy and training; and special projects such as BME young people projects. Some of BVSNW's main funders are WAG, Wales Co-operative Centre, Big Lottery Fund, WCVA, the Arts Council for Wales, All Wales Ethnic Minority Association (AWEMA).

Black Voluntary Sector Network Wales is managed by a volunteer Board of Trustees elected from its membership organisations, and employs 8 paid staff.

Content and accreditation of existing higher level learning

BVSNW delivers between 30 and 50 courses per annum that are attended by public sector and voluntary sector staff as well as volunteers. They also provide training for BME groups across Wales. Black Voluntary Sector Network Wales provides a wide range of training such as cultural diversity and equalities to different groups of stakeholders. All BVSNW training courses are delivered face to face, at venues around Wales, including sometimes at their own offices in Cardiff. The organisation provides three main types of training:

- Courses related to the specific topic of equality of opportunity –with specific focus on race equality. These programmes typically include awareness raising, equality legislation and so on.
- Bespoke training and consultancy. This relates to training and services offered to individual organisations related to race equality.
- Training and development of skills within the BME community

Courses on Equality
These courses are usually 1 day for the public sector. For BME groups they tend to involve a series of three hour sessions during weekends, evenings or whenever is most accessible to the groups. It was emphasised that they would prefer to run more sustained and detailed three-day courses on topics like equalities schemes in order to ensure depth of understanding, reflection, and assessment of impact. However, public sector organisations tend to request only one day - a probable reflection of resource limitations.

Bespoke training and consultancy

BVSNW provides bespoke training and consultancy for organisations in the public and voluntary sector. For example, they have provided courses on implementation of equalities schemes for local authority employees; they have run focus groups for a consultation exercise on voluntary sector and equalities for a local authority; and have provided training for the Arts Council for Wales and Communities First Partnerships. These courses are considered to be potentially at level 3 or above.

Training and development of skills within the BME community

Examples of this category of training for BME groups include building confidence, funding, mentoring, and literacy. These courses are always tailored to meet a group's needs. Workers meet the group first to discuss and identify priorities and relevant interests so that they can be incorporated into the design and delivery of training. These courses would cover the whole spectrum of levels, from basic skills to higher level, reflecting the diversity of participants and their needs.

When providing, for example, equalities training for an organisation they also hold pre-meetings to establish expectations, and draw up a contract. Black Voluntary Sector Network Wales then create appropriate case studies and customised 'examples of evidence' for use in subsequent training. Other courses BVSNW run include topics such as race equality legislation, events management and training regarding the support needs for BME Artists (such as confidence building, profile management). Black Voluntary Sector Network Wales also run the LINK project which is for BME youth, and this includes training on mentoring, and facilitation skills.

BVSNW are currently in discussion with Disability Wales regarding the exchange of training for their respective beneficiaries, to support and inform the implementation of merging equalities legislation and infrastructure organisations, and share good practice.

Accreditation

All BVSNW training courses are currently non-accredited. These are generally delivered by BVSNW staff, and some outside consultant trainers, in a roughly two-thirds to one-third proportion. Black Voluntary Sector Network Wales also deliver training in partnership with other organisations (for example VAC, Welsh Assembly Government, or consultants). the organisation does not currently engage in APL or APEL, but would be interested in exploring this.

Scope for accrediting existing and future programmes/learning

There is evidently great potential for accreditation of courses both for public and voluntary organisations' staff, and BME groups. Black Voluntary Sector Network Wales identified the importance of cultural sensitivity, and language and literacy skills' needs of many of their learners. They highlighted the need for English for Speakers of Other Languages and Computer Skills as being two key areas for BME groups. There is potential for both basic skills and higher level skills training for their trainees and for planning a sound progression route to higher education accreditation processes. There is also potential for credit-rating the range of training they provide for larger public and voluntary sector organisations, which is higher level.

Case Study 4
British Red Cross

Organisational profile
The British Red Cross (BRC) was founded in 1870, and is part of the largest independent humanitarian network in the world, the International Red Cross and Red Crescent Movement, offering unconditional help to all people in need. The British Red Cross is a very large organisation providing a diverse range of services throughout the UK - from first aid to medical loan, skin camouflage to transport services, home from hospital to care in the home. The British Red Cross also provides two new services: support for

refugees and support for older persons. Support services are provided in the form of practical and emotional assistance to vulnerable asylum seekers and refugees in the UK.

The Red Cross responds to hundreds of emergencies every year and has a special role to play in supporting emergency services, as the organisation is included in local authority emergency plans for every county in the UK. All the charitable work carried out by the Red Cross is based on seven fundamental principles: Humanity, Impartiality, Neutrality, Independence, Voluntary Service, and Unity. The British Red Cross' funding primarily comes from fundraising activities, trading and some service generated funding, although it does receive some grant funding for projects - such as Big Lottery Awards for All. British Red Cross relies on volunteers as its largest resource for service delivery, co-ordination and training. In 2007 the British Red Cross had 28,857 volunteers active in the UK, including 1,863 in Wales. The British Red Cross has 182 employees in Wales's branches, as well as a number of staff employed directly by HQ based in Wales.The British Red Cross has divided the UK into four Territories with four Directors, (and an HQ in London), and these consist of twenty one areas. Services in each area are driven by the need in each area. Wales is one of these areas, and is unique in that it is split into four localities.

The British Red Cross do not have a collective union agreement, (although staff are free to belong to unions), but they do have a Joint Consultative Committee on to which staff are elected. Training needs are identified by individuals and line managers through human resource processes such as supervision and appraisal.

Content and accreditation of existing higher level learning

The Red Cross delivers more than 150 different courses to its staff. Most training is nationally controlled from head quarters in London. Uniquely, in the South West Wales locality, there are some local courses designed locally where they have identified a gap in training - such as infection control. These are now being considered by head quarters to be rolled out nationally. Training courses are run across the country, and most are provided locally for each sub-region in Wales in venues suitable for the training (for example Chepstow race course is used as outside grounds are needed to set scenes for first aid and emergency response, as well as using internal training rooms).

The Red Cross provides a range of training to all its staff and volunteers, as well as providing first aid training to the public. The majority of courses are delivered face to face, although initial pre induction and induction courses (for example *Introduction to BRC*) are offered on line or via a workbook, followed by a two hour workshop. In addition BRC have bought a number of external training packages which are available on line that also form part of the induction process. The majority of training is delivered internally by paid staff or volunteer trainers. All of the First Aid training is accredited. Volunteer Management courses have been designed for paid staff who manage volunteers and volunteer team leaders. They have eight modules, and each one lasts for a half-day and has been written by BRC head quarters using Institute of Leadership and Management (ILM) standards and frameworks. They are currently looking at the possibility of accrediting this course through ILM as a full diploma. The critical issue is the cost of registering and accrediting each student. Developing Management Skills is a four-day residential internal course for paid staff only. This is currently non-accredited.

Each Red Cross service has its own core training. *First Aid Service –* seven days Induction to First Aid – is accredited by BRC itself. The programme covers:

- Standard First Aid
- Manual Handling
- Radio Communication
- Infection Control
- Automated External Defib.

All are half or one-day competency based training courses. Further courses for enhanced skills are on offer - such as *Resuscitation Advanced* and *Trauma Management*. After that there's an additional option of Crew Ambulance training which involves a one-day exam including a written paper, and a practical scenario on resuscitation. This is accredited by the Institute of Health Care Development IHCD, as well as BRC, so participants receive a double certification of Red Cross Ambulance Crew and IHCD qualification.

BRC use volunteers to act as "casualties" in First Aid training, and provide training for these casualties. This involves eight different modules:

- Basic skills
- Technical acting
- Expedition training
- Drugs
- First aid at Work
- Role play
- Portrayal of disabled people.

All BRC staff are trained through NVQs in Care. Staff and volunteers have to gain qualifications to teach the first aid courses. BRC provide an internal Train-the-Trainers four-day certificate: three days on how to train, and one day assessing. APL is on offer for doctors as well as paramedics (with, for example, PGCE qualifications). Once they have done the four days training they work with a designated BRC mentor trainer, after which they are monitored whilst actually training. This leads to an assessment which, if successful, finally allows them to train for BRC. Following this they can do separate courses if they want to specialise - *Trauma* being one popular area.

Scope for accrediting existing and future programmes/learning

Some staff do currently engage in APL or APEL, for example in relation to criteria competencies for a variety of First Aid courses. If a doctor, nurse or medic testifies to previous experience, then they are asked to read through guidelines, and then interviewed in order to check for competency and understanding. They may be asked to demonstrate a particular skill (to prove they do it in their job), and a successful outcome leads to exemption from parts of the course. Certificates from an earlier course or qualification can also be accepted. There is significant potential for including APL or APEL in any new accreditation processes introduced with BRC.

Another service area is Emergency Response – involving a one-day Level 1 *Awareness* course , a one-day Level 2 *Emergency Response (ER)* (where volunteers help manage a rest centre) and a two-day *Providing Emotional Support* course. This programme was designed by a consultant in conjunction with BRC, and is internally accredited.

The BRC's new unique and developing training services include *Support for Refugees*, and *Support for Older Persons*. Some external courses are provided (such as POVA, delivered by the Council at levels 2 and 3) although they are difficult to access due to over subscription. National Vocational Qualifications in Care are needed for some workers as well as an NVQ 4 for managers. The Benefits Agency support BRC in the delivery of training in this area of work. Private sector providers are also commissioned – such as POVA and *Child Protection* - in order to complete the NVQ. Other non-accredited one-day internal courses are provided:

- Refugee Awareness
- Ideals in Action
- Equality & Diversity
- Promoting Diversity

These are areas of potential accreditation in the future as well as a course entitled *Developing Management Skills*. This is a four-day residential course for paid staff only and is not currently accredited.

Case Study 5
Llamau

Organisational profile
Llamau was founded in 1986, and has grown from a small, local charity into a small to medium sized organisation. The organisation

currently works across 9 Local Authority areas in South Wales to improve the lives of socially excluded, homeless people. It is a specialist provider of advice, accommodation and support to homeless young people with exceptionally high support needs. Some of Llamau's funders are Big Lottery, The Esmee Fairbairn Foundation, Arts Council of Wales, and the Oakdale Trust. Llamau is managed by a volunteer Board of Trustees.

Llamau run a number of different schemes – for example, mediation services, supported housing projects for individuals aged between sixteen to eighteen or eighteen to twenty one, tenancy support services (including young mums), women only projects, Young Person's Advisors schemes, bond scheme and learning centre. Llamau currently employs 190 paid staff. Staff learning and development needs are identified through a combination of approaches, from informal discussions with line managers, to formal performance management reviews.

Content and delivery of higher level learning

Llamau delivers more than 54 different courses to its staff. It has a Core Competency Training Matrix, which covers knowledge, skills and behaviour learning experiences. The development areas are either at an organisational level or job specific. Examples of the organisational level include:

- Health and Safety
- First Aid
- Equal Opportunities

Job specific examples include:

- Child protection
- Housing management
- Substance misuse awareness
- Basic counselling techniques
- Motivational interviewing

- Team management
- Anger management
- Presentation skills.

The content of these courses is designed to reflect the level of the individual's role (responsibility for staff or a project) and the learning needs of the individuals (taking into account their previous experience, training and qualifications). The majority of the courses are offered to staff within the first 18 months in post. The Core Competency Matrix also covers the learning needs of the Support Services function which includes Finance, Human Resources, and Fundraising.

Llamau provides training on a range of subjects to its staff, all are delivered face to face, most are non-accredited and the majority take place at Llamau Head Office in Cardiff. Courses last for a half, one or four-days. Most are delivered by external providers, by private sector consultants and companies but with some public sector involvement via local authorities. Providers include Housing Benefit Consultants, Conflict Solutions (who deliver Anger Management, Lone Working, Protection of Vulnerable Adults), Newlink Wales (Drug awareness, Drugs Education Training Level 1,2 and Advanced), and WIFA (Carpentry Skills).

Llamau provides training for service users through its Learning 4 Life project, which delivers level 1 – 3 OCN units in its Learning Centres in Cardiff, Newport, Caerphilly and Barry. Topics include Introduction to a Training Environment and Introduction to Cookery, as well as film making projects (allowing participants to work towards completing OCN units in Creative Arts and Leisure & Recreation). In 2006/07 Llamau also delivered 126 OCN units to 201 learners in the community.

Accreditation

Accredited courses on offer include First Aid, Manual Handling, Fire Safety and Mediation. They range from levels 1-4. Llamau do not currently engage in APL or APEL, but would be interested in exploring this possibility further.

Scope for accrediting existing and future training
There appears to be plenty of potential to work with Llamau to develop accreditation. Llamau are keen to accredit their learning and development programme and have indicated that they would definitely be interested in working in partnership with HE providers. The interesting challenge would be the added dimension of partnership with a range of potential training providers, both private and public sector in developing these processes. Llamau felt that offering accredited routes to support workers would be particularly beneficial, as they have extensive experience and knowledge but often have not followed traditional formal qualification routes.

A range of accredited courses would be beneficial not just for Llamau but for other organisations in the Housing Support sector. As a result of this suggestion, contact was made with Community Housing Cymru (CHC), the membership body for housing associations in Wales, which are all not-for-profit and provide around 95,000 homes and housing services throughout Wales. CHC provide a range of services including conferences, training, consultations, and promotional opportunities. They agreed that there was a need for accreditation for housing management and higher level staff, in particular because of the new Welsh Housing Quality Standard, on which the Welsh Assembly Government is focussing heavily. Housing support management staff need to implement such new areas of legislation and consider the accreditation of training (for example, in providing training and advice to clients) as very beneficial to the Housing sector. They identified scope for accrediting job-specific trade skills and professional and management skills for higher level senior staff. It appears that this is an area with plenty of scope for development of accreditation and progression routes for the housing sector.

Common Themes and Issues

The research identifies some common themes and issues which would need to be addressed by the HE sector in order to further develop accreditation and work-based learning processes with the voluntary sector successfully. Key issues identified were the need for:

- flexibility of provision
- diverse, appropriate and tailored methods of delivery and assessment
- greater understanding and knowledge of the voluntary sector and its culture, in particular the 'volunteer' dynamic and its impact on provision
- a multi layered approach for working with BME voluntary networks to encompass both basic and higher skills.

The challenge for the HE sector will be to explore future meaningful consultation methods and strategies with stakeholders within the voluntary sector in order to inform the development of accreditation processes, thereby ensuring that diverse needs are addressed.

References

Black Voluntary Sector Network Wales (2006) *Annual Report 2005 – 2006,* Cardiff: BVSNW   www.bvsnw.org.uk

British Red Cross (2005) *Volunteer Handbook* , London: BRC www.redcross.org.uk

Llamau (2007) *Annual Report 2007,* 'A step in the right direction'; *Training programme January 2007 to June 2008*; *Core Competency Training & Additional Training*; Cardiff: Llamau www.llamau.co.uk

Voluntary Action Cardiff (2007) *Annual Report 2006 – 2007, Training and Events Programme September 2007 – March 2008*; Cardiff: Voluntary Action Cardiff   www.vacardiff.org.uk

Wales Council for Voluntary Action (2007) *Annual Report 2006 – 2007, Training and events October 2007 – 2008*; Cardiff WCVA www.wcva.org.uk ;   www.coursesforcommunities.org.uk

Business Facing Skills Through Workbased Learning – A Higher Education Framework for Success

Alec Forsyth, H A Forsyth Consultancy,
Mike Goodwin, University of Wolverhampton, UK

For the purposes of this paper the term Business Facing Skills reflects the perceptions employers have of the range of knowledge, skills and employability attributes of employees to successfully support and continuously sustain their organisations. The ability to demonstrate the effectiveness of higher education to develop people with a wide range of relevant business facing skills (through graduation and continuous professional development as their careers progress) is becoming of increasing importance. (Forsyth and Goodwin, 2006, 2008a). In the United Kingdom vocational education is increasingly expected to provide up-to-date work-ready graduates (Department of Education and Employment (DfEE), 2003; Lambert, 2003; Little *et al.* 2003). Additionally, Universities are increasingly asked to: "Prove to us that your awards are relevant to our industry or my business".

The result is an increasing requirement for demand led learning frameworks, which support the development of employability through the acquisition of appropriate business facing skills, emotional competencies within the individual and indicate capability within the world of work. A high level of capability, through an up to date range of relevant business facing skills, will enhance the agility of an organisation to effectively respond to the continually rising expectations of its customers.   (Department for Children, Schools and Families (DCSF), 2007; Department for Education and Skills (DfES), 2005; Department of Innovation, Universities and Skills (DIUS), 2008; Harvey *et al.*, 2002; Leitch, 2006)
In order to reinforce industry credibility and develop the range of business facing skills, vocational higher education should focus on the following three key industry drivers:

- The use of best professional practice.
- The application of relevant up to date knowledge, skills and technologies.
- Successful innovation of products, services and problem solving.

An increasing focus by Higher Education on innovation as a key business facing skill is expected (DIUS, 2008).

Vocational learning incorporating these three key industry drivers will encourage University-employer collaboration at a range of organisational levels so supporting workbased learning. During the normal reflective and improvement cycles the value of, and opportunity for, innovation and its application should be explored - so enhancing a person's ability to respond to change. Developments in technology, socio-economic, market and competitive pressures both from within the UK and overseas, as well as career progression, will continually affect the constitution of each of these drivers and composition of business facing skills. The level of learning and consequent priority given to each of the drivers should be related to academic level descriptors, which could be used in conjunction with National Occupational Standards so enhancing industrial knowledge. Consequently lifelong learning through workbased continuous professional development will be required to maintain relevant up to date business facing skills for both the individual and the organisation. The determination of the acquisition and the successful application of these continuously updated business facing skills is through their assessment:

- self assessment
    - by the individual reviewing their own performance against given standards;
    - by organisations reviewing their own performance against given standards, including the performance of individuals contributing to the organisation.
- peer assessment
    - to determine an independent measure of performance and fitness for purpose against standards;

- o to develop parity of performance of both the individual and organisation across the network;
- academic assessment.
  - o offers learners the opportunity to advance to higher levels of achievement, effectiveness or quality of performance through negotiated programmes located within a workbased learning framework.
  - o is rigorously assessed, externally referenced and quality assured against national academic descriptors and standards.
  - o the development needs of both the individual and organisation, in the context of their work and of the wider framework of advanced knowledge and scholarship , are encompassed.

While accredited certification may not be a requirement for continuous professional development, the users of the products and services offered may demand it as a measure of the importance they attach to evidence of the capability of the organisation or individual. It also supports the development of the individual who may wish to progress to a higher level award enabling him/her to develop and evidence high level skills, the ability to cope with highly complex situations and the ability to effectively analyse, evaluate and reflect. This enables all involved to have confidence in the system, and will reassure new and current participants. Such accreditation by an independent awarding body demonstrates overtly that the learning and acquisition of business facing skills are fit for purpose. This will support or enhance the brand image of an organisation.

Continuous professional development that takes place that does not lead to an accredited award can be valuable in itself, provided that its value to the individual and the organisation can be evidenced, and providing that a lack of accreditation does not open the door to variability in standards and a loss of focus and or rigour.

The ability to make fair and rigorous self and peer assessments are important business facing skills. They should supplement both the reflective and improvement cycles so as to measure the appropriateness and effective application of current skills and identify future lifelong learning.

The purpose of this approach is to provide appropriate business facing skills in order to evidence and develop learners through workbased learning with:

- An ability to identify the components of and cope with complex situations
- A determined confidence to succeed based upon prior learning
- The flexibility and experience to both collaborate with others and think creatively
- An enhanced ability to anticipate and cope with change
- The knowledge and skills to:
  - act as an agent of appropriate change, innovation and knowledge transfer
  - both challenge and effectively apply their learning in the workplace
  - demonstrate relevance and learning progression to the benefit of both organisation and individuals
  - through the above evidence the up to date capability of the individual and employing organisation

It is increasingly difficult for would be participants to be released from work on a regular basis to attend traditional courses (The British Chambers of Commerce (BCC), 2007). Consequently workbased learning needs to accommodate a wide range of geographically dispersed persons and organisations.

Workbased learning not only takes learning to the workplace for those in work, but also provides relevant meaningful work experience to those on traditional programmes of study. It provides an opportunity for a range of business facing skills to be developed within a variety of contexts. It can take the participant out of the traditional class room into a learning environment where the participant is expected to cope with unfamiliar activities. Alternatively, the learner may be familiar with the work place environment but not with the learning processes and experience.

This mode of study should not only accommodate participants' preferences as to their learning style, but also combine and apply the theoretical with the vocational practical. It should also excite both the employer and employee by the relevance, academic and industry credibility of the learning on offer. (Forsyth & Goodwin, 2006; 2008a).

Vocational higher education through workbased learning should bring about a knowledge community, bridging the worlds of education and work (Boud and Solomon, 2000), and considerably reduce the significant differences between the academic and employment environments which militate against learning transfer (Candy and Crebert, 1990; Chalkley and Harwood, 1998), and satisfy the need to build skills through subsequent practice via a range of contexts (Cherniss and Goleman, 1998). This approach is compatible with the notion that motivation and interest are particularly important in learning transfer and sustained transfer of interpersonal skills to the work place (Axtell et al., 1997; Alexander and Murphy, 1999). It should widen the range of contexts through which learning occurs as well as encouraging learners to question, to innovate and to interact with others in order to create the knowledge and soft skills that will identify their capability. This is also recognised by enlightened employers, universities plus current government policies.

The flexible workbased learning framework should be designed to accommodate the expected range of participants. It should provide a framework that:

- is quality assured, flexible and highly responsive;
- scaffolds and supports Lifelong Learning in a workbased context;
- enables and empowers the individual to become an autonomous Lifelong Learner who plans, manages, reviews and develops her/his professional learning and functioning;
- provides a flexible learning environment where the needs of both the organisation and participant are central;

- meets the specific needs of individuals and their employers with respect to learning, training and professional development;
- encourages the enhancement of skills, knowledge and general personal abilities relevant to participants' context, aspirations and responsibilities;
- focus on both essential professional skills and also high-level "soft" skills such as initiative, self-management, creativity, innovation, emotional competences;
- develop in the learner confidence as an essential foundation of professional development;
- enhance the employability, professional effectiveness and business competitiveness of the learner in the context of rapidly changing employment, career and business demands
- be capable of rigorous, independent assessment against clear, appropriate and nationally accredited standards, encompassing a range of criteria appropriate to and able to accommodate the growing demands of the world of work.

Additionally performance indicators provide a tool to be used by employers, learners and tutors. They provide guidance in relation to:

- Deciding on an appropriate academic level of qualification
- Exploring the feasibility of making a claim for academic accreditation on the basis of prior experiential learning
- Setting aims and formulating objective.
- Designing learning activities
- Undertaking formative 'self checks' to ensure the programme is on track
- Encouraging productive dialogue among employers, learners and tutors so developing a common understanding through a common language. National Occupational Standards may offer a foundation for the development of a common language and understanding between employers and academics.

The success of workbased learning is reliant upon the tripartite partnership of employer, leaner and tutor. All must develop a common understanding of their individual roles and responsibilities (Goodwin and Forsyth, 2007) as well as those of the other partners in order to provide agreed meaningful workbased learning facilities and environments compatible with academic levels, assessment criteria, learner expectations and the continuous updating of business facing skills. Such tripartite relationships should prevent any partner working in isolation to the detriment of the workbased learning experience and outcome. Consequently the needs of each should underpin the learning on offer (Forsyth and Goodwin, 2008b) through the categories of needs;

Employer needs

- Cost effective training/learning programmes within the workplace with discernible pay back in terms of time utilisation, work relevance and cost benefit relations. Such programmes must support the three key drivers and up-to-date business facing skills.
- Staff development, which is vocationally relevant but is also flexible enough to meet the changing needs of the employer and organisation during the study period. Short lead times to implement any such associated changes in learning content, assessment and delivery are vital.
- To home grow the latent talent of their staff through 'tailor made' programmes to meet both employer needs and competitiveness plus employee aspirations.

Tutor needs

The tutor will need to utilise fexible workbased learning frameworks, as described above, within the workplace in order to:

- Identify and elicit the required information using appropriate sources and methodologies.

- Use the reflective and continuous improvement cycles (Goodwin & Forsyth, 2005a) to ensure that the leaner reflects upon the effect of previous activities and uses what is learned in future activities, to develop a range of business facing skills.
- Produce measurable outcomes to meet academic levels, assessment and emotional competencies all informed by the three key industry drivers. This requires analysis, evaluation plus reflection upon progress and its application for future learning. This goal-based approach has been found to be useful (Forsyth, 2002a, 2002b; Forsyth & Goodwin, 2002, 2004, 2005, 2008b; Goodwin & Forsyth, 2003a, 2003b, 2004a, 2004b, 2007).
- Be assured that the quality assurance aspects including facilities, learning environments, and both employer input plus criteria for learning assessments of any learning in the workplace are fully understood by both learner and employer before any workbased learning occurs.

Learner needs

- To be fully cognisant of the respective roles and responsibilities of the tutor, employer and learner so reducing any feeling of isolation.
- A cost and time effective workbased learning framework based upon the current and or future job functions of the learner.
- The assurance that the learning framework is able to accommodate prior, current, planned, unplanned and future learning while retaining a high degree of relevance to the candidate and employer.
- Employability through the attainment of an appropriate range of knowledge and skills providing continuing benefits to the employer.
- The conversion of aspiration into attainment.

- An appropriate level of learning support provided within the agreed learning framework in order for the learner to succeed. Such learning support should provide the transferable learning tools and skills appropriate for learning in both higher education and the workplace.
- The development of a safe learning environment so that the learner may take risks and learn from mistakes without loss of status with their tutors or managers and peers within the workplace.
- The synchronisation of the academic and experiential learning so as to fully support the learning environment, delivery and availability of facilities, tutor and employer inputs within the agreed time frame.
- Recognition by employers and peers of the value of the learning and qualifications attained.

Conclusion

The identification and inclusion of the appropriate components of business facing skills, coupled with the successful partnership of employer, tutor and learner within the workbased learning framework, enhances the opportunity to both evidence and develop learners with the abilities put forward within this paper relevant to their job, career aspirations and employer needs. Such collaborative work based learning should provide the agility, through continuous professional development, to respond to, and provide for, future business facing skills. It offers a self sustaining cost and time effective workbased learning framework, utilising the job functions of the learner. This sustains its relevance and effectiveness in a changing work environment now and in the future.

References

Alexander, P.A. and Murphy, P.K. (1999) Nurturing the seeds of transfer: A domain specific perspective – Rethinking mechanisms of a neglected phenomenon *International Journal of Educational Research* 31, pp. 561-576.

Axtell, C.M., Maitlis, S. and Yearta, S.K. (1997) Predicting immediate and long-term transfer of training *Personnel Review.* 26, pp. 201-213.

BCC., (2007) *UK Skills: Making the Grade* London, UK: The British Chambers of Commerce.

Boud, D.L., and Solomon, N. (2000) (eds) *Work based learning: A new higher education?* Buckingham, UK: Open University Press.

Candy, P.C., and Crebert, R. (1990) *Teaching for Now, Learning for Later; Transfer of Learning Skills from the Academy to the Workplace.* Paper presented to the 8th Australian conference on Language and Learning Skills, Queensland University of Technology, 11-13 July.

Chalkey, B. and Harwood, J. (1998) *Transferable Skills and Work-based Learning in Geography.* UK: Cheltenham Geography Discipline Network.

Cherniss, C, Goleman, D. (1998) Bringing Emotional Intelligence to the Workplace. In *A Technical Report issued by the Consortium for Research on Emotional Intelligence in Organisations.* USA: Graduate School of Applied and Professional Psychology, Rutgers University.

Connor, H. (2005) Workforce Development and Higher Education. London UK: Council for Industry and Higher Education.

Davies, P. (1999) Student retention in further education: a problem of quality or of student finance?
Access, www.leeds.ac.uk/educol/documents/00001257.doc

DCSF (2007) *Building on the Best. Final report and implementation plan of the review of 14-19 Work-related Learning. 14-19 education and skills.* Department, for Children, Schools and Families. Crown copyright UK.

DfEE. (2000) *Frameworks for effective work-related learning* Produced by the University of Cambridge Programme for Industry. London, UK: Department of Education and Employment.

DfEE. (2003) *21ˢᵗ Century Skills Realising our potential* Cm 5810 Presented to Parliament by the Secretary of State for Education and Skills, July 2003. Crown copyright. UK.

DfES. (2005) *Skills: Getting on in business, getting on at work.* London, UK: Department for Education and Skills. Cm6483-I, II, III..

DIUS. (2008) *Innovation Nation.* London UK: Department for Innovation, Universities and Skills, Cm7345 March 2008 Crown Copyright.

Forsyth, H.A. (2000) 'The Role of Benchmarked, pre computed National Catering Business Games (NCBG) in encouraging effective business decisions and lifelong learning'. In *The International Simulation and Gaming Research Yearbook, Vol. 8. Simulations and Games for Simulation and Change.* Saunders D & Smalley N (eds) London: Kogan Page, pp. 176-186.

Forsyth, H.A. (2002a) 'The contribution bespoke National Catering Business Games (N.C.B.G.) offer to study at undergraduate and postgraduate levels via Negotiated Work Based Learning (NWBL)' in *The International Simulation and Gaming Research Yearbook Vol.10, Employability: the role of Games, Simulations and Case Studies.* Maggie Boyle and Yvonne Smith, (eds) Edinburgh: Society for the Advancement of Games and Simulations in Education and Training, Napier University, pp. 209-216.

Forsyth, H.A. (2002b) 'A role for the National Catering Business Games (NCBGS) to offer parity of experiential learning for Graduate Apprentices (G.As) in hospitality' In *The International Simulation and Gaming Research Year Book Vol.10, Employability: the role of Games, Simulations and Case Studies.* Maggie Boyle and Yvonne Smith, (eds) Society for the Advancement of Games and

Simulations in Education and Training, Edinburgh: Napier University, pp. 202-208.

Forsyth, H.A. and Goodwin M.G. (2002) Games and Simulations; Their added value to Negotiated Work-based Learning (NWBL) and Emotional Competence Development. *Knowledge Work and Learning, Conference Proceedings of the Work Based Learning Network of the Universities Association for Continuing Education.* Middlesex University, London: National Centre for Work Based Learning Partnerships. pp. 74-89.

Forsyth, H.A. and Goodwin M.G. (2004) Higher Education – Does it meet employer's needs? A response. *International Conference on innovation, good practice and research in Engineering Education.* University of Wolverhampton, June 2004. Pub. University of Wolverhampton, Vol. 2, pp 213-218.

Forsyth, H.A. and Goodwin M.G. (2005). Should a University be involved in work-based learning? - A UK perspective. *Challenges for Integrating Work and Learning, Conference Proceedings of the 4th International Conference of Researching Work and Learning.* University of Technology Sydney, Australia www.oval.uts.edu.au/ and click onto (RWL 4 papers)

Forsyth, H.A. and Goodwin M.G. (2006) The University Alumni- a force for making a difference to lifelong learning through the workplace. *Proceedings of the The International Conference on Innovation, Good Practice and Research in Engineering Education 2006.* University of Liverpool July 2006. The Higher Education Academy Subject Centres for Materials and Engineering. UK. pp. 110-114.

Forsyth, H.A. and Goodwin M.G (2007) Widening Access and the Transition to Higher Education: A Catalyst for Development. *Transformation, Progression and Hope: What ever happened to lifelong learning?* International Conference Proceedings, July 2006, University of Swansea. Forum for Access and Continuing Education, UK, pp.135-143.

Forsyth, H.A. and Goodwin M.G (2008a)) The Development of Employability and Capability for Sustained Workforce Development through Vocational Higher Education. *Social Justice and Lifelong Learning: Diversity, Globalisation & Transformation.* International Conference Proceedings, July 2007, University of East London, Forum for Access and Continuing Education, UK.

Forsyth, H.A. and Goodwin M.G (2008b) Quality Assurance for Learning Brokers of HE – an Outline Proposal. *Social Justice and Lifelong Learning: Diversity, Globalisation & Transformation.* International Conference Proceedings, July 2007, University of East London, Forum for Access and Continuing Education, UK.

Goodwin, M.G. and Forsyth, H.A. (2000) A Development Of Professional Studies By Negotiated Work Based Learning (NWBL). *The Impact of Work Based Learning, Conference Proceedings of the Work Based Learning Network of the Universities Association for Continuing Education.* National Centre for Work Based Learning Partnerships, Middlesex University, London. pp. 13-23.

Goodwin, M.G. and Forsyth, H.A. (2003a) Negotiated Work-based Learning (NWBL) as a mode of learning designed to contribute to sustainable economic development (An UK model) *Work and Lifelong Learning in Different Contexts, Conference Proceedings of the 3rd International Conference of Researching Work and Learning.* Department of Education, University of Tampere, Finland. Proceedings Book II, pp. 51-58.

Goodwin, M.G. and Forsyth, H.A. (2003b) Enhancing Negotiated Work-based Learning (NWBL) by utilising third party private providers – a model. *Work-Based learning opportunities for Lifelong Learning. Conference proceedings November 2003 of the Work Based Learning Network of the Universities Association for Continuing Education and Intercollege, Nicosia, Cyprus.* National Centre for Work Based Learning Partnerships and Intercollege, Cyprus, pp. 43-51.

Goodwin, M.G. and Forsyth, H.A. (2004a) The impact of a work-based learning framework on University external relationships and internal structures. *Learning Transformations - Changing learners, organisations and communities* International conference proceedings July 2003, University of Stirling. Forum for the Advancement of Continuing Education, UK, pp. 206-214.

Goodwin, M.G. and Forsyth, H.A. (2004b) A work-related Foundation Degree framework – its concepts, nature and scope. *International Conference on innovation, good practice and research in Engineering Education*. University of Wolverhampton, June 2004. Pub. University of Wolverhampton, Vol. 2, pp. 29-33.

Goodwin, M.G. and Forsyth, H.A. (2005a) The role of reflection in supporting a continuous improvement cycle – A University Model for work related learning. *Access, Retention and Employability: Transforming Higher Education* International conference proceedings July 2004, University of Portsmouth, Pub. Forum for the Advancement of Continuing Education, UK. pp. 39-45.

Goodwin, M.G. and Forsyth, H.A. (2005b) Preparing the worker for work based learning - A successful approach. *Challenges for Integrating Work and Learning, Conference Proceedings of the 4th International Conference of Researching Work and Learning*. University of Technology Sydney, Australia www.oval.uts.edu.au/ Click on (RWL 4 papers)

Goodwin M.G., and Forsyth, H.A. (2007) Work Place Learning: Building a sustainable framework. *Transformation, Progression and Hope: What ever happened to lifelong learning?* International Conference Proceedings, July 2006, University of Swansea. Pub. Forum for Access and Continuing Education, UK, pp.154-163.

Harvey, L. Locke, W. and Morey, A. (2002) *Enhancing Employability – Making links between higher education and the world of work* A report prepared by Universities UK and the Higher Education Careers Service Unit (CSU) Universities UK, London.

H.M.Treasury (2004) *Skills in the global economy*. HM Treasury, UK.

Laing, C. and Robinson, A. (2003) The Withdrawal of Non-traditional Students: developing an explanatory model. *Journal of Further and Higher education,* 22.2

Lambert, R (2003) *Lambert Review of Business – University Collaboration (Final Report)*. H.M. Treasury, UK, Crown Copyright.

Learning and Skills Research Centre (LSRC) (2004) Learning Brokerage: Building Bridges between learners and providers. LSRC, UK.

Leitch, S. (2006) Prosperity for all in the global economy-world class skills (Final Report). H.M.Treasury, UK, Crown Copyright.

Little, B., Connor H., Lebeau, Y., Pierce, D., Sinclair, E., Thomas, L., and Yarrow, K. (2003) *Vocational Higher Education – does it meet employer's needs?* Learning and Skills Development Agency, London UK.

Taylor, S. (2001) *Getting Employers involved – improving work-based learning through employer links*. Learning and Skills Development Agency, London, UK.

Quinn, J., Slack, K., Casey, L., Thexton, W., & Noble, J. (2005). From life crisis to lifelong learning. Rethinking working-class "drop out" from higher education. York, UK: Joseph Rowntree Foundation.

How Can Work Based Learning Address the Needs of the Isolated Worker?

Professor Geoffrey C Elliott, University of Worcester

Introduction

This paper draws on lessons from the current development at the University of Worcester of a work based learning framework for higher education qualifications. This initiative was developed, in part, to address the needs of an isolated rural workforce, often employed in small and micro businesses in Shropshire, Herefordshire and Worcestershire, and is part of the University's drive to extend and enhance employer engagement. As well as including employer partners, the framework has drawn in the Chamber of Commerce, Learning and Skills Council, FE Colleges and Private Training Providers.

The paper focuses on aspects of programme design that give centrality to the workplace and the employee, overcoming the need for the employee to be away from the workplace to achieve a higher level qualification. It draws upon the 'practice of knowledge creation' (Gibbs et al, 2007) across the higher education and employment fields, to indicate how different this higher education venture is from conventional practice.

Implications for higher education development are explored, and the project is located in the context of the regional higher level skills action plan developed by the Regional Development Agency, and the local Lifelong Learning Network.

Purpose

This paper draws on lessons from the current development, led by the University of Worcester, of a work based learning framework for higher education qualifications. The framework, comprising academic awards at all levels from foundation degree through to professional doctorate, is learner centred and experience-led, and falls within the paradigm of lifelong learning (Elliott, 1999; Boud and Soloman, 2001). Hence its unique appropriateness as a mechanism for continual professional development for the isolated worker and others for whom the traditional university degree course is, for whatever reason, inappropriate.

The University's major objective over the next five years is to build on its reputation as a high quality University, widely recognised for excellent, inclusive higher education. (University of Worcester, 2007). Within the University's portfolio of courses, the work based learning scheme is a new arrival, introduced specifically to meet the learning needs of those who work in the University's immediate region of Herefordshire, Worcestershire and the surrounding area, a significant proportion of which are employed in small and micro businesses and enterprises and up to thirty miles away from any higher education provider. So it is necessary to explain something of the regional context before developing in more detail the drivers for the WBL scheme and the potential impact upon isolated workers and businesses.

The context of the University of Worcester's immediate region

The University's immediate region includes two County Council areas: Herefordshire, which is a unitary authority and Worcestershire, which comprises five District Council areas, and one Borough Council – Bromsgrove, Malvern Hills, Worcester City, Wychavon, Wyre Forest and Redditch. The two counties have a mixture of rural and urban areas. Herefordshire is predominantly rural with concentrations of population in a number of market towns and Hereford City. In Worcestershire, rural areas are more extensive in the south, west and north-west of the county. The remainder of the county, although interspersed by rural pockets, is more urban, particularly Worcester City and the districts to the north-east of the county adjoining Birmingham.

The sub-region is included in two of the regeneration areas identified by the Regional Development Agency – Advantage West Midlands. The Central Technology Belt, which runs along the M5 corridor from central Birmingham to Malvern in south Worcestershire and the Rural Regeneration Zone that includes all of Herefordshire and a very small area to the north-west of Worcestershire.

The overall size of the total residential population is nearly ¾ million, and projected to grow by 3% to 2014. Population density decreases as you move westward across the sub-region. In Herefordshire, the estimated population density in 2006 is 82 people per square kilometre, whereas in Worcestershire, the estimated population density is 319 people. Herefordshire is one of the most sparsely populated counties in England.

The local learning and skills council plan provides comprehensive data on population and workforce demographics in its local plan, from which the local economy metrics in this paper are sourced. The adult working age population (16-65 years old) accounts for 64% of the total residential population. Future projections indicate that the size of this age-group is likely to remain virtually constant in terms of overall size up to 2014.

In 2004, almost 8,000 residents in the two counties reached the age of 65. Using current economic activity rates as a guide (81%), potentially 6,500 people in this group were economically active and thus will have left the workforce. This level of retirement represents a significant loss of skills and experience from the workforce, which in many instances will need to be replaced. Forecasts for the next ten years show that both the volume and proportion of the resident population reaching 65 will continue to grow. By 2014, the proportion of the population reaching 65 will have grown by close to one third (a 33% increase since 2004).

The rurality and isolation of Herefordshire has proved, especially in recent times, a positive attraction for those moving into the county. There is a real trend of 'lifestyle-changers' who are attracted to the county in search of the rural idyll. Much of the industry base in

Herefordshire is connected to quality of life products such as food and drink, from small specialist food produces such as Tyrrell's Crisps to large multi-nationals such as Bulmers, now owned by a Carlsberg and Heineken consortium. Sustainable development is a significant local priority, and many related initiatives such as transition towns find a warm reception.

Work based learning as a field of study

The WBL scheme development group, as experienced Higher Education practitioners, were highly aware of the HE context in which the scheme would be developed, and equally aware of the potential for the scheme to bring isolated businesses in the University's immediate region into Higher Education. So the WBL scheme was developed in the context of wider changes in HE, responsive to new work practices and cultural logics within societies. For example, change in organisational practices has meant flatter structures in terms of management hierarchies and individual practitioners taking greater responsibility. Arising from this are new ways of making meaning and new ways of framing questions and making enquiries into meanings. A higher education response is to construct programmes of learning that enable practitioners to take a critical, reflexive and evidenced-based approach to change and development at work.

In surveying the work based learning field in preparation for a forthcoming text on WBL research methods (Costley et al, forthcoming) it has become clear that multi-disciplinary approaches to knowledge are now necessary to answer the questions of complex societies. It is with this background in mind that work based learning as a field and mode of study in higher education took up a unique approach to programmes of study or particular work-based modules in the UK about 15 years ago. Many of these programmes or modules are not developed from a subject disciplinary perspective, they use generic assessment criteria and focus on practice that has a particular work context. Work–based and professional studies usually have a multi-disciplinary and inter-professional approach to their learning programmes even if they are developed in a particular subject area. This kind of practitioner–led research and development has now become a principal means of developing organisational learning and enhancing the effectiveness of individuals (Barnett and Griffin, 1997; Rajan, 2000) and an essential capability for people at work. Both government and employers have highlighted this area of knowledge and skill in their key skills initiatives (DfEE, 1998).

The curriculum in work based learning is a new and emerging field of study in higher education (Jary and Parker, 1998; Boud and Solomon, 2001). Universities are now beginning to establish a research infrastructure that promotes and develops practitioner-led research and development and apply quality assurance to the delivery mechanisms of research and development at work. Approaches to work based learning as a 'field' of study, e.g. in programmes of Work Based Learning Studies as well as a 'mode' of learning, e.g. in subject discipline degrees that meet at least some of the learning outcomes through WBL, have some differences. Despite the differences in the implementation of work based learning across the UK and internationally, programmes that include elements of work based learning as a mode of study still have much in common with those that treat it as a field. We share similar approaches to knowledge and understanding that is generated outside of the university in a context of practice. We share similar pedagogical approaches, where students are 'experts' in the sense that they are or have been in a particular work situation and have understanding of its nuances, micro-politics and so on. Students researching their own practice are a common scenario in WBL programmes of study.

Drivers for the Worcester WBL scheme

In 2005, the University initiated a comprehensive curriculum review, identifying strengths and weaknesses, and areas for potential growth, which in turn led to the formation of a number of Curriculum Innovation Groups (CIGs), comprising academic staff from the University and its college partners. The Leadership and Management Curriculum Innovation Group identified the need to have a WBL Scheme within the University. There were at least ten key drivers for this:

1. Scale. Most private companies in the immediate region are SMEs – small and medium size enterprises with less than 250 employees. In fact many employ considerably fewer, and the majority under 25 employees.

2. Rural isolation. Herefordshire, Worcestershire and the surrounding areas of Shropshire, and Gloucestershire are key local markets for the University. All are significantly rural in character, with associated issues of infrastructure, communications, transport etc.

3. Skills agenda and employer engagement. The regional skills partnership has identified significant skills gaps in the region surrounding the university, and the University's own research and that carried out by the local Lifelong Learning Network, has established that employers require bespoke education and training provision tailored to their immediate and longer term needs.

4. Lifestyles. Combining the various demands of work, family, leisure and study means that, for most learners, a flexible mode of delivery is essential to successful HE participation, retention and completion.

5. Progression. Many employees have a depth of prior experience which can be a launch pad for higher level study. Effective approaches to recognising and accrediting this were seen as a high priority.

6. Knowledge Transfer, Innovation and Enterprise (KTIE). Discussions with employers and employees identified the need to link higher education more effectively with KTIE in the workplace. The traditional model that located course design in the academy and overlaid work placement / experience onto the academic programme needed revisiting.

7. Precedent. Through academic collaboration, links had already been established with the National Centre for Work

Based Learning at Middlesex University, and a successful model of WBL programme development identified.

8. Inter-professionality and knowledge exchange. The tradition of developing separate courses in separate departments no longer reflected the external reality. Inter-professional structures and practices were becoming the norm, particularly in the public sector, for example in Children's Services where professionals from different professional and discipline backgrounds routinely worked closely together.

9. Continuing professional development. The work based learning scheme spans Foundation Degree through to Professional Doctorate, allowing for participation by all levels within the workforce from associate / professionals to senior executive / practitioners. And an academic progression route available to any employer/employee, in any sector, through flexible, part-time study.

10. Coherence and compatibility. The WBL programmes sit well with other academic programmes designed for specific sectors and levels. They offer a flexible and radically different alternative, centred around a different form of knowledge creation, whose locus is in practice, application and utility. However integrating the new qualifications within the University's portfolio is achieved by embedding the awards within the existing undergraduate and postgraduate regulatory framework. (These frameworks had themselves been recently revised to be more flexible, making integration of the WBL qualifications a realistic proposition.)

How the WBL scheme supports other initiatives in addressing local and regional skills needs

Synergy between curriculum development, regional skills priorities and the strategic objectives of partner institutions is, in general, central to unlocking government and institutional resources and commitment, both of which are fundamental to sustainability. Therefore it was important to ensure that the WBL scheme was well-integrated with the Regional Skills agenda, led by the Regional Skills Partnership, an arm of the West Midlands Regional Development Agency, Advantage West Midlands (AWM 2008). The regional skills action plan is highly focused on partnership delivery, and one of its key objectives is to achieve a LSC/AWM Skills Strategy agreed and supported by regional partners. It highlights the need to identify higher level skills needs to support and grow regional economy, to identify appropriate funding regimes to support activity (especially ESF and ERDF), to agree a strategy to attract and retain more graduates in the region, to ensure that LLNs, HEIs and FE providers work within local partnerships to widen participation and sustain employment , and to achieve demand led provision developed through LLNs, Fdf, HEIs and FE providers interaction with employers. By placing the employer, the employee and the workplace in which they interact at the centre of curriculum development, work based learning programmes are uniquely well placed to support increased higher level skills through better university employer engagement. Both as a mode and as a field of learning, WBL is particularly well suited to learners in remote locations as the need to travel to a university or college centre of learning is avoided – the workplace itself becomes the centre of learning, with educational resources directed towards supporting remote learners to study in their own setting.

The role of the local Lifelong Learning Network in supporting learner access and higher education curriculum development in Herefordshire and Worcestershire has been very significant. The LLN comprises, the University of Birmingham, Open University, University of Worcester (lead HEI), the local FE Colleges, and other local providers of higher education. The LLN is well supported by the LSC, the local authorities, and other regional government bodies. The WBL framework has been seen by the LLN as a key mechanism for delivery of its key aims, to support vocational learner transition, develop new vocational programmes, improve access through guaranteed progression arrangements and credit agreements, and strengthen provider collaboration.

A strategically important local development which the WBL scheme will support is the *HE for Herefordshire* project, which was formally launched in the wake of a HEFCE funded HE demand study (HEFCE 2005) that looked at options for higher education across the three areas of the Marches: Herefordshire, Shropshire and Powys. The study concluded that whilst there was insufficient demand for a traditional university in Herefordshire (primarily due to issues of rural demographics and infrastructure), there was considerable scope for a managed collaboration between existing providers of higher education, to increase provision and stimulate new demand for higher education, particularly in the local workforce.

HE for Herefordshire is a managed network, led by the University of Worcester, as the lead HEI. It forms a distinct part of the structure of the Herefordshire and Worcestershire Lifelong Learning Network, with its own Management Board. The key priorities for *HE for Herefordshire* are to develop a credit accumulation system within the framework of the Lifelong Learning Network, to help to fill regional skills gaps, and to improve collaborative working with a range of partners in Herefordshire. The aim of *HE for Herefordshire* is to focus on HE provision in and for the people of Herefordshire. This includes improving the range of provision, both locally and remotely delivered, and ensuring improved take up and progression opportunities for all people who might benefit from them. It also involves extending the vocational curriculum, including work-based learning, and working more closely with employers.

Some issues and approaches

Thinking particularly about the needs of learners in the isolated rural communities of Herefordshire, Worcestershire and the surrounding areas, especially those in work, effective approaches to recognising and accrediting prior experience and learning (APEL) were felt to be a high priority for the WBL scheme. The team developing the scheme recognised at the outset that a systematic approach to APEL would be required, following QAA guidelines, and that there would be a resource implication in terms of staffing and administration costs. Similarly, the personalised learning approach required in a

WBL programme requires extensive use of individual and small group interactions with tutor-supervisors, which would form a major element of the costing model. Conversely, WBL programmes would move away from traditional learning and teaching methods, with their associated costs. From both perspectives, the WBL programme seemed ideal to meet the needs of a predominantly rural population.

Because it is often easier to attract businesses and learners to targeted, unitised module-based learning programmes, it was important to agree also that short CPDcourses and interim awards could also be encompassed within the WBL framework, and suitable nomenclature, consistent with University regulations, applied to these. The interim awards, typically Certificates and Diplomas, would be recognised and promoted as pathways to full award, with full credit allocated towards the next level degree award. Equally, it was important to confirm that individual modules within a WBL CPD framework could be funded by the HE Funding Council, and to then ensure that the institutional returns for these programmes of study were made to HEFCE correctly. Proper funding recognition for this work is absolutely key to its viability and sustainability, particularly where the market has high sensitivity to financial costs.

The needs of academic and support staff within the University were considered from the outset, with plans for a full staff development programme to familiarise colleagues with the range of WBL awards and routes through them. This investment was considered crucial, given that the WBL scheme was quite different from a typical University course. Those developing the WBL programme were keen to ensure that consistent terminology was used to describe the stages of the scheme, and that its accessibility should be easily recognised. It was anticipated that, in common with the experience at Middlesex, some of the first participants on the WBL scheme could be employees of the University, which provided a further instrumental reason for thorough internal promotion of its features and benefits.

Equally important was the need to communicate the Scheme to employers. The Steering Group planned a conference for employers to hear about this development and how it could be of use to both them and their workforce. Local public sector employers, such as the local authorities, NHS, police, were individually targeted as significant clients for the WBL programme.

Conclusion

In this short paper I have tried to draw out some significant lessons learnt from the current development, led by the University of Worcester, of a work based learning framework for higher education qualifications, and to show how work based learning is particularly appropriate to meet the needs of isolated rural workforces. I have suggested that the success of WBL programmes depends in great part upon the active co-operation, from the earliest planning stages, of employers, other HE providers, and appropriate agencies who can provide funding and other support. For example, in the University of Worcester WBL scheme, the local Chamber of Commerce has participated on the Development Working Group and promotes the scheme to its members, many of which are the SMEs and micro-businesses that the WBL scheme particularly targets.

The scheme has given a cutting edge to the university's desire to become more closely engaged with employers. Whilst not in any way replacing traditional courses designed for one particular sector or employee group, the WBL scheme allows for the needs of diverse employers and employees to be met through a higher education programme of workplace-rooted knowledge creation practice. In practical terms, the programmes, which span all HE levels from Foundation Degree to Professional Doctorate, give centrality to the workplace and the employee, overcoming the need for the employee to be away from the workplace to achieve a higher level qualification. As Gibbs and Costley (2006: 346) correctly summarise, in work based learning, 'Students are the primary agent of control and the exercise of this agency within critical academic and professional environments is the basis of the impacts that WBL programmes can have upon individuals and their work situations or professional area'. These attributes will form the centre of the marketing promotion of the scheme, which is the next phase of development. The planned evaluation will assess the extent to which the scheme is successful in engaging isolated businesses and employees.

References

Advantage West Midlands, *Skills Action Plan.* Accessed 2nd June 2008
http://www.advantagewm.co.uk/Images/Skills%20Action%20Plan%20Document%20final_tcm9-10743.pdf

Barnett, R. and Griffin, A. (1997) (eds) *The end of knowledge in Higher Education*, London: Cassell.

Boud, D. and Solomon, N. (2001) 'Future Directions for Work-based Learning: Reconfiguring Higher Education'. *Work-Based Learning: A New Higher Education?* Boud, D. and Solomon (eds), N. Buckingham: SRHE and Open University Press.

Costley, C., Elliott, G. and Gibbs, P. (forthcoming) *Doing Work Based Research*, London: Sage.

DfEE (1998) *The Learning Age*, Green Paper, February, 1998, London: HMSO.

Elliott, G. (1999) *Lifelong Learning: the politics of the new learning environment*, London: Jessica Kingsley.

Gibbs P., Dickerden, M., Elliott, G., Garnett, J. (2007) 'Introduction to Work Based Learning' Special Issue of *Research in Post-Compulsory Education*, 12 (3), pp. 277-278.

Gibbs, P. and Costley, C. (2006) 'Work-based learning'. *Research in Post-Compulsory Education* 11(3) pp. 341-350.

Herefordshire and Worcestershire Learning and Skills Council, *LSC Plan 2006-2007*. Accessed 10th May 2008, http://readingroom.lsc.gov.uk/lsc/2006/ourbusiness/strategy/nat-herefordshireandworcestershireannualplan200607-pl-may%202006.pdf

Higher Education Funding Council for England, *Options for higher education in Herefordshire, Powys and Shropshire.* Accessed 2nd June 2008 http://www.hefce.ac.uk/pubs/rdreports/2005/rd07_05/

Jary, D. and Parker, M. (eds) (1998). *The new higher education: issues and directions for the post-Dearing university.* Stoke on Trent: Staffordshire University.

Rajan, A. (2000) *Employability: Bridging the Gap between Rhetoric and Reality. Employers Perspective,* London: Create/PDF/IPD.

University of Worcester (2007) *Strategic Plan 2007-2012*. Accessed 9th May 2008, http://www.worc.ac.uk/documents/Strat_Plan_FINAL.pdf

ANNEX 1

The University of Worcester Work Based Learning Scheme

Foundation Degrees

LEVEL 4	CREDITS	LEVEL 5	CREDITS
Portfolio Development (including Academic study Skills)	30	Portfolio Development	15
Reflective Practice	30	Choice of existing modules	1/2 x 15
Choice of existing modules	1/2 x 15	Enquiry – Project Preparation	1 x 15
Enquiry in Practice	1 x 15	WBL Modules	2/3 x 15
WBL Module	1/2 x 15	WBL Project	30
TOTAL	120		120

BA/BSc (Hons)

LEVEL 4	CREDITS	LEVEL 5	CREDITS
Portfolio Development	30	Portfolio Development	15
Reflective Practice	30	Choice of existing modules	1/2 x 15
Choice of existing modules	1/2 x 15	Enquiry – Project Preparation	1 x 15
Enquiry in Practice	1 x 15	WBL Modules	2/3 x 15
WBL Module	1/2 x 15	WBL Project	30
TOTAL	120		120
Level 6		"Top up"year	
Portfolio Development	15	Portfolio Development	15
Research and Enquiry	30	Research and Enquiry	30
WBL modules	2/3 x 15	WBL modules	2/3 x 15
Independent Study	30	Independent Study	30
TOTAL	120		120

Masters degree

LEVEL 7	CREDITS	
Portfolio Development	20	
Methods of Enquiry/Project Planning	40	
Reflective Practice	20	Option
WBL	40	
WBL	20	Option
Dissertation	60	
CREDITS	**180**	

Postgraduate Certificate

Portfolio Development	20	
WBL **or**	40	
Portfolio Development	20	
Reflective Practice	20	
WBL	20	
CREDITS	**60**	

Postgraduate Diploma

120 credits made up of the Post Graduate Certificate modules and a further three modules not including the Dissertation	120 made up of 20 or 40 credit modules	
CREDITS	**120**	

LEVEL 4	CREDITS	
University Certificate award – any 2 modules	30	
University Diploma award – any 3 modules	45	
LEVEL 5		
Intermediate Certificate – any 2 modules	30	
Intermediate Diploma – any 3 modules	45	
LEVEL 6		
Advanced Certificate – any 2 modules	30	
Advanced Diploma – any 3 modules	45	

Section Three :

Formalising the Informal

Looked After Children and Educational Achievement

Deirdre Lynskey, Aimhigher Greater Merseyside

Introduction

Children in care are one of the most vulnerable groups in our society. Currently there are over 6,000 children placed within the care system in England. Sixty two per cent of those in care are there because they have endured abuse or neglect. This evidently has a profound impact on their development. Forty five per cent of 5 – 17 year olds in care are assessed as having a mental health disorder (this is four times higher than in other children) and 28 per cent of children in care have a statement of special educational needs (SEN) which compares to only three per cent of all children.

It is therefore not surprising at all to find that the outcomes for children in care are extremely bleak. Data for 2006 highlight that only 12 per cent are gaining five GCSEs at A – C compared to 59 per cent of all children. Twenty nine per cent of children who had left care were not in education, training or employment (NEET) at the age of 19, compared to 13 per cent of all young people. Children in care are three times more likely to have some dealing with the criminal justice system, and between 25 per cent - 50 per cent of children in care end up in custody as adults.

The current care system dictates that a child who is in care should, by the age of 18 be living independently. The role of the 'Corporate Parent' who up until then has been responsible for the child, stops and the 'care leaver' is then extensively responsible for themselves. Any of us who are parents knows only too well that parenting never ceases! How many of us say, 'We used to care for him/her, now we don't'! Many Local authorities do offer support to care leavers within their leaving care service, social workers or personal advisors provide support to find housing and or financial support if in the young person remains in education. Some young people continue to live with their foster carers and many find accommodation in supported lodging schemes.

With such stark statistics it is no wonder that so few children who have had experiences of the care system are continuing into further and higher education. A number of legislative acts and guidance has been issued since 1989 but within those 19 years very little improvement has been made in terms of the outcomes of looked after children and care leavers . This paper attempts to highlight some of the reasons why legislation and guidance has not proved effective and what current practice is now beginning to be implemented to counteract this.

Local Authority Research

Discussions with three local authorities (Sefton in Greater Merseyside, Westminster, and Kensington and Chelsea in London) highlighted that local authorities face very similar barriers recognised by the Government's White Paper: Care Matters: *Time for Change* (2007) which sets an ambitious strategy for transforming the life chances of children in care. Presently, the White Paper is informing the structure and content of the Children and Young Persons Bill, which is part of its comprehensive package of system reform. Comparisons between these authorities shows that although structured very differently, their issues were in the main similar. There was one major difference however which did make a huge impact on resource and time, and that is the number of looked after children placed out of authority care, i.e. living in foster or residential care in another borough. This particularly affected the two London authorities, Kensington and Chelsea and Westminster.

Very often, when a child has been placed in care, they will have already missed a considerable amount of schooling due to their disruptive and traumatic lives. Because of the lack of foster and residential placements in the local authority a child can be moved to a different school in a different town. This is a particular issue for the two London authorities, where they have introduced policies which   support children to stay within the families whenever possible, with appropriate support, or for the child to enter a family with   Special Guardianships,   giving the special guardian legal parental responsibility for the child until they reach 18. This is different from an Adoption Order, as it does not remove parental responsibility from the birth parents, however they would only be able to exercise this in exceptional circumstances.

In practice, this means that the child is no longer the responsibility of the local authority; the special guardian will have responsibility for all day-to day decisions about caring for the child and for taking important decisions about their upbringing, for example their education. And, importantly, although birth parents retain their legal parental responsibility, the special guardian only has to consult with them about these decisions in exceptional circumstances.   More often than not Special Guardianships are members of the child's family.

In Westminster, where the majority of their looked after children are placed out of borough, the team have to deal with over 40 local authorities and their respective schools. This incurs a major drain on resources in terms of social worker time and travel commitments. More significantly it affects the child who not only has to deal with the trauma of leaving home but also   community and familiar surroundings.

The new Children's Bill attempts to ensure that there is more stability for children in care in relation to their education, for example it states that social workers will not be able to move a child at key stage four (years 10/11) unless under 'exceptional circumstances'. Currently 15 per cent of looked after children (LAC) start year 10 outside of the normal admission process compared to just 3 per cent of all children. All three authorities welcomed this provision. For many children, where their placement has broken down and as a consequence they have had to move school, the impact is enormous. The curriculum in the new school may be very different and being delivered at different stages, and making new friends and explaining why you have moved can be extremely distressing for a young person. In one authority it was revealed that the placement had broken down so badly that the child was unable to reclaim their GCSE course work from the house - this obviously had a devastating impact on their overall GCSE grades.

The tracking and sharing of attainment level data for LAC is an issue for all three authorities: all argued that this could and should be given high priority. However, collection of data is still very difficult and there are still many cases where data is incomplete (for example schools not being able to provide test scores because the child has not been able to complete and follow up assessments); this results in gaps in attainment resulting in inaccurate target setting. All three authorities are currently investing considerable time and resources to ensure that correct data is obtained and shared between the relevant teams. This becomes especially difficult where children are schooled out of authority, where schools have not always seen the priority of sharing such information. As part of the government reforms, Local Authorities are creating 'Virtual Schools', for LAC. A Head teacher will manage this by liaising with schools and other educational establishments to ensure that LAC are receiving the correct level of educational support and that the relevant attainment and target setting data is collected and analysed.

The three local authorities within this study are all at different stages within this process.

- Westminster has for the past two years been developing the role and is therefore more advanced. Situated within Children's Services the team is headed up by an Education of Pupils in Care manager, two case workers, responsible for specific case loads and an Educational Psychologist. The team also works closely with other professionals within the children's services portfolio. The team has over the past two years been able to embed itself within the authority and the virtual head teacher sits on a number of strategic and operational groups to ensure that the outcomes for LAC are prioritised.
- In Kensington and Chelsea the part time head teacher has been in place since September 2007. The team is also

comprised of one part time primary and two full time secondary teachers.

- Within Sefton, the team is comprised of an education worker, a learning mentor and a multi agency youth worker. The Head teacher for the virtual school will be in place in September 2008, and a consultant works part time in preparation for this post, i.e. gathering data, setting up systems and structures.

All three authorities agree that the process of completing the Personal Education Plan (PEP) is in need of drastic improvement. It is statutory that when a child becomes 'looked after' the local authority draws up a care and a placement plan that should be reviewed and assessed at regular intervals. The 1989 Children Act further emphasised the importance of assessment and review of these plans. The DCSF 'Education of Young people in Care' Guidance (2000) states :

> *Every child and young person in public care needs a personal education plan which ensures access to services and support: contributes to stability, minimises disruption and broken schooling; signals particular and special needs; establishes clear goals and acts as a record of progress and achievement. (5.17)*

In the guidance point (5.17) is underlined, obviously emphasising that the DCSF strongly recommend that the PEP should be a priority for social care and educators. Yet this has not been the case in practice. The plan has four areas that it should concentrate on: 'An Achievement Record' (academic or otherwise), 'development and educational needs', (short and long development of skills, knowledge or subject areas of skills), 'short term targets' (including progress monitoring), and long term plans and aspirations (targets including progress, career plans and aspirations).

Past practice has relied on social workers being responsible for initiating and ensuring that PEPs are completed as they are incorporated within the care and placement plans. Schools have jointly been responsible for the PEP's content ie that what it contains is relevant and up to date. However it is now recognised that this is not working as effectively as anticipated. During the consultation process for the Care Matters Green Paper, a group of young people highlighted that the review process was extremely diverse: One young person commented:

> 'I didn't know I was able to go to my review.'

A response from another young person:

> 'My social worker phoned me up afterwards to see how I felt it went and whether I felt ok about it'.

All three local authority representatives have placed the monitoring of the PEP process as a high priority, because of the lack of information contained in them at present. Training and support packages have been developed and delivered to enable social workers to come up to speed on educational areas:

> 'it is very difficult to expect a social worker to report on educational progress when they don't even know what the key stages are!'.

Multi agency forums and conferences are just two examples of how authorities are attempting to ensure that all professionals working with LAC are kept fully informed of developments in areas of education and social care.

Emerging Issues

In most circumstances the number of LAC within a school is small compared to total population. However, the support and resources that are needed to support these young people will vary according to their particular circumstances. The new Children and Young Persons Bill will for the first time place the role of the designated teacher' (DT) as a statutory responsibility for all schools ensuring, *that the needs of children in care are treated as a priority by all schools and that educational support for children in care is effectively co-ordinated including by establishing stronger relationships between schools, social workers and carers.* (Impact assessment of Children and Young People Bill 2007)

However, this statutory responsibility does not address the issue comprehensively. It is suggested in the guidance that this role is undertaken by someone with seniority within the school. A fundamental weakness involves there being no stipulation for allocated time within the school day to fulfil this role.

To ensure that DTs are undertaking their role effectively there must be recognition and a commitment to enable this to be done within the school day/year. If the DT is a staff member who has a timetable that restricts access to them for the main part of the working day and no time to collect, analyse, record and share appropriate attainment and attitudinal information, then looked after children will not be a priority as the Bill states and the status quo will remain. For the Bill to have a positive impact it relies very much on additional support being carried out at authority, not school, level- which is the current situation, and as the statistical evidence shows does not work. Schools need to ensure that the staff member who is the DT person will be able to commit their time in and out of the scheduled school day. As the Corporate parent and employer the local authority needs to determine how this can be delivered to ensure that their 'children' are provided with quality education.

Placement of looked after children remains a very big issue. Twenty seven per cent of care leavers leave care at 16. The quality of placement care is critical to how a young person is supported through their informative years. Only a quarter of children's homes currently meet 90 per cent or more of the National Minimum Standards, and many foster carers are not provided with the level of support and training to cope with children with multiple trauma related issues. Historically, educational support has not been a priority for foster carers, and as a result Parents Evenings and other school information events were not attended by the majority of carers. It is important to look at the language used by schools and institutions, focussed around the 'traditional' family, i.e. father/mother/brother /sister. Schools have not acknowledged the different ways in which children live, 'parents' evening is a typical example of this. Looked after children are likely to feel excluded, children in care develop beautifully crafted scenarios and excuses for why they or their 'parents' are unable to integrate into school life.

The Bill recognises that the potential benefits to the young person and society can be improved by supporting the educational agenda of care leavers. It is estimated that someone with five GCSE A* –C grades earns over a lifetime £249,705 more than someone with no qualifications. (Department for Children Schools and Families, Impact Assessment of Children and Young Persons Bill, Section 44)

The Proposal that every care leaver will have an appointed personal adviser until the age of 25, if they remain in education, and the assurance that their views will be listened to in relation to staying within a secure foster/residential care placements appear a positive way forward. Appropriate training and awareness raising for the Personal Advisor will be crucial if they are to provide effective information advice and guidance to care leavers.

For these support services to provide quality information advice and guidance it is vital that they are aware and able to access the many wider initiatives and services available to support vulnerable people. For example, in 2006 The Frank Buttle Trust launched its Quality Award for higher education. It is currently held by over 40 institutions and sends the very clear message to current or prospective students that they are committed to supporting care leavers both in undergraduate and post graduate study. Provision of 52 week accommodation, bursaries and peer mentoring are just some examples of how universities are looking at ways to support care leavers. Institutions complete an annual action plan stating how they are implementing their commitment and the Frank Buttle Trust will monitor this. This seems to be a very supportive process of monitoring, with the opportunity for institutions to learn and share best practice in order to meet the very individual needs of the students within their educational communities. The introduction of the tick box on the UCAS form, means that universities will need to be more proactive and responsive to the needs of care leavers.

A National Voice (ANV) is a Charitable organisation set up by and for young people who have had experience of the care system. They deliver and support a number of campaigns that aim to empower its members. One such campaign is 'This is not a bin bag'. Too many LACs end up having all their belongings 'stuffed' into bin bags when having to be moved to emergency accommodation following the break-down of a placement . This campaign highlights this injustice and urges local authorities and other supporters to sign up to support the ending of this practice.

Conclusion:

Looked After Children are one of the most vulnerable groups within our society and the majority have consistently been failed at every stage of their lives. The Government is recognising this and is starting to put into place strategies to overturn such injustice.

However, for this to happen effectively it needs a major shift in practice and understanding of those dealing directly and indirectly with LAC and care leavers. The 'Corporate Parent,' has a responsibility to ensure that any institution, sector or agency working with this vulnerable group are provided with the support and understanding of how to best support them.

Social Work practice reform is crucial to ensure effective change. Universities will be a major part of this, as they will be one of the key delivery agencies . Those universities currently in possession of the Quality Award could ensure a more comprehensive staff development programme supported by the social work practice reform. Institutions where teacher training takes place could also utilise this award to support further staff awareness and understanding. Anecdotal evidence from universities where the award is being disseminated amongst staff has shown that some staff, themselves graduates of the care system, have made themselves known and wish to provide support to students.

The care planning and review system needs to adopt a more multi agency approach but without it becoming too unmanageable. Consistently, the young person must be involved and comfortable enough to express their views. More autonomy to Social Workers (as recommended in The Bill) in allocating a sum of money for educational/aspirational experiences (£500 per child) gives the opportunity for LAC to explore their dreams and aspirations.

Stability, and recognition of the importance of education, is a major factor in determining success. The Bill aims to ensure that LAC do not suffer from disrupted education and constant change of school. Schools themselves will need to be more proactive in their support of LAC. Schools and agencies working in partnership with them must re–evaluate their practice, ensuring that LAC are actively involved in process and activity. In effect there should be 'a Champion' for LAC and care leavers in every workplace. For example, after much lobbying to the government and the Higher Education Funding Council (HEFCE), LAC are now part of the Aimhigher cohort, meaning that they should all be targeted for Aimhigher interventions.

This paper highlights just a fraction of the issues faced by LAC and how improving outcomes involves major reform for many sectors. We have a responsibility to question our own institution's policy on supporting vulnerable young people/adults. There is a need to scrutinise language use, staff development and awareness practice in order for reform to truly take place. As the Government wish for a closer working relationship between schools, colleges and universities materialises, we can all ensure that the most vulnerable of our society are prioritised within our working practice to ensure equality and justice for all.

References

Department for Children, Schools and Families, Impact Assessment of Children and Young Persons Bill (2007)

Social Exclusion Unit, Cabinet Office, a Better Education for Children in Care (2003)

Department for Children, Schools and Families, Care matters: Time for Change (2007)

Department for Children, Schools and Families, Care Matters: Transforming the lives of Children and young people in Care (2006)

Department for Children, Schools and Families, Education of Young People in Public Care, Guidance (2000)

Jackson, S., Ajayi, S., and Quigley, M. (2005) Going to University from Care, Institute of Education.

Sergeant, H. (2006) Handle with Care, Centre for Young Policy Studies.

Working in Partnership: Developing a Cross Sector Widening Participation Care Programme across Four Boroughs

Maggie Mclinden, Andrew Lowing, University of East London,
K. Bee Ong, London East Thames Gateway Aimhigher,

The recent Department of Children Schools and Families (DCSF) White Paper *Care Matters: time for change* (DfES 2007) outlined the UK Government's policy intention to increase the numbers of young people with a care background succeeding in education. Recent statistics demonstrate a small proportion of eligible 19 year olds, who have previously experienced care, progressing into higher education; in 2007 this amounted to 350 out of a cohort of 5,800 (ONS 2007). Organisations such as The Frank Buttle Trust reporting through the 'By Degrees Study' (Jackson, S. et al. 2005) and the Rainer Charity are championing the educational progression within the higher education sector of those leaving care.

This paper takes a practitioner perspective to explore development work based in East London which aims to increase the numbers of young people with a care background entering higher education. This is of note as the programme is being informed by a number of partnerships between colleagues internal and external to the higher education sector. It draws on the experiences of Aimhigher partnerships and London borough education care teams.

The programme focuses on four London boroughs and targets: those in care, care leavers, their foster carers, social care professionals and trainee teachers. It is informed by previous Aimhigher, European Social Fund (ESF) and core funded widening participation activity. This paper discusses work in progress with the aim of exploring some of the challenges faced when developing a project with a hard-to-reach group, and to share good practice.

Background

Care leavers are one of the most under-represented groups in higher education. Figures released by the Office of National Statistics (ONS) indicate that this is not a new trend. In 2007 from a total number of 5,800 19 year olds who had been in care 350 had progressed to higher education; this amounts to 6% of the population. This percentage has also remained fairly static; back in 2003 the percentage was 5.7 percent (ONS 2007).

UK Government recognises and is working to address change. Following on from an earlier consultation (DfES 2006) 2007 saw the release of the White Paper *Care Matters: time for change* (DfES 2007). This paper painted a picture of a significant number of looked after young people who were not attaining educationally, were experiencing poor health, found difficulty accessing positive activities and were at times disengaged. A commitment was made by the Government to developing a co-ordinated approach by improving the role of the corporate parent. It was anticipated that this role would support a number of measures including delivering 'a first class education'. Earlier the *Children Leaving Care Act 2000* research commissioned by the Joseph Rowntree Foundation had clearly linked education attainment to later life success (Allen 2003).

Latest figures released in 2008 from the DCSF show a limited improvement in level 2 educational attainment for those in care from previous years. In 2007 13 percent obtained at least five general certificates in secondary education (GCSE) at grades A*- C compared with 62 percent of all children of a similar age. In 2006 this figure was 12 percent compared with 59 percent.

In addition to the Government the agenda is being supported and championed by other, often third sector organisations; see, for example, work to promote learning through educational mentoring led by the Rainer Foundation (Wellings 2008). But perhaps the most vocal advocate in the area of higher education has been the Frank Buttle Trust. In a seminal study commissioned by the Trust entitled 'By Degrees' Jackson and her fellow researchers noted the centrality of the attitude of the placement foster family to education as being key to educational success, as well as the failure of the higher education sector to support these young people to make informed choices. The study also identified a number of critical areas to remaining in higher education. These were: access to and managing finance, coping with previous care experiences, relationship problems, isolation and lack of support, accommodation and academic concerns. Jackson *et al.* conclude by noting that despite the attempt to widen participation this under-represented group remains persistently under provided for and hard-to-reach (Jackson, S *et al.* 2005).

The position of the Frank Buttle Trust is supported by the continuing priority of care leavers for the Higher Education Funding Council for England (HEFCE) in their recent guidance for Aimhigher partnerships planning for the 2008-2011 programme (HEFCE 2008/05). There is beginning to be much good work developed and embedded by a number of partnerships (Action on Access 2007) and it is our experiences as a group of widening participation practitioners operating in East London that we bring to this paper.

Building on Experience

The project Aiming High drew on direct experience of delivery with students integrated into existing activity, action research with an identified group, a literature review of research and good practice and consultation with four East London boroughs local to the university.
Our experience of working with those working in care happened by chance - a phone call from a colleague based within a local borough education team acting as an advocate for year 11 students in care wanting to apply for ESF summer school places. This led to a 'did you know you're working with…. and perhaps we could do this better' conversation. Following a visit by university staff to meet the education team, we started to unpack issues at the end of the summer term 2007 and from this a university campus visit was hosted. This gave a group of care leavers an opportunity to consider higher education and some of the challenges they faced. It emerged later that the colleague who had initially fired our enthusiasm to engage

more effectively with this group was based in the Borough of Barking and Dagenham, a borough which had been previously awarded best corporate parent.

From this initial exploration we carried out a literature review and consulted with looked after children education teams in three other East London boroughs. The rationale for the borough selection was that they were known to have a high percentage of young people in care or leaving care as a proportion of their under 18 population.

The Partners

The partnership was drawn from educational institutions and boroughs across East London. Boroughs have a statutory duty to young people in care as corporate parents and educational institutions an interest in developing work with looked after children, care leavers and key gatekeepers as part of their commitment to widening participation. There was a relationship between the boroughs and the educational institutions through the work of Aimhigher.

The educational partnership focuses on the London East Thames Gateway (LETG) Aimhigher relationship; the lead higher education institution for the care leaver work is the University of East London with the bulk of support coming through the Information Advice and Guidance (IAG) strand of LETG Aimhigher. There was consultation with London North Aimhigher to ensure that the East London offer complimented the care leaver developmental work being led by Middlesex University.

London Boroughs approached and responding to the consultation fell within the LETG Aimhigher geographical area. These were; Barking and Dagenham, Hackney, Newham and Tower Hamlets. These Boroughs also provided the programme with its geographical boundaries as the programme of activities was targeted at the young people and their gatekeepers who are both living and studying there. Boroughs were in an interesting position of being gatekeepers to the target groups, stakeholders with an interest in the programme and partners in delivery.

The Programme

The programme offer was developed as part of the consultation process, research and good practice outlined above. It was underpinned by an ethos of inclusivity and recognition of a number of critical gatekeepers and stakeholder groups.

There were a number of groupings that the programme needed to articulate between in order to be successful. These were identified as: young people who had experienced care; universities, boroughs and Aimhigher partnerships; gatekeepers including boroughs, teaching staff, foster carers, care professionals.

The programme offer was developed with the intention of running the first year as a pilot followed by evaluation and revision of the offer at the end of this cycle. Key to this was collection of monitoring and evaluation data collected at the point of consultation and at a number of delivery points in each intervention, ultimately will be the need for tracking data. In the short term, success is judged by forming relationships (between the stakeholders, gatekeepers and the cohort) and getting the programme offer 'right'. In the long term it will be judged on the numbers of young people engaging in the programme and increasing the borough numbers progressing on into higher education.

The programme offer fell across eight strands. This offer was presented at the consultation phase as a menu for individual borough education teams to buy into. Colleagues' awareness of the main Aimhigher programme and individual institutions widening participation interventions were also raised at this point.

1. Mentoring Scheme - targeting years 12 and 13 students, aimed to recruit 20, funded through the IAG strand of LETG Aimhigher

2. <u>Young People in Care Event</u> - targeting years 10 and 11, aimed to recruit 30, funded through the aspirations strand of LETG Aimhigher (an event targeting older learners was run by Middlesex University)

3. <u>Foster Carer's Event</u> - targeting foster carers, aimed to recruit 30, funded through the IAG strand of LETG Aimhigher

4. <u>Care Professionals Event</u> – targeting social workers and other care professionals working with looked after children/care leavers aimed to recruit 25, funded through the IAG strand of LETG Aimhigher

5. <u>Trainee Teacher Event</u> – targeting trainee teachers in Schools of Education within the Aimhigher LETG area, targeting 30, funded through the IAG strand of LETG Aimhigher

6. <u>Work Placement</u> – targeting care leavers on Borough work placements over the summer vacation, funded through UEL

7. <u>Transition Summer School</u> – targeting years 10 and 11, aimed to recruit 30, funding application to a third sector organisation

8. <u>Evaluation and tracking strand</u> – to monitor uptake and focus of the programme offer and to track the target cohort, funded through UEL

A detailed examination of each of the programme strands is beyond the scope of this paper.

Slow Progress

Progress was slow against milestones both in terms of identifying named gatekeepers, setting up meetings and gaining access to events where the programme could be promoted. For example, it took a number of months to get in touch with foster carers networks, access was then gained to a sub regional event where the foster carer intervention was well received, there was an immediate impact on recruitment.

Funding had been secured for all strands through Aimhigher or core university funding streams with the exception of the transition summer school. After an initial approach to a third sector organisation a decision was made to seek funding in the next year of the programme.

Early conversations, research and funding applications had been made the preceding academic year 2006/07.   At the point of writing we are approaching the start of delivery of the programme offer in the pilot year.

Points of Learning

There have been many points of learning for the partners involved. Here we are reporting on the development of the programme prior to delivery of activity. Learning can be broadly categorised into two areas related to access and to the programme offer:

Access
There was an under estimation of time needed to identify and make contact with the key gatekeepers e.g. foster carer co-ordinators, borough education teams. This was felt to be a reflection of the lack of previous relationship.

There was also an under estimation of the layers of gatekeepers, and time it would take, to orientate ourselves to care structures which vary in each borough. These structures lay outside our previous widening participation knowledge/relationships. In addition to the key gatekeepers in the borough teams, there were also new gatekeepers within the borough educational structure – the designated teaching staff.

Once we had negotiated the gatekeepers we were then faced with bringing a new piece of work into an existing structure and challenged with developing a relationship with a very vulnerable and hard-to-reach group. We recognised that although welcomed, developing this baseline would take time. In consequence we sought to dedicate more time in developing meaningful ties with these gatekeepers who could act as advocates for programme activities. Thus we revised our over ambitious initial target numbers downwards for the pilot year.

Getting the Offer Right
The challenges of access shaped the programme offer; we recognised at an early stage that for the pilot year, the scope and scale of the initial menu was overly ambitious.

We found that "one size doesn't fit all". Different boroughs favoured different aspects of the programme. For example the higher education mentoring scheme complimented an existing mentoring programme in one of the Boroughs. Some boroughs ruled out segregated interventions for the target cohort, preferring to raise awareness of the main Aimhigher offer with their students (the inclusion agenda).

Strand 1 mentoring – The mentoring strand aimed to target years 12 and 13. The rationale of this was to support the cohort at a point of transition as they moved into higher education thus aiding retention. We found, however, that this year group were extremely hard-to-reach and take up was very slow. Advice from key gatekeepers (designated teachers) was twofold. Firstly, that younger students in Years 10 and 11 would also benefit from mentoring as they prepared to undergo transitions into post-16 education and started thinking about their future. Secondly, the mentors could also be a source of encouragement as these young people prepare for their GCSEs. This approach did yield more success and it was decided to extend the mentoring programme to the Year 10 and 11 cohorts through the designated teacher network within secondary schools.

Strand 2 young people in care event – Low recruitment to the young people in care event appeared to be less to do with learner disinterest and more a reflection of the fee status of many of the care leavers. Despite their aspirations and attainment levels, these students had no entitlement and were classified as international students therefore facing full fee status in higher education. Issues of slow recruitment have been detailed above. This strand had the least uptake, despite the call from care leavers taking part in the action research. There were mixed perspectives on the value of offering a segregated intervention from stakeholders and funders, based on largely on fears of labelling. A decision to run this strand had been based on tailoring content to match needs identified by research and the focus group (the provision of specific housing and financial information).

Strands 3 and 4 foster carers and care professionals - This offer was uniformly well received. There were a number of aspects of the programme that overlapped and a decision was made to deliver these interventions as one event. The programme has been planned to include sessions standard to existing parent/carer events such as finance and accommodation with the focus on the needs of those leaving care. Additional funding has been gained to enable individual IAG sessions to be offered to foster carers who wanted to support their looked after child.

Strand 5 trainee teacher – This strand has been well received by the lead institution's School of Education and the borough based education team approached to deliver the event. Approaches are currently being made to other Schools of Education within the Aimhigher LETG area.

Strand 6 work placement– The work placement opportunity was part of an existing programme offered by a number of the boroughs. This strand is on schedule to be delivered for the first time using the university as a venue.

Strand 7 transition summer school – was deferred to a following year, see section on slow progress.

Strand 8 evaluation and tracking – this is beyond the scope of this paper reporting on the development of the programme.

Conclusions: Next Steps

We feel that the above has confirmed that we were right to see the first year as a pilot with the opportunity to: develop stakeholder, gatekeeper and target group relationships, to refine the programme offer and to build capacity. We are also looking to secure further funding, to begin work within the lead institution on meeting the needs of care leavers through embedded processes, and looking to the Frank Buttle kite-mark as an example of good institutional practice.

The past two years have been a roller coaster. We thank our funders and managers for being supportive and recognising that developing a widening participation pre-entry offer for a hard-to-reach group is a long and testing journey, heavy on resources, especially at the outset. We believe however, based on our own experience and the good practice of others, that in the long term this area of work is a worthwhile investment.

References

Action on Access (2007) *July 2007: issue 42 e-bulletin* available at http://www.actiononaccess.org

Allen, M. (2003) *Into the Mainstream: care leavers entering work, education and training.* York: Joeseph Rowntree Foundation.

DfCSF (2008/08) *Statistical First Release: outcome indicators for children looked after: twelve months to 30 September 2007, England* available at http://www.dfcsf.gov.uk/statistics

DfES (2007) *Care Matters: time for change* available at http://www.dfes.gov.uk/publications/timeforchange/

DfES (2006) *Care Matters: transforming the lives of children and young people in care.* available at http://www.dfes.gov.uk/publications/carematters/

HEFCE (2008/08) *Guidance for Aimhigher partnerships: updated for the 2008-2001 programme.* Bristol: HEFCE.

Jackson, S, Ajayi, S. and Quigley, M. (2005*) Going to University from Care: a final report of the by degrees study.* London: Institute of Education.

ONS (2007) SFR27/2007: *Children Looked After in England (Including adoption and care Leavers) Year Ending 31 March 2007* [online] http://www.statistics.gov.uk

Wellings, S. (2008) *Mentoring for Looked after Children: dissemination manual.* Westerham: Rainrer.

An Institutional Response To Students Leaving Care

Joy Clews, and Phil Davis, Bishop Grosseteste University College, Lincoln

Introduction

Statistics demonstrate the stark differential in educational achievement between children in public care and the wider population. In 2007, 12.6% of young people in Year 11 who had spent at least one year in care achieved five or more GCSEs grades A*-C, compared with 62.0% of all young people. An estimated 1% of care leavers progress to higher education, compared with around 40% of the total population. During recent years, at national level, there has been greater acknowledgement of the unacceptable underachievement of children in public care and the need to address the underlying issues. In his Foreword to the White Paper, "Care Matters: Time for Change", Alan Johnson, Secretary of State for Education and Skills, states:

> *Education is crucial. Too often, a child in care will possess innate talents or abilities that are squandered through system failures. We will improve opportunities at every stage ... ensuring that they have the opportunity to go to the best schools ... and to aspire to university.*

In its most recent guidance, the Higher Education Funding Council for England has instructed Aimhigher - the national programme which aims to widen participation in higher education by raising the aspirations and developing the abilities of young people from under-represented groups - to include children in public care as one of its priority groups (HEFCE, 2008)

This paper describes the experience of a University College's institution-wide approach to providing an enhanced level of support to care leavers at every stage of the student journey - from aspiration-raising to registration and through to graduation. This has been achieved largely through effective communication and debate at a senior management level, where consideration of the University College's ethos, as well as the operational implications of offering effective support, has given rise to a constructive response to the needs of care leavers. This process brought the additional benefit of establishing new relationships for successful dialogue on how the institution might develop more effective responses to the needs of other vulnerable groups.

Bishop Grosseteste's approach

Bishop Grosseteste University College Lincoln (BG) is a small HEI with approximately 1650 students. BG has a long-standing commitment to widening participation in higher education and a history of success in its recruitment and retention of students from under-represented groups. Since 2006, BG has been working pro-actively to address the needs of care leavers, and the barriers they face, through partnerships with local organisations and the development of strategies within the University College.

BG has played an instrumental role in establishing a working group dedicated to improving the educational outlook of children in public care in Lincolnshire, and facilitating opportunities for them to continue their education. The Children in Public Care progressing to Further and Higher Education Working Group is chaired by a member of BG's Directorate and brings together a number of key agencies from the county to examine relationships and opportunities which exist or might be developed to further the interests of children in public care and encourage their progression to further and higher education. This group has been successful in facilitating dialogue between the Local Authority, schools, Further and Higher Education Institutions, Aimhigher and agencies representing care leavers. In addition, consultation with the group improved BG's understanding of the needs of care leavers and helped to shape the package of support developed by the University College.

Within the University College, BG's Extended Senior Management Group has been fundamentally involved in BG's decision to adopt an institutional approach to meeting the needs of care leavers.

Research by "A National Voice" (2007) indicates the following key barriers are likely to have a negative impact on care leavers entering higher education:

Stable accommodation:	Students who move around may be unable to build or maintain relationships with their peers – the insecurity of not knowing who you will be living with, or where, can have an adverse impact.
Finance:	With an absence of parental support, care leavers are often dependent upon their Local Authority for financial support. They are usually debt averse and less likely to embrace support available from the Student Loans Company as a result.
Professional support:	A care leaver's potential is unlikely to be realised in the absence of effective and professional practical support.
Self esteem:	Care leavers often lose interest in pursuing their education, as they feel that success is beyond them – this can lead to social exclusion, and cause even lower self esteem.

The Social Exclusion Unit (2003) cites similar reasons for students dropping out of higher education, with the most frequent reasons given being financial difficulties, accommodation and lack of support from a named person.

In providing a response to the needs of care leavers identified above, and in formulating its submission to achieve the Frank Buttle Quality Mark for Care Leavers, BG recognised the implications of the above barriers were not only the responsibility of its Student Support Team, but of all departments within the University College. We were cognisant of the recommendations made by Jackson et al (2005) following their longitudinal study of care leavers who progressed to higher education. Particular note was taken of their suggestion that 'all HEIs should have a comprehensive policy for recruitment, retention and support of students from a care background.' By adopting an institution-wide approach, our aim was to develop an encouraging and supportive environment for care leavers at each step of their journey towards and within the University College.

BG's Extended Senior Management Group was the principle resource for devising a strategy for addressing the barriers for care leavers, and its members facilitated consultation with the key teams that would play an important role in addressing these barriers. These included Student Support, Academic Registry, Finance, Estates (for Accommodation), and Academic Schools. The Students' Union was also involved in discussions.

Stable accommodation
The Student Welfare Working Group, chaired by the Head of School of Culture, Education and Innovation, acted as champion for 365 day on-campus accommodation for care leavers. The group brought together key personnel from the Estates, Student Support, Academic Registry and Academic School teams, to provide a forum which would allow all perspectives to be considered within a comprehensive review. This resulted in an agreement that care leavers would be a priority in the allocation of on-campus accommodation together with a guarantee of 365 day on-campus accommodation for all care leavers, if required. On-campus support is available through a network of senior residents and the warden, as well as a buddy scheme operated by the Students' Union. In addition, arrangements are now in place for BG's Student Support Team to provide continuing support, including liaison for the continuation of existing foster care arrangements, as appropriate, where care leavers wish to continue to draw down on their established support mechanisms. Effective assistance is also available in securing private sector housing, if required, with housing rights advice available from the Student Support Team.

Finance
Members of the Extended Senior Management Group (representatives from Directorate, Finance and Student Support) convened to discuss plans for a comprehensive package of financial

support, focussing on BG's existing Bursary Scheme which was introduced with the aim of encouraging and supporting students from widening participation backgrounds into higher education. Direct liaison with the Finance Team allowed budgetary models to be considered, and an immediate assessment made of the extent of financial commitment that could be afforded by the University College. This expertise, together with the knowledge of the statutory funding system available through the Student Support Team, allowed a targeted bursary to be developed and included in the University College's Access Agreement for 2008/09. This bursary package for care leavers is worth £3,500 each year of their undergraduate course. The extent of this support is expected to reduce the need for care leavers to be reliant on the maintenance loan and can realistically be expected to significantly reduce the amount of debt they accrue during their time in higher education. In addition, it was agreed that care leavers would be eligible to apply for up to £500 from the University College's Discretionary Fund, as well as the £1,000 Accommodation bursary payable from the Access to Learning Fund.

Professional support
The Extended Senior Management Group was instrumental in embracing the opportunity to apply for the Frank Buttle Trust Quality Mark for Care Leavers. In developing its outline project proposal, numerous support mechanisms within BG were identified and the process of applying for the Quality Mark facilitated discussion between those teams responsible for their delivery: Student Support, Learning Advice, Schools and Colleges Liaison, Academic Registry, Academic Schools, the Students' Union and BG's Directorate all played a part in this process. The professional teams involved in dialogue recognised the need to deliver to care leavers reliable, accessible services with consistency and continuity. The admissions cycle, progress throughout the course, and graduation were all taken into account. The links between relevant teams were considered so that seamless support could be given, using a minimum of named contacts to ensure continuity for the individual. This resulted in the introduction of a range of practices including those identified below:

- actively encouraging care leavers to disclose their background using the opportunity on the UCAS/GTTR application form, during the registration process, or by asking their Local Authority or Personal Adviser to make a disclosure on their behalf

- use of the disclosure to alert care leavers to the comprehensive package of support available to them

- providing opportunities for a disclosure to be made at any time during a care leaver's time at BG

- liaison with the Local Authority in order to provide impartial and non-judgemental information to the care leaver at an early stage, with the expectation that this approach will enable a detailed and comprehensive response to individual circumstances

- development of materials detailing the information and services available to care leavers, including pre-entry guidance on funding, assistance with admissions procedures, and information on housing issues

- introduction of a 'named contact' member of the Student Support Team for care leavers to provide support through the admissions process and beyond.

Self esteem
BG has a strong commitment to raising the aspirations of people from non-traditional backgrounds and encouraging them to consider, and be successful in higher education. Such aspiration-raising is especially important for young people in public care. A survey undertaken by A National Voice indicated that 97% of young people in public care consider their education to be important but many feel that achieving a good education is beyond them. BG's Schools and Colleges Liaison Team, and the University College's partnership with Aimhigher, has provided new opportunities for children in public care and their personal advisers to gain a first-hand experience of higher education through visit days, taster days and

residential summer schools. Furthermore, BG is committed to developing strong links with agencies involved in the support of care leavers and aims to explore opportunities for student ambassadors to communicate their experiences of higher education to care leavers. These opportunities give individuals the chance to experience first hand the University College's ethos and its commitment to offering effective support, thus demonstrating that BG is capable of offering a constructive response to the needs of care leavers.

In order to ensure the ongoing development of support for children in public care, it was agreed by representatives of Directorate, Student Support and Academic Registry that this would be a standing agenda item at meetings of the Widening Participation Team and that progress against the Team's Children in Public Care Action Plan would be reviewed at the meetings.

Conclusion

The approach used by BG to enhance the support offered to care leavers considering progression to higher education involved extensive engagement with departments across the University College. The extent of this involvement was significant. Student Support, Finance, Academic Schools and the Directorate have each played a lead role in the project so far. These lead departments have liaised with the Students' Union, Chaplaincy, Estates and Academic Registry. Whilst Human Resources, the Centre for Learning and Teaching, Library and Knowledge Services, and the Research Department have yet to make a direct contribution, their senior managers have had the opportunity to contribute to discussions which have taken place within Extended Senior Management Group meetings. This is seen as a vital means of cascading the University College's commitment to students who have been in public care.

The departmental relationships which the University College aims to achieve through the implementation of its project plan are as follows: the Estates, Students' Union and Chaplaincy teams are expected to become members of the core due to their direct involvement with accommodation-related issues and the provision of

buddying schemes. The Academic Registry is expected to continue playing a supportive role, largely in the dissemination of information relating to disclosures from care leavers. The Human Resources department will be expected to respond to the staff development needs of team members, whilst the Centre for Learning and Teaching, and Library and Knowledge services will be expected to provide similar responses to the needs of the care leavers themselves, e.g. by providing advice on independent learning, and ongoing induction/orientation sessions to help individuals feel more comfortable accessing learning resources. In turn, the Research Department, through the introduction of the Centre for Education for Social Justice, will provide new avenues for the dissemination of the project's findings, thus completing the complement of departments involved in the institution's approach to students leaving care.

It is our view that the time spent in discussion with various departmental groupings was worthwhile, resulting in a range of benefits, some of which were expected, but others that had not been anticipated. Anticipated benefits included the high level of ownership and understanding that was generated. Colleagues in cross-departmental teams, who were active in the detailed work of developing new practices and procedures, recognised the part their department played within the holistic experience of the care leaver and had an increased understanding of the challenges facing this group of students. For example, a representative of the Finance department said:

> 'Our day-to-day activities don't afford us many opportunities to engage with the University College's widening participation agenda, but being involved in the consideration of financial support for care leavers allowed us to make a direct contribution in enhancing the University College's support for this group of students, which was really rewarding.'

A member of the Academic Registry recognised that her understanding of the needs of care leavers had improved considerably and that her department had a significant role to play in the support of students progressing to BG from public care:

> 'My involvement in this process meant that I had a much better grasp of the issues and I now have a greater sense of ownership of the actions that fall in my area. Members of my team have become more proactive and have started to network with relevant external organisations.'

A related benefit of cross-institution teams was the extent to which those colleagues who were seldom engaged in discussions about student support challenged proposals, leading to improvements to the resulting agreed practices. For example, the group which convened to discuss 365 day accommodation for care leavers also provided a useful forum to discuss challenges faced by other groups of students. Issues concerning international students, students reporting ill-health and pregnant students were discussed and actions agreed. This was achieved largely as a result of giving colleagues the opportunity to meet together in the context of providing supportive mechanisms for students.

The initial focus of our work was quite narrow in that it related to BG's support of a defined group of people in their journey to and within the University College. However, the process has helped to establish new relationships for effective dialogue about how the institution might better serve its students. Already these relationships have proven valuable in developing more effective responses to the needs of other groups of students. The Student Support Team in particular has benefited from welfare related discussions with various teams, which have opened up new relationships with other departments. For example, Student Support's dealings with the Finance Office had previously been matter of fact in terms of processing payments to students in hardship, but the approach used for care leavers has facilitated opportunities to discuss support arrangements for students in general. Discussions in the Student Welfare Group in turn led to the creation of a dedicated Accommodation Working Group adopting a similar approach in considering the support needs of students, and this is now a central theme in the University College's review of its accommodation provision.

Before it was submitted, the Frank Buttle document was considered and endorsed by both BG's Extended Senior Management Group and the Children in Public Care progressing to Further and Higher Education Working Group. These two groups will be involved in the review of BG's progress against identified actions and will be consulted in the development of annual evaluative reports. We believe that this ongoing involvement of a wide range of colleagues – both within and beyond the University College – will enhance the support offered to care leavers at each stage of their student journey.

References

A National Voice (2007) *Please Sir! Can I Have Some More?* Manchester: A National Voice.

Department for Education and Skills (2007) *Care Matters: Time for Change*. London: The Stationery Office.

HEFCE (2008) *Guidance for Aimhigher Partnerships*.

Jackson, S., Ajayi, S. and Quigley, M. (2005) *Going to university from care: Summary of findings and recommendations*. London: Institute of Education, University of London.

Social Exclusion Unit (2003) *A Better Education for Children in Care*. London: Social Exclusion Unit.

Foster Parents Reflection on their Experiences within Widening Participation

Jasbir Panesar, University of East London

Fostering services recognise the need to carefully match foster children from similar cultural and ethnic backgrounds with suitable foster carers. Foster carers are required to have regular training as outlined by the Office For Standards in Education Children's Services and Skills and regular supervision with their social workers. The University of East London has run a series of information, advice and guidance workshops with foster carers, predominantly from Afro-Caribbean and a minority from South Asian communities. These workshops inform foster parents of the range of educational routes available to foster children. In addition, there is an exploration of how the standards required by the Children's Workforce Development relate to foster carers' own learning. The aim is to enable fostering to gain a more professional status.

The workshops enable foster carers to gain understanding of how to support the educational progress of their foster children as well as the care leavers. Equally, the foster carers, who have been fostering for a number of years, may gain a qualification in social care, which is becoming a requirement by Office For Standards in Education Children's Service and Skills. The foster carers become aware of the various educational routes they could follow in the United Kingdom in achieving childcare qualifications, where skills gained within their own area of work would be taken into consideration. Such an approach enables foster carers to reflect on their educational progression, and to assist the fostering agencies in following the Office For Standard in Education Children's Services and Skills recommendations.

The Fostering Regulations 2002 aim to ensure that the standards of the Commission for Office for Standards in Education Children's

Services and Skills are maintained. The new requirements within the training, support and development standards for foster carers - developed by Children's Workforce Developments - give guidance on support to foster carers who should receive an induction, training, and continuing professional development. From April 2008 foster carers are expected to complete the Children's Workforce Developments standards to assess their skills, knowledge and experience. There are seven standards consisting of:

- understanding the principles and values of working with young persons,
- understanding one's role as a foster carer,
- being aware of health, safety and health care,
- communicating effectively,
- understanding the specific development of young persons,
- keeping young persons safe and the foster carers yourself.

The Children's Workforce Development recommendations are in line with the Department for Education and Skills guidelines to develop the Training Framework for Foster Care for England. The Children's Workforce Development standards are to be incorporated in the National Minimum Standards for Fostering Services. Foster carers will need to complete the Standards and achieve the Children's Workforce Development certificate of successful completion by April 2011. Furthermore, the Children's Workforce Development has incorporated the United Nations Convention on the Rights of the Child. This has a framework on the right of the children and young people in the participation, protection and provision of the specific services which nurture and assist them in reaching their full potential. (Children's Workforce Development 2007).

Fostering agencies have to ensure their services provide foster children with the opportunity to express themselves in a supportive and controlled environment. The aim is to empower the young person in their emotional, educational, social and cultural needs within a safe family environment. The service has to be sensitive to the foster child's religion, ethnicity, and culture and provide a placement which respects the racial and religious origins of the child.

The training framework for foster carers has three stages: Stage one is pre-approval which has to be completed within six months of an application being submitted for the foster carer. Stage two is based on the induction, which has to be completed within one year of approval as a foster carer. Stage three consists of foster carer development which has to be completed within two years. The Children's Workforce Development Council Certificate is given on completion of Standards. All training received must comply with the equal opportunities and anti-discriminatory practice specified within the Training Framework for Foster Care (Children's Workforce Development Council 2007). The workbook, which has to be signed off by the supervisory social worker or an appropriate person, is a key tool which will demonstrate that the foster carer has received the required competency to practise in the fostering service. The foster carer's competency to foster has to be reviewed and updated regularly via annual reviews. The fostering panel requires a couple in the same household who are caring for the approved foster children together, to complete the workbook individually and achieve the Certificate of Successful Completion as each will have differing learning needs, skills and knowledge assessment.

The workshops which UEL has run recruited fifteen Afro-Caribbean and five South Asian foster carers. They had been fostering from two to seven years. Literacy skills varied. Many foster carers had not previously had to produce lengthy reports and were wary at the prospect of having to produce academic course work. The fact that the documents, such as fostering approval reports, annual review reports, supervisory social workers reports and education plans, were to be used as evidence of their fostering skills relieved the foster carers anxiety.

The foster carers were experienced and this meant they had ample evidence which could be used for their workbook - which includes social workers reports, annual reviews, reflective diaries, review meetings, feedback from support groups and training and a personal induction plan. However, some of the foster carers had yet to gain proficiency in the English language. Therefore, the fostering services need to ensure the type of assessment methods adopted will take account of this. For instance, assessment methods such as witness testimonies, oral professional discussion, with taped questions and answers and observation could be deployed. Local authority social workers can be asked to fill in tick box questionnaires after completing their review meeting with the foster carer. It is likely that second language foster carers will take a longer time to complete their workbook than the time scale required by the Department of Health Fostering Service and National Millennium Standards. Completion of the workbook has to be agreed with the supervising social worker and support from the fostering agency is required. The supervising social worker is familiar with the foster carer's strengths and weaknesses and is aware of the type of support which will be most effective to demonstrate the foster carer's competency related to the Standard requirements.

Some foster carers welcomed the Standards as it meant they did not have to attend further education colleges or training centres to gain a National Vocational Qualification in childcare or social care qualification, as time was a problem for them. This arrangement meant they will be required to attend training, support groups and have regular supervision with their allocated social worker to progress their workbook. Foster carers were also attracted by the fact that evidence demonstrating the accomplishment of Standards requirements can be transferred to other qualifications. The Standards evidence can be used against meeting the required knowledge within the core units of the National Vocational Qualification at each level. Similarly, those studying at National Vocational Qualification level can transfer the evidence from specific National Vocational Qualification units to the Fostering Standards units.

In service training can be used to generate evidence based material which can be used in the portfolio against the units within the standards laid down by Office For Standards in Education Children's Services and Skills. The training covers a wide area which includes: confidentiality, equal opportunities, legislation, children's rights, health and safety, working within a team, direct work with children, health promotion, education, culture/identity awareness, drug/alcohol awareness, engagement in recreational activities, presenting reports writing (log books), working with challenging behaviour, family contact, gender awareness, semi-independence living, life story work with children, neighbourhood and community, dealing with aggression, handling meetings, new arrivals resettlement to the United Kingdom, liaising with agencies and first aid. This level of training is intended to give the foster carer the skills, knowledge and competency to carry out their agreed responsibilities along with the multi agency support and accountability. The review meetings will ensure that the required standards and expectations are met, difficulties are addressed, further training needs are assessed and specific support packages are considered, as well as any changes which need to be made in the foster carer's approval.

Apart from the essential training the fostering service also provides social events, workshops, support groups, allowances and regular visit to help with foster carers with the day to day care of the looked after child. It is essential the foster carer provide quality care to the foster child; understand their role, responsibilities and duties as outlined within the contractual Foster Care Agreement which is part of the Fostering Services Regulation 2002. The support groups are important where they give foster carers an opportunity to share experiences, gain advice and information.

The educational workshops at UEL were able to provide foster carers with information on the range of educational and training courses at further education colleges, universities and training centres available to the foster child once they reach semi independent living. The Access course programmes and National Vocational Qualifications were viewed to be suitable for the foster child as within fostering some would have a disruptive education history where they may not have achieved qualifications. In addition, at the workshops, foster carers felt it was more appropriate for those foster children who did not perform well in their General School Certificate Examinations to be given preference in undertaking the BTEC First course programme running at another institution.   It was felt that a the range of student service support should be available - from financial, disability, accommodation to counselling in colleges and universities.   This was thought to be an essential component in keeping the retention rate of foster children in further and higher education. The life story work book which the foster child will take away with them after leaving care, contains the written records of the looked after child's progress, life with the foster carer, incidents, changes in behaviour, photographs, and school reports.   This gives the young person an opportunity to reflect on the past, present and future goals.

In conclusion, the foster carers found the workshops enabled them to gain a better understanding of the range of educational opportunities available which made them, and to be better informed as to how to assist their foster children in their self development. Also the foster carers were able to assess how the new Standards from the Children's Development Workforce will help carers themselves to improve their fostering skills and knowledge, as well as give them a wider perspective on how they can use this experience to engage in other areas of employment, and undertake further and higher education course programmes.

References

Borthwick, S., and Lord J. *Effective Fostering Panels*. London: British Association for Adoption and Fostering.

Smith, F., Braun, C., Cullen, D. and Lane M. *Fostering Now – Current Law Including Regulation Guidance and Standard (England),* London: British Association for Adoption and Fostering.

Learner Support For Vocational Students In Higher Education

Sue Cordell, Jane Barker, Caroline Beasley, and Nick Hooper,
Yorkshire & Humber East Lifelong Learning Network

The context

The government's demands on the higher education (HE) system have clearly changed. A plethora of reports between 1997 and 1998, including the Kennedy Report (1997), the Dearing Report (1997), the Fryer report (1997), and the consultative paper *The Learning Age* (1998), which aimed to build on them, signalled 'a shift in policy towards lifelong learning'. (Tight, 1998: 473). Over the following ten years or so change has been steady. A number of key issues now indicate that swifter action is expected.

The pledge by Tony Blair's Labour Government that fifty per cent of 18 to 30 year-olds (Greenaway and Haynes, 2003: 152) would go into higher education (HE) is still some way from being realised. This shortfall was recently highlighted by David Willetts, Shadow Universities Secretary, who claims that 'at the current rate it would take until 2124 to reach the 50 percent target'. (Attwood, 2008: 17). Whilst his claim clearly has a political bias, it shows the increased impetus that would be needed to reach the participation target. Simultaneously the demographics for 2011 to 2020, show a fall of 15 per cent in the number of 18 to 20 year-olds in the UK and of around 17 per cent in our sub region. Therefore, any strategies will have to drive even harder to compensate for this reduction in potential student numbers.

The Leitch Review of Skills *Prosperity for all in the global economy – world class skills* (2006), has also had an impact on the new agenda. Leitch's rhetoric calls for the nation as a whole to invest more in learning and improving skills to recover and progress the UK's position in the global market place. The objective for higher education is for 'exceeding 40 per cent of adults qualified to Level 4 and above', (Leitch, 2006:3). This is a substantial increase from 29% in 2005, but still falls short of the 45 per cent that Lord Dearing predicts is needed to improve the UK's uncompetitive skills base. (Dearing, 2008: 3). Even the achievement of the 40 per cent target would mean something in the order of five million more students. From an analysis of the Office for National Statistics Labour Force Survey this would mean 75,103 more students from the Yorkshire and Humber East sub-region. (Dearing, 2008).

One response to the achievement of this target was from the Higher Education Funding Council for England (HEFCE) who by June 2007 had invested some £100 million in around thirty lifelong learning networks (LLNs). (Whitston, 2007). The Yorkshire and Humber East Lifelong Learning Network (YHELLN) is just one of the networks and is a sub-regional partnership involving eight Further Education Colleges (FECs), one Higher Education Institution (HEI) and associate partners. Its central mission is to increase opportunities for vocational learners in higher education. In order to fulfil this mission the key areas of activity for YHELLN are:

- Progression agreements
- Credit accumulation and transfer
- Curriculum development
- Learner support and IAG
- Research and CPD

These activities take place within four priority curriculum areas, namely, Business and Logistics, Creative Arts and Digital Media, Health, Education and Social Care and Construction and Engineering, and should play a key role in meeting these ambitious targets.

To reach the targets there will have to be a massive increase in participation in higher education. In his speech on 29 February 2008, John Denham made the point very clearly: '[n]ot only will there be more older students. There will be more studying part time and…I certainly expect there to be more students from non-traditional backgrounds'. (Denham, 2008). The term that is generally used to refer to such expansion is widening participation, but, as Ben Lewis (2002: 205), rightly, highlights there is 'no definition of widening participation in HE that is used by all stakeholders in the sector'. He then states that for the purpose of his article the meaning from the HEFCE (2001) document 'Strategies for widening participation in higher education: a guide to good practice' will be taken as a 'starting point'. (Lewis, 2002:205). Lewis states that 'the HEFCE means "policy initiatives to target the individual groups that higher education institutions (HEIs) have identified as under-represented and to ensure their success"'. (Lewis, 2002:205). Greenbank opens his article by suggesting that '[w]idening participation encompasses issues such as ethnicity, gender, age and disability' (Greenbank, 2006: 141). Labelling learners with 'issues' seems to highlight potential areas for problems rather than focusing on the strengths and diverse cultural capital that all learners bring to HE. However it is defined, widening participation is an important factor in contemporary HE and appropriate learner support is vital to its achievement.

Why is Learner Support Important?

Much of the widening participation debate and agenda has been focused around support for the learner. Learner support needs include academic support relating to the curriculum, delivery methods and study skills as well as personal support, such as counselling, accommodation, disability, financial and health. HE should be seen as a part of a continuum of learning. For all students, entry to level 4 can be seen as a significant point in their decision making or alternatively as a trigger point which may form a barrier, or an opportunity, to progression to further study. Universities and Colleges have traditionally selected students that they assess to have the ability to react to that trigger point as an opportunity. Widening participation has offered access to students who may have more diverse skills and experiences, which can be viewed as equipping them differently to deal with the challenges of HE. Recent education policy has placed great emphasis on widening participation, but the recent report of the Public Accounts Committee has suggested that retention and achievement of students who have been described as 'non-traditional', is not as healthy as it should be. Such high profile analyses show that, not only for our students' sakes, but also for the successful future of widening participation in HE, the need to get student support right is a crucial and urgent one. (House of Commons Public Accounts Committee, 2008).

Post-transition Support

For some students transition to higher education forms a natural progression from level 3 (A level/BTEC National Diploma or equivalent) at school or college. This has, for many years, been the accepted route into university for the majority of eighteen-year-old students. Historically, it is a rite of passage that has been supported by activities both within schools and colleges that have a strong tradition of progression to HE, and by families who themselves have a history of attending university and can, therefore, empathise with the transition to higher education of the young people taking this step. It was, and often is now, generally assumed that these students were equipped to cope with study at university by the education they had received to date and by the support of families, friends and peers who also had the cultural knowledge and experience to support them. If these students did face difficulties, academic or otherwise, most universities would put into place 'post-need support', which will be referred to as model 1.

Such support might be academic or more general, perhaps covering financial or pastoral support. For some, this would be too little, too late, which could reinforce feelings of inadequacy and low self-esteem. It can also give the feeling of being 'singled out' and, therefore, exacerbate rather than ameliorate the situation.

Pre-transition preparation

However, for some, and perhaps a growing proportion, it is a less obvious progression and may involve a decision which marks significant changes in their lives. They may have given up a job, made childcare arrangements or be attempting to balance employment and domestic arrangements to enter a world that is completely outside their comfort zone and that of those around them. For many, entering education or progressing between institutions or levels poses a challenge that they are unable or unwilling to face. The established approach to widening participation, and the policies derived from it, seeks to help learners face this challenge by identifying specific groups with particular needs and developing policies to meet those needs. In effect, this puts learners into boxes and creates special paths for each box, so that those in the box can meet the needs of the education system. Aiming strategies at specific groups of students can potentially have a negative effect, as dominant discourses can be reinforced and students can be compartmentalised and labelled as having problems. The LLNs have been introduced with an agenda of making the vocational HE offer more widely available. This can be seen to rely upon further development of widening participation in study at HE levels.

Up to the present, with generally good intentions, the widening participation agenda has led to the identification of groups of potential students anticipated as likely to see entry to level 4 as a barrier - the grouping of potential students into boxes. The students identified as being in these boxes are often offered support before entry to increase their likelihood of successfully transferring into level 4 and completing a programme of study at HE level. Examples of pre-entry support include Aimhigher initiatives and statutory school curriculum support which are often found within the 14-19 institutions. These initiatives realistically begin by introducing the concept of further and higher study rather than assuming this is part of the overall progression route being considered by some students. A recent study by a number of Aimhigher Partnerships and Action on Access have, in their interim report, concluded that the activities that are delivered to learners move towards an agreed continuum of experience, rather than a series of activities that have been accessed via a menu approach. (Aimhigher, 2008).

Additionally, access programmes and summer schools could be available, all of which are designed to raise aspirations and bring the idea of HE within the frame of reference of those groups of students who previously would not have considered it. This method of promoting and supporting participation in HE is referred to as model 2. For about thirty years numerous FE colleges have contributed a variety of initiatives to improving access to HE; good examples can be seen in practice across the YHELLN partners and studies suggest that this is widespread. Examples are included in Macdonald and Stratta (2001) and Bingham and O'Hara (2007). The recent ESCalate conference (April 2008) also highlighted the good work that has been done, both in the FE sector and in the universities. The focused nature of this response may mean that many will still slip through the net of this model, not realising that HE is an accessible and relevant route for them.

Removing the Barrier

This approach (model 3), which forms the basis of many current initiatives, including some of the work of YHELLN and other LLNs, is the one we contend can attract and retain students from the so-called 'non-traditional' backgrounds. It aims to remove the barriers, whether real or perceived, and encourage an assumption that HE is relevant, appropriate and open to all, as well as accessible and readily available by making the opportunity to access it simple and transparent. It is based around breaking the very large step of entering HE into a series of smaller and, hopefully, more manageable and less threatening steps. Inherent in this approach is the need to reconsider the way in which HE has traditionally been delivered.

A model that we have called 'Staged Engagement' has proved effective so far, although a longitudinal study has yet to evaluate the long term usefulness and sustainability of the strategy. It is essentially a three stage model for participation in HE, although the model is by no means solely linear. The model comprises 2-hour Expert Sessions, 10 credit Bitesize Modules and beyond to foundation, honours, masters and doctoral levels. Students may progress in a linear fashion if it is appropriate for them. There is also the potential for them to mix and match or to take breaks between modules. As the modules are validated by the University of Hull they may also be built into a 60 credit University Foundation Award, which has provided a potential entry route to HE for some time. Some modules may be used to claim advanced standing against other qualifications. There are also examples where an employer has attended the Expert Session and subsequently arranged for employees to take the Bitesize Module.

It is anticipated that this model will eventually fit into the 'Flexible Framework' that is being developed at the University of Hull. There will also be opportunities for accrediting work place learning, which should benefit students who are already in work and bring a great deal of skills and experience to underpin and enhance their academic studies. This is an area which seems to have previously been neglected, but could encourage employees to engage in HE. Although the model is probably more focused on mature learners who are already in the workplace, there will also be benefits for younger learners following a more vocational route. Breaking down learning into more manageable chunks and encouraging employers to support staff engaging in HE will benefit many learners, not just those designated as widening participation learners.

The model also encourages the use of more innovative pedagogy. Necessitated by the fact that most employees are not available in what would be considered usual teaching times, there is a move to providing sessions at times to fit in with the working day. Locations can also include delivery at local colleges or the work place and can also involve employers. Teaching strategies can also be varied, relying less on the traditional lecture/seminar model, and incorporate more kinaesthetic methods. Importantly, assessment methods can also be innovative and more appropriate to practical subjects. Writing lengthy essays or sitting exams often do not allow students from vocational backgrounds to show their skills and knowledge. However, these options could be of benefit to all students, as more flexibility can improve the learning and teaching experience for students and tutors.

It is hoped that by successfully enjoying a shorter, more manageable learning experience and recognising existing skills and experience, people will be encouraged to venture further and construct a programme of learning appropriate to their needs. However, it is very clear that most students will need very informed and focused support in the form of information, advice and guidance, which could be delivered through a variety of sources, such as information leaflets, websites and personally from tutors and guidance professionals. This should help them make the right, well-informed decisions to maximise the benefits of the opportunities available to them. The support however, may, on occasion, include advising against enrolling on a programme of study where it is clear that it would not be in the student's, or potential student's, best interests at that time. This model relies heavily on objective and realistic student support.

Implications for Widening Participation

It is clear that very diverse reasons influence the decision whether to participate in HE or not. These may vary at different points in a person's life cycle and will be affected by their early experiences of schooling. For the young, schools, families and peers are strong factors. Later, pressures of work and family responsibilities may be the main priority and may dictate the need for flexible provision, closer to home.

However, it is not just the decision to enter HE that is important. Recent statistics show that 'while participation in higher education has more than doubled since the mid-1980s, the non-completion rate remains broadly unchanged'. (HEFCE, 2008). In the light of this £245.9m of HEFCE's £356.3m widening participation allocations in 2007-08 have been designated as 'funding for improving retention'. (HEFCE, 2008). This suggests that the challenge of widening access to HE and encouraging a wider student constituency is starting to be met. The tougher task is now to help them complete and achieve.

The strategies outlined in model 3 can help accomplish this in a number of ways. Firstly, bitesized chunks of learning should be more palatable for many learners and give them the opportunity to access HE at a gentler pace, without facing the fear of 'dropping out' of a full programme. Secondly, success breeds success and other learners may be encouraged to access HE by seeing the success of others. Once people know peers and colleagues who have achieved qualifications it can remove some of the mystique that can surround universities. This is further broken down by the extended use of more accessible pedagogy. Good learner support can add value to the university experience by ensuring that learners understand what HE is about, where it can lead to, and are equipped with the skills to get the greatest benefit from it.

Universities should endeavour to create a 'habitus' where the vocational learner can be at ease to learn and achieve. Reece and Walker adapted Abraham Mazlow's hierarchy of needs, suggesting that we should 'help students feel good about themselves and they may learn that much more effectively'. (Reece and Walker, 2003: 79). Good learner support can ensure that conditions conducive to deep learning can be created for everyone. Over the centuries universities have evolved and taken on a set of discourses of their own, which can be quite exclusive and excluding. Many will have been amused by the example of Arthur Quiller Couch, first professor of English at Cambridge University in the early twentieth century. He persisted in Addressing his students as 'Gentlemen' when the class consisted mainly of women. (Eagleton, 1983: 28). This illustrates the evolution needed to make HE more accessible. The third model of learner support offers one way of promoting an inclusive learning environment.

Evaluation of Effectiveness

At its simplest, widening participation will be reflected in an increasing number of HE students. However, there may be many reasons behind a rise in student numbers. Although increased numbers can be taken to reflect increased participation, it may still be difficult to ascribe this to a change in policy and even more difficult to prove a link to a particular policy.

Demonstrating widening participation can be broken down into a number of steps. Firstly, evidence is needed of an increase in the number of HE students, expressed as a proportion of the population to control for changes in the population size. Secondly, an assessment of policy should take into account the support measures to which the increased participation is being linked. Such an assessment should consider the nature and extent, as well as the appropriateness of the support measures in place.

Finally, an assessment of impact should consider not only the quantity and quality of the effect on the learners, but also the extent to which the outcomes are appropriate. In this context the outcomes would be judged in relation to the academic, employment and personal development needs, both of the individual and society. An important aspect of this assessment would be the dynamic impacts - the extent to which the policies have not only increased the numbers of students gaining an HE qualification but also whether further learning opportunities have been created. An evaluation of how the policies have helped extend an academic learning culture into the work place and the wider society. Such a learning culture is the true embodiment of widening participation and lifelong learning.

References

Aimhigher, (2008) *Learner Progression Framework Feasibility Study Interim Report,* 22 January 2008.

Attwood, R. (2008) 'University Entry Reaches Plateau', in *Times Higher Education,* 3 April 2008.

Bingham, R. and O'Hara, M. (2007) 'Widening participation on early years degrees: 'I realised I could, and would, do this - and I have!' In *Journal of Further and Higher Education,* Vol.31, No.4, November 2007, pp.311-321.

Dearing, R. (1997) *Higher Education in the Learning Society, Report of the National Committee,* London: HMSO.

Dearing, R. (2008) 'The Challenges and Opportunities facing the University', keynote address to the University of Hull Learning and Teaching Conference, 17 January 2008 (unpublished).

Denham, J. (2008) 'Speech at the Wellcome Collection Conference Centre, London', 28 February 2008. Accessed on 26.05.08 www.dius.gov.uk/speeches/denham_hespeech_290208.html

Eagleton, T. (1983) *Literary Theory: An Introduction,* Oxford: Blackwell.

Fryer, R. (1997) *Learning for the Twenty-First Century: Report of the National Advisory Group for Continuing Education and Lifelong Learning,* London: National Advisory Group for Continuing Education and Lifelong Learning.

Greenbank, P. (2006) 'The Evolution of Government Policy on Widening Participation'. In *Higher Education Quarterly,* 0951-5224, Volume 60, No 2, April 2006, pp.141-166.

HEFCE, (2008) *How we fund widening participation* Accessed 03.06.08 http://www.hefce.ac.uk/widen/fund.

HM Government (2007) *World Class Skills: Implementing the Leitch Review of Skills in England,* London: DIUS.

House of Commons Public Accounts Committee (2008) *Tenth Report Staying the Course: the retention of students on higher education courses,* HC322 House of Commons Public Accounts Committee.

Kennedy, H. (1997) *Learning Works,* (Coventry: Further Education Funding Council.

King, M (2007) *Workforce Development: how much engagement do employers have with higher education?* London: CIHE.

Leitch, S. (2006) *Prosperity for all in the global economy – world class skills,* London: HM Treasury.

Lewis, B. (2002) 'Widening Participation in Higher Education: The HEFCE Perspective on Policy and Progress'. In *Higher Education Quarterly,* 0951-5224, Volume 56, No.2, April 2002, pp. 204-219.

Macdonald, C. and Stratta, E. (2001) 'From Access to Widening Participation: responses to the changing population in Higher Education in the UK'. In *Journal of Further and Higher Education,* Vol. 25, No. 2, 2001, pp.249-258.

Reece, I. and Walker, S. (1992) *Teaching, Training and Learning,* (2003, 5th edition), Sunderland: Business Education Publishers Limited.

Tight, M. (1998) 'Education, Education, Education! The Vision of lifelong learning in the Kennedy, Dearing and Fryer Reports'. In *Oxford Review of Education,* Vol.24, No.4, 1998.

Whitston, K. (2007) 'HEFCE has invested £100 million in 28 networks' in *Lifelong Learning Networks*, Bristol: HEFCE.

Re-visiting Community Based Adult Learning Approaches to Learning

J. Bradley, University of Stirling

Introduction

Part of the focus on widening access to learning in Scotland has been on learning transitions. In the main, however, this has been transition from school to college or university or from college to university. Little attention has been paid to community to college/university transition and this lack of focus can be said to reflect the limited attention paid to community based adult learning (CBAL) as part of widening access. However, this may now be changing prompted by a research carried out by the Centre for Research in Lifelong Learning (CRLL) entitled *Understanding and Enhancing Learning in Community–based FE*. This research focuses on the nature of community based learning as provided by Scottish FE colleges with a view to improving learning experiences.

The CRLL research has now prompted further activity in this area with the most recent being a series of consultation events focusing on developing a greater understanding of community based adult learning, and to develop ideas that might contribute to more effective learner transitions. These events are being led by the Scottish Further Education Unit's (SFEU) Transitions Reference Group. SFEU are joined in this group by partners from across a range of providers and support agencies involved in CBAL. Among these partners are Professor Jim Gallacher and Paula Cleary from CRLL who undertook the CRLL research. This paper has been informed by this current activity and will hopefully add to the current discussion on community based adult learning. However, this paper is not intended to be read as a critique of the provision of community based adult learning in Scotland. Nor is it an examination of the policy and strategy, both current and previous, that informs the provision of community based adult learning in

Scotland. Rather it is an attempt to add to the current debate and discussion on the nature and development of CBAL as it looks to meet the needs of the people in the communities it serves.[1] Community based adult learning can represent for many an opportunity to progress to further learning that can have a life changing effect for them and their families. However, I would argue that there has been a failure to enable more adults to progress from community provision to campus based learning and from there to professional careers.   The failure to significantly raise the number of adults from the lowest participation communities progressing to campus based learning has led me to re-examine my approach to the provision and delivery of CBAL.

The role of community based adult learning in Scotland has always been contested.   Is it a vehicle to regenerate and re-energise communities? Is it a method for radicalising the population? Is it a 'drive to reconfigure the relationship between the individual and the welfare state', as Vernon Galloway argues that it was under the last conservative government? Or, is it that community based adult learning has been subsumed within lifelong learning, and learning now 'is not a right but rather an obligation that is the responsibility of the learner to engage with?' (Galloway, V., 2004:280)

Community-based Adult Learning in the Scottish system

Community based adult learning has always been the poor relation of the adult education sector in Scotland. The Scottish FE college sector and the Scottish HEI sector have always been led by government policy and strategy that focuses on the nature of the provision of learning signified by formal, accredited award programmes. CBAL on the other hand is seen as an informal learning provision where success can be gauged in a number of ways including being judged against community objectives.   Further, success in learning in CBAL provision is also not always reflected by linear progression as it is elsewhere. Learning programmes in

---

[1] The view expressed here is a personal one, informed by my (almost) twenty year involvement in community based adult learning.

Scotland are levelled against the Scottish Credit Qualifications Framework (SCQF) and students on campus based provisions move, in the main, up the Framework. In contrast community learning staff talk about learner progression involving moving *across* the Framework rather than up it. This is contrary to how we view progression through campus based programmes, and in the school qualification systems, of standard grades and higher grade qualifications.

There is no doubt that community based learning does act as a point of entry for adults returning to learning after a significant break. It also acts as an entry point to learning for those who had a negative experience of formal, school-based learning. Community based adult learning can, then, by use of this provision of informal learning, enable adults to return to, and progress with, their learning. The significance of this approach has been recognised by the Scottish government:-

> *Community learning and development is the third strand of our work on raising participation in learning. Informal and community-based learning plays a crucial role in supporting people to engage in or to return to learning and can often be a first step back into more formal further or higher education for people who have become disengaged from learning.*
> (Life Through Learning; Learning Through Life, 2003: 40)

Yet in the last major Scottish Funding Council report on widening access, *Learning for All*, community based adult learning rates a very limited mention and in most places is glossed over in favour of working with the so-called 'NEET' group of young people even though the report recognises that 'people from the most deprived areas are particularly unlikely to attend HEIs …' (Learning for All, 2005: 13)

Much of this difference of approach to the provision of learning in the community may be down to the development of community based learning in Scotland. The most significant change to the community learning provision in Scotland in the last forty years was the Alexander Report produced in 1975 which recommended that the three strands of work in the community - youth work, CBAL and community work - be brought together as community education. For adult learning the hope was that:

> *...an adult education service less attached to formal institutions would be more responsive to local need. The driving concepts of disadvantage and educational need shifted the emphasis of adult education policy from the provision of curriculum in a formal setting to one which set out to address individual need in a non-formal context.* (Galloway, V. 2004: 205/6)

Within the last few years, though, community education has been superseded by Community Learning and Development.

Community learning and development (CLD) is learning and social development work with individuals and groups in their communities using a range of formal and informal methods. A common defining feature is that programmes and activities are developed in dialogue with communities and participants...(CLD's) main aim is to help individuals and communities tackle real issues in their lives through community action and community-based learning. (Working and *Learning* Together to Build Stronger Communities, 2004)

CBAL and Progression

One of the main areas of community based adult learning in community learning and development is adult literacy and numeracy (ALN). Although it may appear that a literacy provision is aimed at enabling individual learners to improve their level of literacy, ALN has a community focus,

> *The Scottish approach to adult literacies adopts a social practice model, which sees literacies as a key dimension of community regeneration and a part of the wider lifelong learning agenda.* (Scottish Government, 2007)

Progression from ALN to other learning opportunities does not seem to feature highly on the list of key principles and, indeed, none of the seven key principles listed in *Literacies in the Community: resources for practitioners and managers* mentions learner progression. These seven principles are:

- Promoting self-determination
- Developing an understanding of literacies
- Recognising and respecting difference and diversity
- Promoting participation
- Developing equitable, inclusive and anti-discriminatory practice
- Developing informed practice
- Drawing on partnerships

(Literacies in the Community, 2000: 5)

This lack of a wider focus on the provision of community based adult learning, (and progression from there to campus based learning), is at a time when adults from the most deprived communities are still not accessing learning in significant numbers. 'Mature participation changed less markedly and increased marginally in the most deprived class'. (Learning for All, 2008:5). Even when learners from the most deprived communities progress to campus based learning, they still face difficulties in completing their programme. 'While overall retention remains high in colleges and universities, students from deprived areas…continue to be more likely to drop out'. (Learning for All, 2008: 5)

The Scottish Funding Council (SFC), through its instructions to the four wider access regional forums, does have a focus on community based adult learning but this does not propel CBAL to the forefront of mainstream providers. 'There are no incentives for community-based learning particularly in the light of the loss of European Structural Funding'. (Stevenson College, 2006)

Indeed it is extremely difficult to find any Scottish government or SFC policy or strategy document which views community based adult learning as a provision which enables individual learners to re-enter learning and to progress to mainstream learning. In Scotland, community based adult learning is inexorably linked to community learning and development and community regeneration. However, this view of learning is not shared by other adult learning environments.   In both the Scottish FE college sector and in the Scottish HEI sector, learning is an individual undertaking with a focus, mainly, on enabling the learner to successfully achieve the qualification that their chosen programme offers. This approach to learning in these sectors is largely accepted and little time is spent debating the individualised nature of the learning that takes place in these environments. Although it may be mentioned in mission statements or strategic plans, the link between adult education in colleges or universities and community regeneration is generally weak and, even though colleges and universities will be part of community planning partnerships, their learning provision is focused on the individual achievement of their students.

Community based learning though is uniquely placed to enable adults to re-enter learning, and with encouragement and support, progress to all levels of further and higher education and then onto professional careers.   Veronica McGivney has said that 'Non participation (in post sixteen learning) is an indictment not of public apathy but of an education system which still projects a narrow and elitist image' (McGivney, V. 1991: 175). Despite focused work in widening access to learning in Scotland since 1999, within the Scottish FE and HEI sectors this situation largely remains and figures relating to participation in campus based learning programmes of those from the lowest quintile reflect this view. We have made limited headway in engaging with low participation communities and have seen their participation in campus based learning fall overall.

Those from the most deprived areas of Scotland were about 94 per cent as likely to attend university or college as those from other areas in 2005-06. Although the gap has narrowed since 2001-02, this is due to a decline in participation amongst the less deprived rather than an increase amongst the most deprived. (SFC, 2008: 1)

I believe then that in order to bring about a significant rise in participation in learning for those in low participation communities we need a concerted effort on behalf of funders, learning providers, learning support organisations and government. The lack of clarity surrounding the purpose and focus of community based adult learning has a negative impact on community based adult learning. Further, the linking of community based adult learning to community regeneration and not to individual achievement and progression can act as a barrier to the involvement of potential learners as learning achievement may not be linked to individual attainment which is the focus in all other learning sectors.

The nature of CBAL provision in Scotland

The community based adult learning sector is also populated by different providers who are informed by different government policies and strategies and who are funded by different methods. These differences curtail standardisation of outcome and activity and prevent a clear and coherent policy focus for CBAL. Further, this lack of standard approach to the provision of community based adult learning impacts on the practice of staff in CBAL and here there is a lack of standard qualifications. Community based adult learning in Scotland is the only adult learning sector where staff do not need a professional level teaching qualification and where staff delivering learning may hold no qualifications at all. Indeed, even where there are relevant qualifications in Scotland they are in the main set at SCQF level 8 which is equivalent to HND/Dip HE level.

This is not to undermine some of the provision but only to flag that whereas teaching qualifications have been introduced in the FE and HE sectors, community based adult learning does not have a specific teaching qualification. The main qualification for staff from the local authority or voluntary sector involved in CBAL is more likely to be a community education or community learning and development professional qualification rather than a teaching qualification. Where community based adult learning is provided by a local authority much of this provision will be focused on adult literacy and numeracy and/or employability rather than a wider adult learning provision and the service provider is just as likely to be attached to a department that covers libraries and leisure services rather than being attached to an education department. This is not to underestimate the work undertaken by staff involved in local authority adult learning but often their work is constrained by local authority objectives that do not view adult learning as an integral part of a post-sixteen learning sector linked to individual achievement and progression to accredited progarmmes in colleges or universities.

Concluding Remarks

We need to establish, or re-establish, community based adult learning as the third adult learning sector in Scotland sitting alongside the Scottish FE sector and the HEI sector as a formal adult learning sector with all that this entails.

Secondly, and this has been reflected at the recent SFEU led events on CBAL, community based adult learning requires one single representative body that is not focused on community learning and development but is focused on the provision of learning programmes in the community which places the emphasis in individual achievement and progression of which working within the community is only one of the available outcomes. In discussions with colleagues at one of the recent SFEU events one suggested that this could be achieved by the formation of an adult learning equivalent of the Care Commission. This representative body could enable the development of a common language and of shared objectives and outcomes and act as a champion for the sector. Further, this body would also be a funding partner in, or control funding for, community based adult learning programmes. In this way the sector could develop its own set of shared quality procedures and be much more focused on the standardised provision of community based programmes which would offer multi-exit routes. Among these routes would be one to a campus based learning provision and learners would be encouraged and supported to make this move. All community based adult learning programmes would be learner centred and underpinned by the provision of educational guidance. In this way learners would make an informed choice about their next move and not be directed down one particular route that suited a particular strategic objective.

Thirdly, the sector needs a professional (i.e., degree) level teaching qualification for community based adult learning. This qualification should also be accessible to part time and volunteer staff who wish to pursue a career as a teacher of CBAL in the same way the staff working in the Scottish College sector now undertake a Teaching Qualification in Further Education (TQFE).

The current approach to the provision of adult learning in the community does not seem to be encouraging disengaged adults to re-engage with learning and progress to further learning opportunities at the next level. Despite the Scottish Funding Council's widening access strategy there has been a failure to enable and encourage adults from low participation communities to re-enter learning and this is particularly true for men. Part of the problem could be that the SFC's jurisdiction covers the FE and HEI sectors and not all adult learning sectors in Scotland. Because of the nature of CBAL in Scotland policy and strategy objectives for providers are diverse and this provides little opportunity for a common vision. For Scottish FE colleges and HEIs this has never been clearer than in the local Community Learning and Development partnerships or Community Planning (CP) partnerships. Here the focus of the colleges and universities is still on their students and their individual achievements while the focus of the local authorities who usually lead these partnerships is on community regeneration and this can place colleges and HEIs at odds with the CLD or CP objectives.

The issue of progression from community based adult learning provision is one that I highlighted earlier. Part of the argument that staff working in the widening access field hear often on progression is that which says a degree is not appropriate for everyone and some people may be best suited to other forms of learning. Interestingly in my experience, this is usually proposed by people who already have at least one degree and who probably have benefited from at least three years free higher education. But, in one way, this argument is sound. Higher level study at a Scottish FE college or in a Scottish HEI is not for everyone and this paper does not support the notion that it is.   However, we should be encouraging and enabling people from low participation communities to make an informed choice about their learning in the knowledge that if they wish to progress to higher level study in a college or university then they will be encouraged and supported to reach their goal.   It is making an informed choice about learning that is important. For practitioners that means ruling everything in for learners, rather than starting from a point where we rule out certain options in advance for learners from certain communities.

For many adults returning to learning after a significant break, re-entering learning is a big step and the starting point for many can be, and will be, community based adult learning. Providing learning in the community also enables us to be in contact with those who may have disengaged with learning for whatever reason and we can work hard to encourage these adults to return to learn.   CBAL then is uniquely placed to provide a learning lifeline for adults for whom any form of learning, even that which takes places in the safe environment provided by CBAL programmes, may have many negative connotations. Community based adult learning should be a central part of the post-sixteen education sector in Scotland and is the most appropriate sector to enable adults to re-engage with learning.   The current focus on community based adult learning in Scotland affords us the opportunity to re-invigorate and re-establish community based adult learning as one of the three major learning sectors in Scotland. The failure to grasp this opportunity may sound the death knell for the provision as we know it and see the gap widen between those who access learning across the range and those who don't.

References

Gallacher, J. and Cleary, P. (2006) 'Understanding and Enhancing Learning'. *Community-based Further Education*, Centre for Research in Lifelong Learning. Glasgow Caledonian University/University of Stirling.

Galloway, V. (2005) 'Universal Individualism and Constructions of the Adult Student'. *Scottish Adult Education Policy, Journal of Adult and Continuing Education,* Volume 11 No. 2.

McGivney, V. (1991) Access to education for non-participant adults, Leicester: NIACE.

Scottish Executive (2000) *Literacies in the Community: resources for practitioners and managers.* City of Edinburgh Council and the Scottish Executive.

Scottish Executive (2003) Learning through Life, Life through Learning, The Lifelong Learning Strategy for Scotland.

Scottish Funding Council (2005) Learning for All, The Report of the SFEFC/SHEFC Widening Participation Review Group.

Scottish Funding Council (2008) Learning for All: second update report on measures of success.

Scottish Funding Council (2008) Scottish Participation in Further and Higher Education, 2001-02 to 2005-06.

Scottish Government (2004) Working and Learning Together to Build Stronger Communities, Scottish Government Guidance for Community Learning and Development.

Stevenson College (2006) Stevenson College Edinburgh's Response, SFC/03/2006, Review of college and HEI teaching funding methodologies.
www.scotland.gov.uk/Topics/Education/Life-Long-Learning/17551

Supporting Professionalism in Admissions (SPA): current issues in higher education admissions and student recruitment

Annie Doyle, SPA Senior Project Officer

Introduction

This article follows up the FACE Conference session in July 2008, outlining the role of the Supporting Professionalism in Admissions (SPA) Programme and highlighting key aspects of activity and progress that SPA has made.

SPA is the UK's independent and objective voice on higher education (HE) admissions. The aim of SPA is to lead on the continuing development of fair admissions, bringing together and evaluating existing evidence, data and intelligence regarding fairness and professionalism and providing an evidence base and guidelines for good practice and in helping higher education institutions (HEIs) maintain and enhance excellence and professionalism in admissions, student recruitment and widening participation/ access across the HE sector.

Development of SPA

SPA has its origins in the Admissions to Higher Education Steering Group (Schwartz) report *Fair Admissions to Higher Education: Recommendations for Good Practice,* (2004) (The report referred to England only, but has been used throughout the UK). One of the recommendations was the creation of a central source of expertise and advice on admissions issues. In response to this SPA was established in May 2006. It is a UK-wide programme, funded by all the UK HE funding councils.

The five main principles in the Schwartz Report stated that a fair admissions system should:

- Be transparent, and provide consistent and efficient information
- Select students who are able to complete the course as judged by their achievements and potential
- Use assessment methods that are reliable and valid
- Minimise barriers to applicants
- Be professional in every respect and underpinned by institutional structures and processes

The SPA Programme outputs act as resources for higher education provider institutions which wish to maintain and enhance excellence in admissions practice and policy. SPA brings together and evaluating existing research and encourages the identification and dissemination of effective practice. The Programme supports all staff involved in HE admissions procedures, academic and administrators.

The SPA Steering Group has representatives from Universities UK, GuildHE, UCAS, the HE Academy, UK government (including each of the devolved administrations) and HE funding councils, Association of Colleges, the pre-HE and HE sectors (including expert admissions practitioners). This membership helps to demonstrate the inclusiveness of the Programme – SPA is working for all stakeholders.

Although SPA is not part of UCAS, the Programme is based at Rosehill in Cheltenham and SPA values the synergy of working closely with UCAS staff.

The current work of SPA

SPA is working with practitioners to improve the evidence base for good practice and, using existing networks, to build consensus and identify and disseminate advice and guidance on what constitutes good practice. SPA's aim is to enhance professionalism throughout

the HE sector in admissions, student recruitment and widening participation and access.

Since September 2007 SPA staff have attended 61 meetings with 35 different groups or organisations to talk about SPA's work and share good practice. Since the Programme was established SPA staff have visited over 100 universities and colleges throughout the UK (32% of the 309 HEIs in the UCAS scheme for 2009) chosen to ensure different types, sizes, mission groups and geographical areas.

SPA welcomes these opportunities to discover more about the HEI's strategic view of admissions, student recruitment, widening participation/ access and to discuss how this fits into the HEI's teaching and learning strategy and vision as well as day to day good practice.

To inform the production of good practice guidelines SPA staff learn directly from admissions decision-makers, practitioners, academic admissions tutors and administrators, discussing areas including policies, entry criteria and the admissions decision-making process.

SPA has drafted good practice guidelines on:

- Feedback to HE applicants
- Admissions Tests
- Good practice in interviews
- Applicants with criminal convictions

SPA is investigating good practice around contextual data and holistic assessment for fair admissions, increasing the transparency of admissions policies and what makes a good applicant experience. This latter area in many ways underpins all of SPA's work, as it encompasses each of the four areas that SPA has identified as being part of the applicant experience i.e. coming at the start of the student journey. HEIs need to engage with students before they arrive and ensure that:

- effective pre-application activities and initiatives are in place i.e. widening participation/ access, student recruitment, schools and colleges liaison and outreach;
- provide adequate support to applicants during the application and decision-making–process;
- ensure this support continues post-application and throughout the transition from being an applicant to becoming a registered student.

The relevant sections, units and departments in each HEI need to work closely with each other to achieve this.

An effective applicant experience is becoming increasingly important as the UK faces a demographic downturn in the number of home 18 year olds from 2010, and recruitment in the global market for international students is increasingly competitive.

Current debates include the development of Strategic Enrolment Management (SEM) and Customer Relationship Management (CRM) systems and how these can be used to best effect within the HE sector. SPA is looking at best practice and professionalism in all areas relating to students, beginning with initial contact, moving through awareness raising and actively encouraging widening access and participation, recruitment, admission and transition into HE. This is because 'applicant experience' is seen as a key factor in an increasingly competitive market for institutions admitting students to HE.

In order to be fair admissions decision-makers, those involved in the admission, support and teaching of new students need to be professional and ensure they use good practice in all aspects of the recruitment, admission and transition process. This involves being applicant focussed and having clarity and transparency to demonstrate to potential students: the benefits and value of HE; the specific courses the institution has to offer; what is required for admission and progression into HE; that their application is valuable and will be treated professionally; the support and facilities available to new students.

Doing all of this well has huge benefits for the HE provider and for the applicant as it will be clear what the applicant will need to progress to HE and should also help with retention as the applicant should have a better idea of what to expect from the HEI.

SPA takes into account in all it does the equal opportunities legislation in the UK and its constituent parts, the drive to widen participation and access and the QAA's Code of practice: Admissions to higher education (2006).

SPA has worked closely with Skill, the National Bureau for Students with Disabilities, in requesting the production of a briefing on Competency Standards and Admissions to Higher Education. The briefing is published on the SPA website at http://www.spa.ac.uk/topical-issues/equality-diversity-issues.html.
This paper has also been agreed with the Equality Challenge Unit (ECU) as the first step on the way to the production of a further more definitive statement   SPA takes into account equal opportunities legislation, having established a good working relationship with ECU and Equality Scotland to take forward issues relating to undergraduate admissions. SPA is working closely with ECU on areas including Age and Student Issues and is currently liaising with them in relation to the production of the SPA good practice statement on interviewing applicants for admission to HE. SPA will continue to work with the organisations involved in equality and diversity issues on matters relating to equality of opportunity and how this impacts admissions. SPA also liaises regularly with the Quality Assurance Agency (QAA) and supports the QAA's revised section of the Code of Practice for the assurance of academic quality and standards in higher education – Section 10 – Admissions to higher education that was published in September 2006[1]

---

[1] QAA Code of Practice for the assurance of academic quality and standards in higher education – Section 10 – Admissions to higher education, September 2006 see:
http://www.qaa.ac.uk/academicinfrastructure/codeOfPractice/default.asp

Ensuring good practice and fairness in areas related to admissions such as student recruitment, widening participation/ access and marketing across the HE sector is also part of SPA's remit and links continue to be established and contact maintained with staff involved in Aimhigher, the Lifelong Learning Networks, Learning for All in Scotland and Reaching Wider in Wales. Discussions have included aspiration raising, progression agreements, changes in the 14-19 curriculum, the use of data and statistics and contextual information to support decision-making on applications. SPA will continue to develop its role in good practice, fairness and transparency relating to widening participation/ access and the development of good practice linking schools and colleges to HEIs.

A key area of activity has been to focus on admissions tests and meetings have been held with the organisations offering testing in the UK and a number of universities using admissions tests. The focus has been on collecting information from HE perspectives with regard to the purpose(s) of the tests, their validity and reliability and how the test results are used as part of the decision-making process on applications for particular courses. From pre-HE perspectives SPA has focussed on issues related to the costs, manageability and impact on the 16-19 curriculum for schools and colleges with regards to good practice. Tests are mainly for high demand courses such as Medicine and Law, but other institution or course specific tests are in use, covering subjects as diverse as history, social work, engineering, education, nursing and music.

SPA's research in this area has identified a total of 69 tests of different types and SPA has produced guidance on what is a 'good' admissions test. HEIs must consider the purposes and efficacy and set this against the SPA guidance. SPA is not an auditing or validating body, nor does it comment on the value of the tests. SPA urges HEIs, should they decide to use tests, to do so appropriately and to be transparent about their use. SPA will continue to work with HEIs to help them understand the importance of transparency in the use of tests, particularly an institution's own tests and especially in situations where the HEI does not describe the assessment as a "test". The SPA website has the most up to date information on tests www.spa.ac.uk/admissionstests.html.

The Director of SPA is a member of the HE sector led Delivery Partnership[2] Steering Group which seeks to implement the recommendations in the Government's response to the consultation 'Improving the Higher Education Applications Process' published in May 2006[3]. The work is closely related to SPA's activities; the cooperation is creative and beneficial. The Director is also Chair of the Delivery Partnership Entry Profiles Working Group, encouraging HEIs to develop Entry Profiles. The UK wide consultation recommended that UCAS and HEIs should continue their work on Entry Profiles, with a view to moving towards 100% provision of information for HE undergraduate courses by 2009. The current position is that nearly 79% of courses within the UCAS scheme have Entry Profiles.

Entry Profiles are web-based, written by HEIs and located within Course Search on the UCAS website. They help applicants improve their match between their pre-HE study and HE courses they are interested in, and help them to tailor their post-16 study more precisely to their HE needs. Entry Profiles provide applicants with more information about the courses they want to study: i.e. entry qualifications and levels, other entry criteria required such as personal skills and qualities, relevant work experience, motivation, audition, interview or admissions tests. This information is all together in one place in an Entry Profile.

The provision of this information could be particularly useful for those students who lack the confidence to apply for HE, for example, those from a background with no tradition of HE or for those following non-traditional or vocational routes into HE.

SPA is working closely with HEIs to encourage them to increase their numbers of Entry Profiles, including improving the quality of

---

[2] The delivery partnership was established to deliver a number of improvements to the HE applications process, following a government consultation on Post-Qualification Applications, as recommended by Schwartz.

[3] Details can be seen at http://www.dfes.gov.uk/consultations/conResults.cfm?consultationId=1346

the content of Entry Profiles and to include information on the actual admissions decision-making process for the course.

In order to establish the evidence on the use of Entry Profiles, SPA surveyed applicants and HEIs for their views: 94% of home students and 96% of international students stated that Entry Profiles were either extremely helpful or helpful within the application process.

> 'The entry profiles allowed me to judge the level of care and interest that a university had in students of a particular subject. Those universities that had taken the time to complete their Entry Profiles were more interesting to me as a result'.
> (Home student cited in the *SPA Applicant Survey, June 2007*)

The Government recommendation is that HEIs should develop more information to feed back to students, detailing why their applications have been rejected. In May 2007 the Delivery Partnership welcomed the draft statement of good practice developed by SPA from the JISC scoping study, as a positive model to take forward. HEIs had an opportunity through a consultation exercise to comment on the draft statement and the finalised document now appears on the SPA website at http://www.spa.ac.uk/good-practice/applicant-feedback.html.

The responses to the consultation gave a considerable amount of support to finding ways to provide unsuccessful applicants with electronic feedback via UCAS. SPA has worked with UCAS to develop electronic feedback mechanisms, for implementation from October 2008 for entry in 2009. Reasons for rejection are codified by HEIs and generate some standard sentences/ paragraphs and/ or some free text, which applicants are able to view on UCAS Track. These codes are institution specific and will be reviewed/ updated by HEIs on an annual basis.

The Delivery Partnership believes that feedback, together with the increasing number of clear and transparent Entry Profiles developed by HEIs, should go a long way towards overcoming the perception of a lack of fairness and transparency in admissions.

SPA is exploring with UCAS what data and statistics are available to support good practice and professional decision-making in the HE marketing, student recruitment, widening participation/ access and admissions processes. SPA will also work with UCAS to take forward the use of data for HE admissions from sources around the UK, as well as exploring how data can be used by non-specialists within admissions and other teams in HEIs.

The SPA website is a major feature of the information and communication strategy as are meetings around the UK. To promote SPA's work and encourage thinking on good practice and professionalism by the wider community of HEIs, school and college staff and other stakeholders, SPA staff have attended over 20 conferences, launches and events since September 2007. SPA has run five conferences/ seminars to highlight good practice and to disseminate information relating to the support that SPA can offer HE in promoting professionalism. Each event has been well attended with a total of 436 delegates at the five events. Over 20 people have attended more than one event and over 78% of HEIs in the UK have been to one or more SPA event. Positive feedback has been received including, at the SPA Good Practice Seminar in June 2008, over 92% of participants who completed the questionnaire considering the seminar overall as 'good' or 'very good'. Over 88% commented that the seminar had met their expectations well or very well.

The UCAS Professional Development programme exists to support academic admissions tutors and administrative and support staff involved in admissions, student recruitment and widening participation/ access. SPA meets regularly with Professional Development colleagues to input into their programme. Professional development and training issues are discussed by SPA at visits to HEIs including internal staff development, conferences and training and the 26 professional development sessions which are offered by UCAS.

SPA meets with senior staff across all the UK administrations and education, learning and HE funding bodies to discuss policy and implementation of the SPA operational plan from their perspective and to feed back issues. In Scotland this has included: discussions with regard to Learning for All and Learner Choice; Curriculum for Excellence; the new baccalaureates and wider achievement; articulation; enhancement themes on transition to first year under the Quality Enhancement Framework; equality issues. SPA also presents examples of the possible impacts of decisions in other administrations on Scotland, such as the introduction of the Advanced Diplomas and A*.

Following the introduction of variable tuition fees for HE in England in 2006, it has become more likely that complex interactions between fees, bursaries and other funding assistance will develop. This may vary between subject disciplines, across institutions, perhaps between individual applicants applying to the same course at the same institution, and could add to the complexity of student choice in terms of course, institution and the area of the UK in which the applicant chooses to study. SPA will look at the impact of initiatives implemented by the separate administrations of the UK on this and other cross-border issues with regards to fairness and good practice.

The breadth of knowledge that exists in the SPA team enables cross-border issues to be identified and the voice of HE admissions from the individual administrations to be raised by the team at national meetings as appropriate. SPA has a unique, impartial position in these debates in being able to bring together the various perspectives to ultimately have a positive effect on fairness and good practice across the sector as a whole.

Conclusion: Achievements to date and future plans

SPA was funded for two years initially to 31 July 2008. Funding has now been confirmed by HEFCE on behalf of all the UK HE funding bodies for a further three years. The Chief Executive of HEFCE, of behalf of all the funding councils, stated:

'We are pleased with the progress of the SPA to date and believe that the work undertaken during its first two years of operation has and will continue to give the programme a profile and presence in the sector.'

The SPA Programme has become an objective, authoritative and enduring source of evidence and advice about admissions matters. The SPA Steering Group acknowledged this and the External Evaluator for SPA, Professor Geoff Layer, stated:

'The team is to be congratulated for the progress it has made to date in securing sector ownership.'

SPA aims to promote change in HEIs underpinned by good practice, transparency and fairness and to build on the Programme's success to date as the leader in professionalism in admissions by working with Pro-Vice-Chancellors and senior staff in HEIs, as well as continuing to work with admissions tutors and administrators. The focus was initially on full-time UK undergraduates but this will develop further as the Programme progresses. SPA will take a more strategic leadership role over the next three years, focussing on broader policy and practice, not only in good practice but in raising particular issues with HEIs and the sector in general. The Programme aims to drive policy and be known across the sector as the promoter of good practice. SPA's plans for the next three years include:

i	exploring issues around the 14-19 curriculum relating to good practice in progression and admission to HE;
ii	examining vocational, skills and work-based learning routes into HE, including the role of compacts and progression agreements, foundation degrees and employee/ employer engagement
iii	working with the organisations involved in equality and diversity issues on matters relating to equality of opportunity and how this impacts admissions;

iv continuing to develop the Programme's good practice role, including
fairness and transparency relating to widening participation/ access
and the development of good practice linking schools and colleges to HEIs;

v continuing to explore and develop good practice around what makes a good applicant experience, in order to develop HEIs' recognition of the strategic importance of recruitment, admissions and widening access to the institution;

vi examining admissions processes and procedures for part-time applicants, establishing and analysing an evidence base of current practice to review equality of opportunity and good practice;

vii continuing to take cognisance of the policies and strategies of the individual administrations in the UK.

To support the expansion of the Programme SPA will recruit two new members of staff, a Senior Project Officer and a Project Officer.(for further information about SPA please visit the website at www.spa.ac.uk}

References

Fair admissions to higher education: recommendations for good practice ('The Schwartz report') Admissions to Higher Education Review, (September 2004). http://www.admissions-review.org.uk/ (The report referred to England only, but has been used throughout the UK.)

Section Four :

FACE Development Papers

There's more to learning than earning - the Wider Benefits of Lifelong Learning

Sheila M. Hughes, College of Education and Lifelong Learning, Bangor University

Introduction

Writing in *"The Benefits of Learning"*, Schuller et al (2004) explore how learning makes a difference to people's lives as individuals and as members of their community. Their research covers key questions concerned with the interaction between learning and people's physical and psychological well-being; the way learning impacts on family life and communication between generations and the effect on people's ability and motivation to take part in civic and community life.

The range of factors which are influenced by learning include, wellbeing, health, attitudes and behaviour. Schuller et al (2004) argue that UK research on well-being shows that attainment of at least "O" level or equivalent, reduces the risk of adult depression. In health matters, there is a substantial body of evidence suggesting that positive correlations exist between education and physical and mental health. Evidence has also shown that participation in adult learning has beneficial effects on race tolerance, authoritarian attitudes, political cynicism and political interest. There is further evidence to show that educational interventions have been shown to reduce crime. (Feinstein and Sabates, 2005).

Social capital and lifelong learning

Robert Putnam, explains social capital as:

> *"most generally taken to refer to the networks and norms which enable people to contribute effectively to common goals"* (Putnam cited in Schuller et al, 2004 :17).

Field (2005) argues that social capital and lifelong learning are central to current policy concerns both in the UK and internationally. According to Field the relationship between social capital and lifelong learning is complex but there is sufficient evidence to point generally to a mutually beneficial association between these two domains. The premise is that because social networks and learning are both desirable resources - they both help us to enjoy other benefits and, as well as this, they may help us to think in new ways about economic development and social cohesion.

However, this relationship between lifelong learning and social capital suggests that lifelong learning should be holistic in its approach – one which takes on a wider perspective not only to include work and skills related training, but importantly one which enables individuals to participate in the social, civic and cultural life of society.   In spite of this, there is genuine consternation in emerging discourse that the current Government notion of lifelong learning with its emphasis on skills and work is too narrowly defined and arguably one which does not give equal importance to non-economic benefits of lifelong learning and their valuable contribution to social capital.

The Research Project

The aims of this enquiry into wider benefits of lifelong learning are therefore multifaceted - not only are there questions to be asked about lifelong learning and its wider benefits but also attitudes towards lifelong learning itself.   The research data was drawn from a study conducted in Wales, although the implications of the research has relevance across the UK.

The research firstly considered a range of causal factors that may either encourage or dissuade people to take up lifelong learning. These involved such matters as access, availability, affordability, relevancy etc. and may be vocational or non-vocationally orientated. Questions then needed to be posed to discover whether or not students have experienced personal benefits from their learning and how if at all, those benefits have extended into the community at large.

The Lifelong Learning Institution and the students involved in the research

The School of Lifelong Learning at Bangor University provides flexible, bilingual educational opportunities across North Wales - from individual undergraduate modules to Masters level study. There are centres at Bangor, Wrexham and Mold spanning the north east and north west of Wales and serving a population in north Wales of approximately 675,600 (Welsh Assembly Government, 2006). 1000 students were involved in the sample group consisting of both men and women of a wide age range and living across north Wales.

Methodology

A mixed method approach was employed with a questionnaire and focus groups. The questionnaire included 21 questions. Section 1 asked about educational interest and issues, section 2 looked at some of the practical and logistical issues involved and section 3 of the questionnaire included more personal questions to allow the previous replies to be placed into greater context.

The questionnaire was accompanied with a letter and form to ask participants if they would be willing to take part in a focus group in order that some of the issues raised in the questionnaire could be discussed in more depth. This enabled the researcher to draw together both qualitative and quantitative evidence and allowed a number of measurable variables to be quantified and triangulated. Out of the 329 respondents from the questionnaire sample 90 people indicated their willingness to take part in focus group and participate further.

Three focus groups were arranged in three different locations across north Wales – Bangor, St. Asaph and Wrexham. A total of 24 students were invited to the three venues   Quota sampling shown in the table below, was employed in the selection of the participants taken from the 90 respondents, 35 of which were male and 55 female.

Focus groups

Location	Numbers attending out of 8	Male	Female	Age range
Bangor University - Senior Common Reading room	5	1	4	35-65
St. Asaph – Oriel House Hotel	7	5	2	45-70
Wrexham – School of Lifelong Learning	8	2	6	48-72

Limitations of the questionnaire and focus groups
Data collection   focussed primarily on adults already involved in lifelong learning   and therefore it did not include adults who may have yet to take up lifelong learning opportunities. The response rate of the questionnaires was 329 out of 1,000 surveyed (33%), therefore the numbers of respondents involved in both the questionnaire and focus groups represent a small section of the student population and care must be exercised in the analysis and interpretation.

It was envisaged that age, personal circumstances and life experiences will have a direct bearing on the results. Therefore it is useful to look firstly at the age groups of respondents.

Results of the age group frequencies indicate a distribution which is skewed towards the higher age groups. The largest participant age group is the 65+ group with 114 individuals accounting for 35% of the total distribution. The second largest group is the 55-64 years with 29% of the total distribution and 94 individuals. The 45-54 group is the third largest (19%), followed by the 35-44 group (10%) and the under 24s group (4%). The lowest group frequency was in the age range 25-34.

The frequency distribution indicates that in our sample most people taking up lifelong learning were aged 45 and over, with the highest percentage being in the 65+ bracket. The results appear to suggest that as individuals get older they have few family commitments and more free time, particularly those who have retired, which means they can attend education classes,. It may also be plausible to suggest that as people get older they develop a renewed intellectual curiosity and a desire to improve their knowledge and skills either for continued professional development or personal interest or due to a life-change such as retirement. These issues are expounded in many of the questions below. Alongside this it is interesting to note that according to McNair (2008), there are a growing number of "young old" people, [in the UK] mainly aged between 50-75 most of whom will be in good health and many of them still economically active.

Bearing in mind that the students in the three focus groups ranged in age between 35 and 72, it was apparent from the question asking about their views and experiences of lifelong learning that all were open to the principles of learning for life in its broadest sense. Some students felt strongly that learning should be regarded as a rite of passage throughout the life-span, illustrated in the following quotations:

> 'you never stop learning, learning is not just for the young ones'

> 'lifelong learning is appealing because it seems to suggest that there are no age barriers'

> 'age becomes irrelevant, you benefit from meeting younger people. A lot of older people don't realise how much learning has changed. It's a second chance'.

'I think it means its all encompassing, knowledge and work skills yes.. but also social skills…'

Questions and responses

The following represents a selection of questions directly relevant to wider benefits:

How interested are you in each of the following types of study?
This question asked students to rank their attitudes to three possible types of study which ranged from formal, non-formal through societies, clubs and voluntary organizations and certificated courses relating to a profession, such as a 'Microsoft.

1) Formal (at college or university)
61% of respondents were either very interested or interested in taking up formal study within college or university, 10% were a little interested, 20% were not interested in formal learning and 9% were undecided.   This indicates a distribution which is skewed towards very interested or interested in formal learning as the most popular response to this question.

This suggests that students regard colleges and universities as important domains for lifelong learning provision.   During discussions in the focus groups the idea of 'college values' was raised. Students from all three groups associated lifelong learning with a university or further education college.

There was general agreement that students engaging in formal learning were usually very self motivated and were willing to make a commitment to their studies.   There was some consensus within the groups that mature students saw formal learning as a challenge and a way of developing and realising their ambitions. Over half of the participants said that taking up lifelong learning at the University had raised their self-esteem and confidence and for some, the experience had been life-changing:

'accreditation is important and having a degree … makes you wonder why you haven't done it before. I take what I've learned back to work – tea room conversation has changed, I test out theories on my colleagues'

'..yes, learning gives you the ability to argue, it's empowering'

'I always wanted a cap and gown but no way could I have done this in my teens'

These responses appear to provide strong evidence that lifelong learning offers individuals opportunities to fulfil ambitions or desires and suggest that its appeal and success lies in the fact that everyone learns at different times in their lives and that for some people it is empowering and life fulfilling.

Nevertheless, it must be borne in mind that the survey population all had some experience of formal learning and it is interesting that these results show that 20% were not interested in formal learning and 10% a little interested. This provides an interesting dichotomy in that it suggests that some respondents may have negative attitudes towards formal learning.

The question of negative attitudes towards formal learning was taken up in the focus groups. Some students felt that having assessment deadlines could be stressful especially when there are family problems such as illness or caring responsibilities. One student said that missing deadlines 'really put me off' and nearly made her drop out.

'I felt as though I had failed, I got through it … but I think that this could be a problem for some people'

The negative experiences discussed centred around workload and assessment. These comments do indicate that some elements of formal learning can be stressful to some people and it must be borne in mind that this would have a negative impact on wider benefits.

Overall, the majority of respondents placed a high value in formal education. Some wider benefits can also be linked here to formal learning, such as self-esteem and self-efficacy and self-fulfilment. There are also wider benefits which impacts both the individual and the community. For example, one student recalled how much she had enjoyed the local history classes, not only did she learn new information but she had also got to know other people in the community.

> 'The classes brought up lots of interesting things about the area. There was a good turn out.... I had seen some of the people around but never talked to them before..... two of the women were Polish... the class brought us together.... it was a good experience... we have all gained so much'

2) Non-formal (e.g. societies, clubs)

For 65% of our population there is an appeal to learn without the trappings of accreditation and formal structures. This further suggests that these respondents are slightly more concerned with the concept of learning for itself and prefer an informal approach to learning. Non-formal learning was discussed in the focus groups when sharing students' views about their experiences of lifelong learning. Students felt that there were positive attributes to non-formal learning if the quality of the activity is good. Some students liked the idea of learning for learning's sake and not to gain certificates or accreditation.

> 'I already have a degree, so don't feel the need for accreditation, but I enjoy the learning and keeping my brain active'
> 'I learned to swim when I was 55, it did wonders for my self esteem'
> 'I went to a "Meet the mouse" course a couple of years ago. We learned the basics of using a computer and the internet... there was no exam or test, I really enjoyed it'

Results from the non-formal learning suggest that this type of learning can also bring about wider benefits in promoting health and wellbeing, self-esteem and social inclusion.

3) Courses specifically related to a profession e.g. Microsoft accredited
35% of the respondents were either very interested or interested in professionally related courses, 14% were undecided and 40% were not interested.   This suggests that some individuals may feel that gaining professional certification is important as it is directly linked to employment benefits. It is also worth bearing in mind the age of the majority of respondents when considering that 40% indicated no interest.

A number of the students in the focus groups believed that gaining professional certification was a way of making oneself more competitive in the work place.   One student in her mid forties had taken an European Computer Driving Licence course (ECDL) and found this had helped her to get a new job after being out of the workforce for some time.

> 'Some jobs ask specifically for ECDL qualifications, I was so glad that I had got my certificate'

All three types of learning have their significant values and appeal which suit the needs of the learners. The results would appear to suggest that it is a blending of formal, non-formal and work related learning that is significant here, as it appears that many people are interested in all three types of learning and not necessarily one specific type of learning.

What are you reasons for study?
The next question asked students their reasons for study.   Six possible choices were proposed, ranging from self improvement, interest, professional development, to gain further knowledge of the subject, to meet new people, to keep intellectually active. Students were asked to rate each one in order of importance.

1)Interest
An overwhelming 94% of respondents felt that *Interest in studying* was either very important or important. This suggests that adults are strongly motivated to take up lifelong learning seeing it as an

important way to keep intellectually active, fulfill their potential and foster a spirit of enquiry. During the focus groups, students were asked whether they felt lifelong learning promotes independent thinking and problem solving skills.   Some of the respondents shared their views:

> 'Philosophy has always held a fascination for me... I wanted to find some answers... but there are no easy answers ….. you have to really think about it…….'.

> 'I joined the class to learn Welsh … it takes effort and you have to practice, it's not an easy option!'

> 'Gives you the ability to argue, it's empowering'

> 'I took up creative writing... aiming to be a professional writer.. I've had a poem published! …''

> It is clear that improved cognitive skills build self esteem and confidence.

2) To gain further knowledge of subject
For 92% of respondents, gaining knowledge of the subject was either very important or important. This high score suggests that adults are keen to better their knowledge or perhaps learn new subjects.

As students develop their skills and understanding they become more self-confident and positive in their attitudes to learning. This theme emerged from within the focus groups when discussing how lifelong learning can encourage positive attitudes and values. There was a discussion about school experiences:

> 'I never understood literature in school and my teacher wasn't very helpful and made me feel stupid……. Damaging school experiences can stay with you, people don't understand why it's been difficult for some people to access education.'

Negative experiences of school education can have a lasting effect on self confidence and attitudes to learning. Many adult students may reach a point in the lives when they want to redress or overcome possible gaps in their knowledge in order to feel better about themselves:

> 'I wasn't very good in school at maths, so I went to class as I wanted to help my grandson with his homework.'

Apart from knowledge and learning, there is evidence here of self-efficacy and self-confidence. However, there are strong indications of barriers to learning also which can have negative impact on wider benefits.

3) Self improvement

Self-improvement was also a popular reason for people to take up lifelong learning. For many adults lifelong learning opportunities are and chance to gain new knowledge they may have missed out on in early years.

Discussing how lifelong learning has made a difference to their lives, two female participants, one in her late thirties and the other in her forties commented:

> 'More tolerant now... we had a lot of sudden changes at work which were quite shocking but education helps you understand and be able to express yourself rationally .. makes you more reflective'

> 'I love learning…. all positive….. social time away from the children, has a knock-on effect on the children too'

The male respondents, both of whom were over 50 reported:

> 'I got a new job because of it'

> 'Made me much more knowledgeable'

The wider benefits here are clearly expounded.

4) To meet new people

A total of 57% of respondents said they had taken up lifelong learning to meet new people. This suggests that for many people lifelong learning offers a forum which encourages social networks and social cohesion and in terms of wider benefits provides a good example of building social capital. As one student in the focus group commented:

> ' you meet people who are interested in the same things as you… not just learning but connecting socially'

5) Professional development

46% of respondents felt that professional development was either very important or important. This suggests that these respondents' main concern with accessing lifelong learning centers around their vocational needs, either for their own satisfaction to facilitate their work or satisfy the requirements of professional bodies.

During the focus group meetings, the facilitator asked participants for their views about whether lifelong learning can contribute to the economy. There was a consensus that taking up lifelong learning can aid continuing professional development (CPD) as it builds people's self confidence and self-efficacy by updating and improving skills and knowledge. It also has a beneficial impact on their performance in the workplace.

> 'I'm a self employed graphic designer, so need to keep up with a range of art techniques so that I can offer a better service and get good commissions'

> 'Gives people confidence to engage in meetings, to be able to have their say and more confidence about being able to back up your point of view'

> 'I'm an occupational therapist so know about CDP … it's mandatory in many jobs in healthcare. Lifelong learning fitted in well for me'..

Provision for CDP clearly matters to many adults as it enables individuals to sustain their productiveness. Also there are wider benefits here such as wellbeing and self esteem.

6) To keep intellectually active
A large percentage of respondents (86%) felt that keeping intellectually active was a prime motivator for study. There is a growing awareness that it is sensible for adults of all ages to keep the mind as well as the body active. The results suggest that for many people, taking up lifelong learning is a way of enabling people to become mentally stimulated and challenged by learning something new - vital for promoting cognitive ability.

This was an area of particular interest for students in the focus group, who discussed the importance of lifelong learning activities and the need to keep abreast of new developments happening in the world around them. This seemed particularly important to the older students who felt it was necessary shake off stereotypical images often relating to older or retired people.

> 'Much better communication with grandchildren, keeps you mentally stimulated. Gave me a new sense of purpose and self confidence'

> 'My boss was amazed that I use a VLE (Virtual Learning Environment) on my course.'

This clearly indicates wider benefits. Hammond (2002) strongly argues that lifelong learning contributes to psychological, mental and physical health and generates immediate psychosocial outcomes (such as well-being, efficacy, communication skills, a sense of social responsibility) that have lasting effects upon mental health, and cumulative effects upon physical health.

People have many reasons for taking up study and are motivated by a number of complex factors. The categories discussed show that reasons cited relate directly to non-economic wider benefits such as self confidence, self-efficacy, improved health and wellbeing and greater job satisfaction but also provide a better understanding and

some evidence of how these processes interact and in some cases can link to economic benefits.

What is your preference for style of course delivery?
Students were asked "What is your preference for style of course delivery?" There were four choices to rate in order of importance. These were face to face learning with tutor/student group; distance learning: study packs at home; on-line learning: via world wide web and a blend of face to face and distance learning.

A majority (92%) of the population prefer face to face delivery, 47% rated blended learning as being important or very important, 41% felt that distance learning was very important or important; 38% rated on line learning as being very important or important. This suggests that it is essential for students to have human interaction and contact to help them acquire learning and subject expertise. The social contact is also very important to students.

This sentiment was clearly articulated in the focus groups where the sense of attending a class was linked with belonging to a community and having access to tutors with subject expertise and knowledge they could trust. The peer support from students themselves also makes the learning experience pleasurable and enjoyable and has wider benefits,

> 'The stuff you get up on Google is amazing but I get sidetracked and don't really know if its right or wrong'

> 'Social aspect of classes are good too… laughing is very good for you'

> 'More self confidence now, I'm learning so much ….and new friends – has to be a health benefit from this….'

Nevertheless, there were some frustrations mooted in that provision did not always meet personal requirements. For example, a course was being delivered in a venue which students were not able to get to, or if the timing of the class was wrong.

It follows from this evidence that it is not so surprising that distance learning was not as popular a choice as this normally entails working in isolation and independently.   Students would need to be particularly motivated to work in this way. Although, one must bear in mind that there are very successful distance learning programs that do hold appeal to some students such as those offered by Open University.   The on-line learning option was rated fairly low. This is worthy of note here, particularly as one of the other questions concerning level of skills with computers and information technology showed that the majority of respondents (73%) indicated they were either very confident or reasonably confident using information technology and computers.   This again implies the need for people to engage in face to face delivery.

It was however, interesting to note that 47% of students were interested in blended learning and this is a model that perhaps holds appeal and could prove to be successful for certain students and may also help learning providers to reach a wider audience.

Overall the results suggests that successful learning takes place in environments where there is a human element and the dynamics of dialogue, debate and peer support exists.   Also one must bear in mind that for many students who are returning to learning after a long period, or who may have suffered some form of trauma or life change, interacting with tutors and peers is likely to be preferred to studying in isolation. These are attributes which aid social cohesion and build self confidence and self-esteem.

Previous Study
29% of respondents had taken part in evening classes, 38% in daytime (am/pm) learning, 13% weekend learning, 7% summer schools, 10% work training and 5% online.

These results are interesting in that they provide longitudinal evidence showing individuals have been involved with learning over a **five year period**. Whilst daytime and evening provision is the most popular, it is interesting that work training and weekend learning are being taken up.

These results confirm that lifelong learning is meeting its aims in that it is life long and ongoing. People may want to step in and out over a period of time as this realistically matches up to life events. For many learners this may mean taking courses which are at the same level of accreditation and not necessarily to achieve higher awards.   This "level" provision however, is an area which is currently being affected by financial policies of the funding councils. In England the funding councils have decided that funding will cease for students who take university and college courses for qualifications at the same or lower levels than those they possess already. This is currently not the case in Wales.

How would you describe your health generally?
90% of respondents, the majority of whom are 55 and over, enjoy average to good health and are intellectually active.   This may suggest that being involved in learning activities can stimulate cognitive processes which can have beneficial effects on health and wellbeing. Of course there is also the possibility that because students are in good health, they are able to take up lifelong learning opportunities.

These results were considered alongside the comments from the focus groups where the theme of health and wider benefits of lifelong learning was emotively debated in all three of the focus groups.   Four students, two female, two male, attending three different venues: Bangor, Wrexham and St. Asaph, reported benefits to their own or their partner's mental health from attending lifelong learning courses.

> ' felt very ill and depressed until I did a degree at 40 .. I probably would have been put in a mental asylum.........

> I've suffered off and on for many years with depression, but doing my degree has given me a better focus – its really made a difference to my life and to my family… working at the course has helped me through ….. I feel so much better about myself…

"I retired at 55 .. I found it difficult to cope at first, but worst of all my wife died suddenly soon after. Taking up lifelong learning has enabled me to find some stability and direction - I have a sense of purpose again..learning new things…. I feel part of a community"

These comments strongly suggest that it is because of their learning that students' health and well being has improved.

How would you describe your current occupational status?
The following question asked people about their current occupation status to ascertain how many people were in full or part time employment, those who were unemployed and those who were retired.

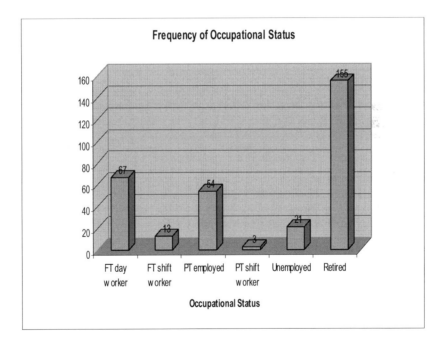

Out of 328 respondents 155 are retired, and 134 are in either full or part time employment and 21 are unemployed.

These figures are particularly interesting when compared to the age of the population where the largest percent of respondents were in the 55-65+ age brackets.

Issues about learning and occupations arose in the focus groups. One student spoke about how he had experienced difficulty in getting work after 55.

> "I sent out over 40 applications, I got a couple of interviews but never got a job .. I think it was because of my age although no one actually said so"

Some in the focus groups felt that employers do not value experience, preferring to take younger people who have may have new qualifications. Only two of the students in all three focus groups were aware of APEL. There was a sense that the work/life experience of older people value is undervalued. Issues such as these can create social exclusion. Finding a new social purpose is important for health and wellbeing and lifelong learning can help to address this.

Main findings and analysis

Peoples' attitudes towards Lifelong Learning
The results have shown that there are excellent benefits to be gained from all types of learning whether this be formal, non-formal or informal which can add to social capital and some of these findings will be further explored in this analysis.

The investigation has found that people have very diverse and complex reasons for taking up lifelong learning. It is clear that once adults engage with lifelong learning they are highly motivated to learn. The research showed that students also have certain expectations, hopes and aspirations about the different kinds of learning that they choose to do and many willingly conveyed that they have experienced profound and lasting benefits from their learning.   The results have also revealed some interesting barrier issues surrounding lifelong learning which may for some people, result in non-participation and isolation.

Health and well being benefits
Students that took part in the focus groups were highly articulate about their experiences of lifelong learning and how it had affected their lives. The majority of the students reported personal wider benefits relating to their health, improved self-esteem, happiness and well being. In some cases students illustrated how these benefits made a direct positive impact on both their family and work-related relationships.

Whilst it is tempting to argue unequivocally that lifelong learning is a panacea for good health, it would be remiss to paint too bright a picture of health benefits as there were issues raised in the research which also point to negative impacts which can for some people, effect their health and wellbeing. For example, some of the students in the focus groups talked about how they had faltered at the amount of reading they needed to do, and another spoke of the pressure of assessments and their deadlines. In both cases the students had lost confidence and this had affected their self-esteem. In these particular cases, students were following part time degree qualifications where support structures were in place to help. However, it does suggest that for some a less intensive qualification may be more appropriate. Hammond (2006) discusses how education can also generate challenges and expectations that are potentially stress-inducing indicating cognitive dissonance explaining that this happens when students aspirations, expectations and reality do not match up and the stress generated from this which may place burdens on students and their families and friends.

Barriers to lifelong learning

Negative experiences can affect many other individuals who may be less motivated to learn because of the perceived expectations it may place upon them. Motivation can be affected if these individuals are at a point or place in their lives where they are vulnerable, or if their confidence and self-esteem is low. This is counterproductive to the aims of lifelong learning in seeking to widen participation and reach the groups of people who may be socially excluded and for whom the right sort of learning opportunity could bring a range of benefits. Jones (1997) identifies these groups as including the unemployed, unskilled, immobilised and carers. However, there are many other disadvantaged people who could be added to this list.

This points to the need for strong advice, guidance and support structures for adult learners who may be isolated and non-participant in learning and perhaps this where taster courses, study skills provision and broad foundation type courses can be of great help, especially if they are of a short duration initially to introduce and encourage new ideas.   It also points to opportunities that can exist between non-accredited and accredited provision as both have strengths and appeal in engaging and fostering educational pursuits and have complementary value for lifelong learners.   In practice such "signposting" would require the skills of a good advisor to ensure that students are aware of the various programmes available to them and are advised about the sort of learning experience they may expect - but more than this, the advisor would need to be sensitive to the circumstances of the individual and in this sense the role should be both advisory and mediatory.

What Lies Ahead for Lifelong Learning?

A response to the UK government's focus on skills and employment has been central to this research, which has shown that lifelong learning *in its broadest sense*, can make a significant contribution in this area. From the point of view of wider benefits, both formal and informal types of learning can improve the skills of individuals and thereby aid sustainable employment levels. However, one could argue that it is through the formal learning domain that people will increase their cognitive and reflective thinking skills, and where people can gain accreditation for their endeavours. Formal accreditation has value to the individual, as it shows achievement and competency which can make them competitive in the marketplace and can have benefits to employment trajectories as adults develop new skills and keep lifelong employment.

References:

Field, J. (2005) 'Social capital and lifelong learning'. In *The encyclopedia of informal education*.

Feinstein, L. and Sabates, R. (2006) *Does Education have an impact on mothers' educational attitudes and behaviours*. DfES Research Brief RCB01-06.

Hammond, C. (2002) *Learning to be Healthy*. Institute of Education, University of London.

Jones, D. (1997) 'Bringing everyone inside the stockade', *Adults Learning* December 1997, pp. 14-15.

Marks, A. *British Journal of Educational Studies*, Vol. 47, No. 2 (Jun., 1999), pp. 157-169, Blackwell Publishing.

Sabates, R. and Feinstein, L. (2004) 'Education, training and the take up of preventative health care', Wider Benefits of Learning Research Report No.12 (on-line) www.learningbenefits.net.

Schuller, T., Preston, J., Hammond C, Grundy., A and Bynner J. (2004) *The Benefits of Learning : The impact of education on health, family life and social capital.* Routledge Falmer, London and New York.

Written Off? Learners' Perspectives on the Efficacy of an Intergenerational Project.

Angela Fish and Kathryn Addicott, Glamorgan Outreach Centre for Lifelong Learning, University of Glamorgan

Intergenerational Practice (IP) can be defined as: Structured activities, projects or programmes that enable younger and older people to work together to their mutual benefit, promote greater understanding and respect between generations and help to build more cohesive communities and promote lifelong learning.

Building on the success of the University of Glamorgan's Widening Access programme and engagement with a diverse range of learners, an intergenerational project was developed and piloted in 2000-2001 as a collaborative venture between the University of Glamorgan, local comprehensive schools and local communities. The *Write-On! Learning Through Life* project was then continued between 2001 and 2007 and further developed as a programme to encompass the delivery of one-off events, and collaboration with sheltered housing complexes. The main aims of the programme were to improve communications between the generations, to break down negative, age-related stereotypes (Keune, 2003), and to inculcate the desire to engage with lifelong learning.

Monitoring and evaluation was carried out for each cohort of learners but the aims and objectives of the research to which this paper relates were to evaluate the long-term impact of engagement with the *Write-On!* programme through the collection and analysis of both quantitative and qualitative data, utilising questionnaires and interviews.

Background to the project:

The initial concept underpinning the project arose from working with schools and in collaboration with groups of older learners. The objective was to address the issues of social exclusion and disaffection as well as the key skills shortages that existed, primarily in Rhondda Cynon Taff (Welsh Office, 1999) where the university is situated. Commitment was sought from individuals to return to and continue learning, and to develop self-reliance, flexibility and breadth of knowledge, in particular through nurturing competence in generic skills, especially communication, through a programme of training, group workshops, field trips, and guest speakers.

The view that lifelong learning has social as well as economic outcomes was fully supported, and the planning of the project addressed the aims of the National Assembly for Wales towards developing an inclusive society, by bringing together members of communities who would not, necessarily, seek each other's company (National Assembly, 2001).

Write-On! was developed within the University of Glamorgan's Centre for Lifelong Learning in 2000 as a European (Objective 1) funding proposal and recruited its first intake (six groups) in September 2001. The project ran for a subsequent five years with a total intake of 264 young people (aged 12-18) and 95 adults (aged 50+), with a yearly number of project groups ranging from three to five. Additionally, two, one-off events were facilitated to gauge interest in the project and to widen recruitment. A total of 130 young people and 66 adults attended these. The overall aim of the project was to widen access and increase participation in lifelong learning by:

- breaking down barriers to learning
- addressing social exclusion
- facilitating the development of a range of skills (with a specific focus on communication)
- making learning fun

The initial recruitment strategy highlighted the sharing of information about common life experiences in relation to local social and economic history, and also personal development. Based on feedback, and on the principles underlying Vygotsky's sociocultural learning theory that social collaboration can enhance the capabilities of human cognition, the focus was shifted to that of a volunteer role for the adults, stressing the value of their input in the young people's development and the shaping of future behaviour and attitudes (Hendry & Kloep, 2002). In recognition of Bruner's theories of cognitive growth and cultural psychology, and to ensure active participation from both generations, a method of bringing two generations together through the investigation and recording of common life experiences through the ages, based on personal testimony was designed (Bruner, 1966 & 1996). There was an underlying theme each year and these were: *Schooldays; Being a Teenager; Leisure Through the Ages; Idols, Heroes & Role Models; Food & the Environment, and Games.*

During the pilot phase participants attended for two hours per week over 30 weeks. This was later reduced to 25 weeks as school examinations, work-experience, and other activities for the older generation, resulted in a falling-off of numbers during the final sessions. During the planning stage of the programme, and based on the theories of educationalists and psychologists such as Kolb, Entwistle and Ramsden, there was a deliberate move away from the tutor delivery mode to interactive workshops, with a focus on group work, discussion and debate, and team building, which stressed peer support, mentoring, reflection, and learning through doing (Kolb, 1984, Entwistle and Ramsden, 1983). (For full details of the background to, development and implementation of the *Write-On!* project, see Fish, 2001 & 2002; Fish & Addicott, 2006. For details and analysis of the effectiveness of the different approaches used, see Addicott, 2006.)

Throughout the project, weekly monitoring and end-of-year evaluations were carried out during the six years of the project's life and modifications were made each year in response to feedback. A number of strategies were employed to gather feedback from participants, partners and facilitators, including: questionnaires; group evaluation exercises/activities; journals and overviews; facilitator logs, and continuous verbal feedback.

Formal evaluation, carried out anonymously, resulted in a 44 per cent response from the pilot year and over 80 percent in consecutive years. This increase was attributed to the fact that, initially, the evaluation forms were distributed by post, whereas subsequently they were distributed during the final sessions. Those who felt that the project met their needs or expectations, adequately through to fully, rose from 83 per cent to 98 per cent, positively reflecting the changes made. Negative responses generally focused on issues such as, transport, retention, and formal/informal structure. The main benefits highlighted were increased confidence; communication skills; team working skills; broadened horizons; new perspectives, and self fulfilment. Overall, results were positive and analysis demonstrated that objectives had been met.

Research Methodology

To assess the extent to which the project has had a lasting effect on attitudes to lifelong learning and on personal and interpersonal skills, together with any impact from engagement with the one-off events, structured questionnaires were used to collect both quantitative and qualitative data. Follow-up interviews were conducted to explore responses in more depth. This approach was designed to 'uncover the interplay of significant rather than produce widely generalisable findings' (Crossan & Osborne, 2004)

Questionnaires
A structured questionnaire was distributed to all former participants of the *Write-On!* programme, who were at a distance of between one to five years from their engagement with the project or event. Learners were asked to reflect (anonymously) on their experience and to assess or comment on any impact on their:

- communication skills
- intergenerational attitudes
- views on lifelong learning

To minimise questionnaires being discarded before opening, or not being returned if undeliverable, a sticker was attached to the envelopes stating that this was not a circular and including a return address.

A letter was included with each questionnaire explaining the aims and the significance of responses. A pre-paid envelope was included to encourage a greater return. Seventy four forms were sent to adult participants and 261 to pupil participants. (A number of adults and pupils had repeated the project and a few adults had passed away, so numbers differ slightly from those quoted for total project participation). At the time of analysis, 23 percent of adults and 7 percent of pupils had completed their forms. Only ten envelopes were returned marked 'addressee gone away'. However, as delivery for 74 percent of letters to the young people depended on being forwarded by the schools, delivery rates could not be verified.

Interviews

An additional form was sent asking for volunteers to take part in follow-up interviews. Former pupils and adults were offered the choice of telephone or face-to-face interviews, as mobility issues or relocation might have influenced decisions if only the latter were available. For current school pupils, interviews were conducted on school premises with an attendant teacher. An additional pre-paid envelope was included, to return separately from the questionnaire, to ensure anonymity. A total of 12 adults and 7 pupils responded.

Semi-structured interviews were undertaken to collect qualitative data. Interviews were audio recorded, with interviewees' permission, so that a full transcript of responses could be made and analysed in depth. This also freed up the interviewer to probe further and follow up interviewees' answers, which would have been restricted by note taking.

It was intended that a cross-section of respondents to the interview request form were to be selected, in relation to: age; project/event; time since engagement with the project/event; tutor; site, and accredited/non-accredited courses. However, given the relatively low number of respondents, all were interviewed. Despite this, interviewees did meet the cross sectional requirements above.

The interviews were designed to elicit illustrative examples of whether, and how, the project or event had impacted:

a) on the bullet points above (questionnaires)
b) in any other aspect of participants'
   life/development/attitudes

and to identify whether, and how, this experience influenced learning activities or engagement with learning.

Hayes (2003) highlights the 'methodological challenges in conducting intergenerational evaluation research' and emphasises the importance of 'developing a multi-pronged approach to gathering data'. Thus, using a combination of quantitative and qualitative methods of research, as outlined above, provided the opportunity for breadth and depth of both data and analysis, and limited the level of bias which might have resulted from the use of a single research method. In particular, the qualitative method described allowed for a flexible approach, which encouraged learners to respond openly and expansively, thereby providing rich data which could not be preconceived.

> *Research that is grounded in concern with meaning and relevance rather than measurement and typology can shift the ground from which we seek to understand experiences of adult learners. It has the capacity to enrich – and to redefine – theory and practice related to adults learning.*
> (Merrill, 1999).

Ethical issues

Due thought was given to the rights and feelings of the learners involved in this study. Learners were informed that participation in the research was voluntary and that they could withdraw at any time. Only one respondent subsequently withdrew from taking part in a follow-up interview. Data protection laws were adhered to and anonymity was assured in respect of the final report. The learners' informed consent was sought and for those under 16 years of age, informed consent was sought in writing from parents/guardians and head teachers. The format of the questionnaire and interviews was appropriate to the diversity of the learner groups.

Results: Questionnaire analysis

Communication Skills
Sixty one percent of both young and adult respondents indicated that they had gained or developed skills or abilities by working on the project. Sixteen point five percent felt they had not, with 22.5 percent being unsure.

The majority of those who identified communication skills as being developed highlighted greatest improvements in: listening and patience; having greater confidence; presentation skills; working with others; team work; helping less confident participants voice their opinions, and understanding different points of view.

Other skills developed were ITC: from overcoming fears of using computers, to making Powerpoint slideshows more creative with artwork. Respondents also pointed to increased: general knowledge; knowledge and understanding of the 'other' generation; ability to connect with young people and identify with 'young ideas', and greater tolerance.

Significantly, 81.5 percent of all respondents stated that they had had the opportunity to use these skills or abilities since leaving the project on a fairly regular basis, in a range of situations. Additionally, having had experience of communicating with another generation, both age groups remarked that they had been able to transfer the skills into their everyday lives. For example, adults had used their improved presentation skills in voluntary activities such as public speaking or chairing meetings, and a number of young people had used theirs in work-related situations.

Intergenerational attitudes
A similar proportion of each age group had or had not heard of the word 'intergenerational' before taking part in the project. Forty one percent of adult and 37 percent of young respondents had heard the

word, while 59 percent of adult and 63 percent of young respondents had not.

Ninety four percent of adult respondents and 79 percent of young respondents felt that the project had developed an understanding of each generation's point of view, giving the opportunity to meet regularly, which they would not otherwise have, and a chance to interact, realise similarities and develop friendships. One young respondent stated that in the sessions, 'both points of view were aired and taken into account'.

The importance of the informal structure of sessions was highlighted as activities and topics such as food and clothes prompted discussions: one young respondent wrote, 'it always keeps people thinking and occupied'. Others pointed to specific activities which were completed together such as computer tasks.

Respondents also pointed to the importance of equality of roles in sessions as opposed to the more traditional senior (expert), to junior (novice) roles. One adult commented, 'we were able to converse on a level playing field'. Another young respondent stated, 'I got to see that other generations don't always have different views on things'. The project had given the different generations a chance to find out what they had in common: it 'bridged the generation gap'.

Ninety four percent felt that the project had had a medium to significant impact on relationships between the generations, and that this impact was positive. All pointed to the level of enjoyment of sessions, shared experiences and activities which built relationships. This had developed over time as people began to feel more relaxed in each others' company. One young respondent commented, 'I felt that I learnt from other generations and that they can learn from us too'. Relationships built as commonality was discovered, and another young respondent stated, 'You realise that they had the same issues but with a different twist on it'.

The project allowed participants to gain an insight into what life is/was like for each other, and facilitated an exchange of perspectives, particularly for the adults. One stated that the project, 'gave me an insight into the low expectations of the less academic and the lack of support they got to achieve what ambitions they had'. Another had gained, 'an understanding how young people coped socially and education wise'. Young respondents indicated that they had had the chance to get to know the adults' feelings and thoughts, and one commented on, 'how refreshing some old people's views were'.

For the minority who did not feel the project developed an understanding or had impacted on relationships, the main reason given was the small number of participants of either generation in their particular group which limited the level of interaction.

Seventy percent of adults felt that their participation in the project had shaped or changed their perception of the different generations moderately or a lot. Forty seven percent of young respondents agreed, with 33 percent feeling it had done so only to a small extent. Thus, the project had more impact on negative views and stereotypical expectations of older people about young people. One adult stated, 'The pupils restored my faith in the young'. Adults commented on discovering how helpful and interesting young people can be and that some youngsters are intimidated by the older generation. This was similar, but to a lesser extent, for the young respondents. They were more surprised to discover that the adults could be so approachable: 'It was good to meet people with open views, keen to learn how the younger generation live'. It was apparent that many of the young respondents already had a positive or neutral attitude to the older generation.

The majority of adults felt this change in perception also applied outside the project group, with a smaller proportion arguing that it had an impact on perceptions and attitudes to family, in particular with grandchildren. Comments included: 'I think it made me more tolerant of young people in general and more confident to converse with them'; 'I now speak to teenagers that I do not know and mostly they will answer'.

For those few respondents who did not feel the project had significant impact, the reasons they identified were poor contributions and attendance from one group of young people, and for another group the boys were cited as being particularly disinterested.

Finally, in answering questions about knowledge gained from the project, one young respondent reflected:

> 'A little time spent with old people showed me that a little time goes a long way. All ages can improve a community, more community activities would improve the areas in which we lived'.

Views on lifelong learning
When asked about their engagement with further learning opportunities, voluntary or paid work since taking part in the project, fifty eight percent of adult and 42 percent of young respondents had done some. For adults this had ranged from computer classes, family and local history societies, calligraphy, craft, first aid, maths, to volunteering at a British Heart Foundation shop, and sitting on a local health board. A number of adults had gone on to volunteer as teaching assistants.

For young respondents experiences had ranged from a Duke of Edinburgh Award scheme; rugby coaching; teaching in an after school nursery work scheme; work experience such as veterinary work, and Saturday or part time jobs in shops, to volunteering to work with international students at a local youth summer centre; with people with disabilities, or in a care home.

For both age groups approximately 50 percent of this engagement had been intergenerational. For 74 percent of all age groups the choice of learning or other activities had been partially or fully influenced by their experience with the project.

When asked if there was anything unexpected that they learned during the project, both age groups highlighted surprising things they had learned about the 'other' generation, thus combating stereotypes. One adult responded:

> 'The vulnerability of the pupils, despite their behaviour as self sufficient young persons.'

Young respondents commented:

> 'We learnt that old people can be fun and don't just knit all the time and their stories are interesting, not boring'; 'I did not expect to become friends with older generations and I did not think that we would have so many similar interests'.

The most important things identified as learned from the project concerned not judging or making assumptions of other generations, giving others the opportunity to express their views and valuing those opinions even if they're different. One adult wrote, 'if treated with respect one receives respect whatever generation one belongs to', while one young respondent argued, 'that it is possible for the older and younger generations to relate to one another and bond'.

Results: Interview analysis

Communication skills
The majority of interviewees maintained that the project had played a part in improving their communication skills. The impact was predominantly on their general confidence: some young people identified that they had been quite shy with anyone they did not know prior to the project, particularly with adults. Comments included:

> 'I've got a bit more confident now when talking to older people'

and,

> 'When I go somewhere new now I'd probably strike up a conversation, whereas before I would not have.'

Since completing the project, one young person has worked as a voluntary assistant at an after school group for primary pupils. She commented that:

'In the *Write-On!* project we were communicating with the older generation but this was the total opposite... (I was) communicating with the **younger** generation, and they were probably thinking what we went through ... I wondered what they were going to be like towards me (the same way) I was towards the older generation.'

Some adults highlighted that they found themselves negotiating with the more vocal, confident, young people to allow and encourage quieter members to have their say, or to facilitate those more able or responsive to take the lead and persuade others to take part. One adult, who described herself as lacking confidence, commented:

'I learned about myself, and I did push myself a bit forward: things that normally I would have let somebody else do'.

A number commented on how freely the different generations were able to communicate by the end of the project and believed its structure and facilitation encouraged this.

Others specifically pointed to the impact on their presentation skills.

'We were encouraged to speak and stand up in front of others, which was a good thing for me because I've always been a bit afraid of standing up in front of a group... it gave me confidence to try that'.

Some adults remembered specific aspects of communication skills they had learned about, such as the need to ask open questions to encourage people to answer and talk.

Intergenerational attitudes
It is clear from the interviews that the project had a significant impact on attitudes from both generations' perspectives. Predominantly, this impact was on the generations expectations of each other, which allowed them to see past the stereotypes. For example, a number of young people indicated that the project had given them an opportunity, that they would not otherwise have had

to get to know older adults, and they were pleasantly surprised that these adults were interested in young people and wanted to get to know them. They commented about pre-conceptions:

> 'Older people are supposed to be more difficult to communicate with, but they weren't, and that's what we found out'. 'It is evidence … that they're the same as us. Just because of age, doesn't mean you haven't got anything in common– just have to discover it.'

Many young people discovered an unexpected, common interest with the adults. This resulted in them becoming

> 'More sympathetic towards them, and more open to listening to them'. One commented, 'They're not ready to be put away … they still should be talked to … it's their community, it's not their time to be really quiet and not have a voice.'

Another young interviewee had been surprised at how in touch the adults were with younger people: 'I don't think there's that much of a gap between the generations as people make out.' He also highlighted that he had gained a lot more respect for the adults because of what he learned from them and the things they had been through in their lives. Significantly, the project had changed this young person's opinion of sheltered accommodation; having read stories of mistreated adults in homes, he found instead that the residents were happy and said 'I'd like to retire somewhere like that'.

Adults were surprised at how interested in them the young people were. They enjoyed finding out the young people's views and commented:

> 'Everybody seemed to want to learn and the ideas were swapped around from older to younger', and '(the project) certainly broadened my outlook on the younger generation … not having any children, and it helped me to talk with them'.

The adults also indicated that getting to know these young people gave them a better understanding of their point of view. As a result, instead of having negative reactions to young people, such as being intimidated by seeing a 'gang' on the corner, they came to understand that 'ninety percent of them are up to no harm: there's nowhere for them to go, and they stand on corners talking'. They learned that young people often experience a negative reaction which in turn makes them view older people negatively. The project gave them a chance to discuss and understand this, increasing their tolerance.

> 'Well, when I see a group of teenagers now, I walk past them and say 'hello', I don't just cross the road';   ' If you talk to them (young people) and treat them with respect, you get respect'.

Some adults already had regular contact with young people, either their grandchildren or through work or voluntary work, and their experience in the project confirmed or reinforced their positive views of the potential of young people:

> 'I think that the project consolidated what I already thought, and felt more strongly that the community wasn't providing outlets for these young people outside of school.'

For other adults with similar contact, the project enabled them to overcome more negative views:

> 'I run a youth club … and I've probably had a slightly jaundiced view about the young generation… I'd almost got to the stage of saying they were a write-off. (However), I came out of there (the project) feeling that I'd re-established links with the modern generation, which I was in danger of losing touch with completely. It made me more tolerant – I'd lost a lot of that.'

Many adults commented on their wish to find out what had happened to the young people they had worked with. Where this contact had continued through a third party, such as the school, the adults identified a continued sense of connection and relationship with the young people and this had prolonged the satisfaction of the experience. Similarly, some young participants were happy when they had 'bumped into' an adult participant, or found out how they were, or attended a follow up event.

Views on lifelong learning
The majority of interviewees had heard the term lifelong learning, and their understanding was similar: that learning does not stop when you finish school or university; you can learn something new every day, and 'learning in life is a journey'. One young interviewee whose project group had worked with residents in sheltered accommodation said, 'When you go in to an old people's home you should not stop learning then … I haven't gone a day without learning something and I don't think those adults in the centre have either.' All of the adults interviewed had been involved in learning or voluntary work since taking part in the project, and were seeking learning opportunities in their retirement.

Most interviewees had gained some insight into lifelong learning through their participation in the project and could see a role for the project in encouraging lifelong learning. One young interviewee said, 'I've learned a lot, and learned from what they've learned in their life as well, and integrated them together'. Another commented: 'I did not really see it like that at the time, but if you look back you remember things they (older people) said and if you repeat it to other people and then they pass it on – it's like a chain, really.' Others were surprised at some of the adults' lack of formal academic education, as their experience of them was as intelligent and 'quick witted'. 'Lifelong learning has served them well and the project showed that to me.'

Some of the adults pointed out specific information they had learned during the project, for example regarding recycling, healthy eating, and local heroes. Others highlighted how much the project had brought back memories and led to further enquiries and learning: 'in looking at things in a different way years after they actually happened, you actually improve your own knowledge, you understand yourself. You're opening a lid to see what you're capable of … it took away the boundaries of 'when you're this age you can only do this' … It showed that at any age in life you can move on, do different things, learn different skills.' The kinds of examples interviewees gave highlighted the role the project had had in learning about social history, particularly on a local level. Most indicated the opportunity the project gave for learning from each other.

Other aspects of their life/ development/ attitudes
A number of the young interviewees highlighted the influence on choices of career and the work or voluntary experience they have sought in order to study for this career. For example, considering a career in medicine, one found the project reassured her that she did want to work in this field and gave her the confidence to communicate with different people and age groups. Describing her work experience: 'I was on some wards with old people … they just love talking … I used to go sit by them and just have a little chat'. She also arranged to do some voluntary work in a nursing home. Some tried to organise work experience in a local care home as a direct result of their positive experience with the project, while others described how it inspired them to choose voluntary activities which involve older people, such as WRVS. The project had given them an insight into what to expect from these experiences as well as confidence.

Others were influenced to work with people younger than themselves, such as a Brownie club, and commented, 'we're teenagers and we tend to just dismiss the other generations but now when I'm talking to the younger ones, they're similar but there's differences as well. So it's healthy to link all the ages.' Another described her part time retail job where many customers were older people: '(the project) … just taught me to have patience … you still should go into the conversation because they may not have another chance to talk to younger people'.

One adult commented: 'The project gave the opportunity to understand other people better … It's easy to criticise people without understanding the buttons you have to press that really affect their lives', and 'I go around giving presentations to schools.

So it's a knock on effect because I would have thought prior to that (project) that to go and stand on a school platform, I might have got beaten up and thrown through the window, but instead I find just the opposite – they want to listen, they're attentive – that's fine'.

Learning activities /engagement with learning.
A number of adults and one young interviewee highlighted that they had gained IT skills through their involvement with the project and they have continued to use and develop them. Adults commented: 'I had to do the research, which made me get on the computer, which had petrified me up until then'; 'After being there, I went to a computer class the next year. Since then I've bought a little laptop. '

Influence on others/ relationships with others
A common theme that emerged from the interviews was the impact the project had on participants' relationships with family and friends outside the project. A few adults discussed how their involvement and relationships built with new young people had improved relationships with their grandchildren.

Interviewees also argued that the project had a wider impact than on project participants. One young interviewee highlighted how the project inspired him to help older neighbours with chores. An adult described seeing a young participant at the supermarket with her mother, who was delighted with the effects of the project, saying, 'we can't stop her talking when she comes home (from the project) 'Mam did you do this, were you dressed like this, did you play 'scotch in the street?'. It's become a talking point in our household'.

A number of young interviewees from the same project group described how their participation had strengthened their friendship, and improved relationships with their grandparents. Relationships with friends who had not taken part were also affected, some becoming encouraged to volunteer similarly with groups such as the WRVS and Brownies. One of these young interviewees commented 'Even my mother was taken aback by all my voluntary work. She will probably look into doing something'.

Discussion

As demonstrated in the project's yearly evaluation processes, there was a limited response to paper surveys once participants had completed the project. However, for this study, no other suitable method of data collection was appropriate given the nature of the population and available resources (Wikipedia, 2008)

The adult response rate of 23 percent was fair, considering the length of the questionnaire (Bogen). While efforts were made to maximise returns, as noted in the Research Methodology section, a number of additional factors have been identified by interviewees as contributing to a disappointing seven percent response from the young people, especially timing, in relation to those still in the education system, whether at school or in higher education. For the adults, factors were cited as relocation to care homes, poor health, or increased family commitments. However, the respondents did represent a cross section of past participants according to the criteria in the research proposal.

Whilst the response rate, especially for young people, limits any significant quantitative analysis, (RDSU) the combined responses allow for a level of qualitative interpretation which, in conjunction with the interview analysis, has provided a rich source of data.

Although there was a high degree of consistency between adult and young people's responses, there were some significant variations. Adults highlighted more change to negative perceptions and preconceptions of young people, than vice versa, as young people were more neutral or already positive about adults before the project.

A greater number of adults than young people felt that they had learned some unexpected facts. These were mainly about the young people's interests and views, and the ease of interaction that the project facilitated. However, a greater proportion of young people than adults felt that the project had had an impact on them since completion.

Responses to both the questionnaires and interviews, clearly demonstrated that engagement with the intergenerational project, *Write-On!* has had a long-term, positive impact on all generations. This was particularly so in relation to communication skills and intergenerational attitudes. This echoed the evaluation responses throughout the project years. However, what has now become evident, is the extent of the long-term, positive impact on the lives of participants, and also on their families and friends.

In the light of interviewees' comments regarding the potential for prolonged satisfaction of the intergenerational experience through continued contact, future projects should include the means to facilitate this, (within statutory protection guidelines both for children and vulnerable adults).

While one of the project aims had been to engender a desire to engage with learning, feedback from the pilot phase clearly indicated that a formal, rigidly structured approach did not work. The project was redesigned to allow a more flexible, student-centred, informal approach, incorporating the principles of learning through doing. This was well received and questionnaire feedback highlighted the influence that the project had had on respondees' further learning or voluntary activities. Interviewee responses likewise commented on the belief that the facilitation and format of sessions an had contributed to positive outcomes, especially improved communication and confidence: '... the atmosphere was there to encourage you to talk ... It came down to creating that environment which made everybody feel comfortable'. Responses also confirmed that this intergenerational approach had effectively engaged young people of a wide range of academic abilities and levels of motivation. While lifelong learning was not overtly highlighted during project sessions, interviewees asserted that, on reflection, they had gained an insight into the role that *Write-On!* played in engaging people of all generations in lifelong learning and in encouraging further participation in a range of activities.

All of the adults interviewed indicated that they had thoroughly enjoyed the project and would have liked to take part in it again. Many of them had not been involved with young people, other than grandchildren, since the project either in voluntary activities or in their community. This highlighted the limited opportunities that exist for adults to meet and get to know young people, and the need for planned, structured and sustainable intergenerational activities, events and projects.

One young interviewee said of the project, 'something like this is really beneficial to you as a person ... you could not learn it in a classroom, even in social lessons ... this is so hands on ... it really gives a good experience of older people'.

References

Addicott, K. (2006) 'Overcoming Barriers to Intergenerational Engagement'. In *Transformation, Progression, and Hope: whatever happened to lifelong learning? FACE Conference Proceedings,* 9-24

Bogen, K. (n.d.) 'The Effect of Questionnaire Length on Response Rates – A Review of the Literature', Census Office Report. Accessed January 2008 www.census.gov/srd/papers/pdf/kb9601.pdf

Bruner, J. (1966) *Toward a Theory of Instruction,* Cambridge, Mass.: Harvard University Press.

Bruner, J. (1996) *The Culture of Education*, Cambridge, Mass.: Harvard University Press.

Entwistle, N.J. & Ramsden, P. (1983) *Understanding Student Learning*, Croom Helm.

Crossan and Osborne, (2004) 'Questions of Access and Participation' in Obsorne, M., Gallacher, J. and Crossan, B. (eds). *Researching Widening Access to Lifelong Learning,* London: RoutledgeFalmer, p.143.

Fish, A. (2001) 'Write-On! Learning Through Life'. In *Challenging Social Exclusion in HE and FE : FACE Conference Proceedings*, pp.63-74.

Fish A. (2002) 'Write-On! An Intergenerational Approach to Lifelong Learning', in *Widening Participation and Lifelong Learning: The Journal of the Institute for Access Studies and the European Access Network*, 4 (1) April 2002, pp.33-36.

Fish, A. and Addicott, K. (2006) 'Write-On Case Study' in *Intergenerational Programmes: An Introduction and Examples of Practice*
(A diversity of intergenerational programmes across the United Kingdom) http://www.centreforip.org.uk/default.aspx?page=820, 159.

Hayes, C. (2003) 'An Observational Study in Developing an Intergenerational Shared Site Program: Challenges and Insights' In *Journal of Intergenerational Relationships*, (1) pp.113-132.

Hendry, L. & Kloep, M. (2002) *Lifespan Development: Resources, Challenges and Risks,* Thompson Learning.

Keune, V. (2003) 'The State of Our Art: Intergenerational Program Research and Evaluation: Part One'. Iin *Journal of Intergenerational Relationships*, 1 (1) p.152.

Kolb, D.A. (1984) *Experiential Learning: Experience as the Source of Learning and Development*, New York: Prentice Hall.

Merrill, (1999: 47) cited in Crossan & Osborne, 'Questions of Access and Participation'. In Obsorne, M., Gallacher, J. and Crossan, B (eds). *Researching Widening Access to Lifelong Learning,* London: RoutledgeFalmer, p.143.

National Assembly for Wales, (2001) *The Learning Country: A Comprehensive Education and Lifelong Learning Programme to 2010 in Wales*, Introduction.

RDSU (Peninsula Research & Development Support Unit, (n.d.) 'Enhancing Questionnaire Response Rates', Helpsheet 14, Accessed May 2008 www.projects.ex.ac.uk/prdsu/helpsheets/Helpsheet14-Feb03-Unlocked.pdf

Welsh Office, (1999) *Future Skills Wales (2000-2003) Report.*

Wikipedia, (2008), 'Statistical Survey: Structure and Standardisation', http://en.wikipedia.org/wiki/Statistical_survey#Structure_and_standardization.